Robert Whitelaw

Sophocles

Translated into English Verse

Robert Whitelaw

Sophocles
Translated into English Verse

ISBN/EAN: 9783337339272

Printed in Europe, USA, Canada, Australia, Japan

Cover: Foto ©Thomas Meinert / pixelio.de

More available books at **www.hansebooks.com**

TRANSLATED INTO ENGLISH VERSE

BY

ROBERT W
ASSISTANT-MASTER IN RUGBY SCHOOL
TRINITY COLLEGE

RIVINGTONS
WATERLOO PLACE, LONDON
MDCCCLXXXIII

I OWE SO MUCH TO THE POETRY

OF

ROBERT BROWNING

THAT HE PERMITS ME

BY INSCRIBING THIS PAGE WITH HIS NAME

BOTH TO RECORD AND INCREASE

MY DEBT.

PREFACE

I THINK it better that this book should have for its preface, in the main, an apology for being unprefaced.

I could find something to say about the genius, the dramatic art, the diction of Sophocles—something perhaps about the several plays and the personages of each; but for such discussions there is no room in a preface, and the systematic treatment of these matters seems to belong rather to the work of a commentator upon Sophocles than of a translator. A translator has undertaken, however unworthily, to be the mouthpiece of the poet, not ('motley on back, and pointing-pole in hand') his showman. The men and the women whom Sophocles created are here, not to be talked about, but to speak for themselves; or else the translation is 'naught.' Whereas Oedipus *was* blind, now he sees. He stands before us, sanctified by suffering; and who shall dissertate about him? The human heart of Deianeira, distracted with love and jealousy, palpitating with hope and fear, torn with remorse and anguish, is laid bare for us; there is no more to say.

Or I could dilate upon the business of the translator, and the principles by which I have been guided in making this translation. But here there is nothing new to be said. All translators must begin with the same principles, though they apply them so differently; the difference arising in part from the various estimates which they form of the conflicting claims to be balanced, in part from the various qualifications, whether of literary or of scholarly faculty, which they bring to their work. But all alike, whatever their achievement, must in the first instance propose to themselves as their aim the utmost fidelity to the thought, the feeling, the form of the original, compatible with perfect loyalty to the requirements of the language into which they are translating. And this, or an approximation to this, the readers of a translation have a right to demand; though, in the case of a writer so subtly perfect as Sophocles, those who know him best will best appreciate the difficulty of achieving such a result. I conceive that the test of a thoroughly good English translation is twofold : it should satisfy both the English reader who cannot read the original, and the scholar who can. It is, I believe, increasingly felt that a good translation is a commentary of the best kind. But, when I have said this, what remains for me to say, but that, whilst hoping that I may have contributed something to the knowledge of Sophocles, I feel profoundly how far I have fallen short of the result at which I aimed?

I have translated the Choruses into unrhymed lines. This seemed to me better in itself, as well as more practicable for me. Mr. Matthew Arnold's fragments of an 'Antigone' and a 'Deianeira' are examples of what can be done in this way. I have only now and then attempted to reproduce the metres of the original. But, lest it should be thought that I may have 'felt the weight of too much liberty,' I have bound myself rigorously, with a few exceptions, by an antistrophic arrangement.

With respect to the spelling of the Greek names, I have been wilfully, and perhaps indefensibly, inconsistent. I could not persuade myself that 'Aias' and 'Teukros' were not pedantic. Yet I have spoken of

'Odysseus.' 'Ulysses,' as I have heard it said, is another person, with Ovidian associations. And 'Odysseus' is sufficiently naturalised. So, perhaps, will 'Aias' be hereafter; but not yet.

I have added a few notes, which seemed necessary, for explanation, or to justify novelties either of interpretation or reading.

I have expressed, in a note on 'Electra' l. 363, my obligations to Professor Jebb's editions of the 'Electra' and 'Ajax.'

R. W.

RUGBY, *November* 1882.

CONTENTS

	PAGE
OEDIPUS THE KING	1
OEDIPUS AT COLONUS	65
ANTIGONE	139
ELECTRA	193
TRACHINIAE	255
AJAX	309
PHILOCTETES	367
NOTES	429

PERSONS.

OEDIPUS.
PRIEST.
CREON.
TEIRESIAS.
MESSENGER.
SHEPHERD OF LAÏUS.
SECOND MESSENGER.
JOCASTA.
CHORUS OF THEBAN ELDERS.

Oedipus the King

Oed. CHILDREN—of ancient Cadmus latest
        birth—
Why in such eager session sit ye here,
With chaplets twined around your suppliant boughs?
And all the city is thick with incense-smoke,
And loud with lamentation and with dirge:
Whereof, O children, choosing not to hear
From lips of others, hither I have come—
I, who am called all-famous Oedipus:
Now therefore tell me, thou, whose reverend mien
Proclaims thee spokesman, wherefore are ye come—   10
What fearing—craving what? In nought would I
Withhold my succour; fearing to be found
Heartless, your suppliant session pitying not.
   Priest. Prince of my people, Oedipus the king,
Thou seëst us, what tale of years we tell,
Who at thine altars sit, some fledged as yet
For no far flight, and some oppressed with age,
Priests—I of Zeus: and lo, with us, of youths
Our chosen: and the general crowd, white-wreathed,
Sit in our squares, and at the temples twain   20

Of Pallas, and Ismenus' prescient hearth.
For Thebes, thyself art witness, sinks beneath
The tempest's stress, and lifts no more her head
Out of the drenching of the deadly surge—
Blighted all fruitful blossoms of the land,
Blighted our grazing herds, and barren births
Of women: and withal the god, fire-fraught,
Grim Pestilence, strikes with his scourge the city,
Whereby the house of Cadmus is made void,
And rich with sorrow and sighing Death's dark halls. 30
Thee therefore, not as equalled with the gods,
Suppliant with these children I entreat,
But chief of men, in casualties of life,
And Heaven's visitations, we esteem thee:
Who, at thy coming hither, didst rid the land
Of that fell songster's tribute which we paid,
Albeit of us no knowledge hadst thou gained,
No prompting, but by aidance of a god
We say and think thou didst redeem our life;
And now, revered of all men, Oedipus, 40
Behold us here thy suppliants: help for us,
Some help contrive, by oracle from heaven
Instructed, or wise counsel of a man:
For oft 'tis seen, that most abiding fruit
Experience bears, when counsellors confer.
O then, uplift our state, thou man of men!
Yea, and beware: for now indeed the land

Hails thee her saviour, for thy former help;
And of thy reign O never be it said,
That thou didst lift us up and cast us down; 50
But stablish thou our state's prosperity;
And, as before deliverance wrought by thee
Was blest by heaven, so help us now again.
For if thou wilt be king in Thebes, as now,
Better a peopled than a vacant realm:
Since neither tower nor ship avails to help,
Empty of men and tenantless within.

   Oed. O woful children, sorrows known too well
To me ye come lamenting. Well I know
Ye all are grieved, and yet, grieve as ye may, 60
There is not one of you hath grief like mine.
For yours is private sorrow, touching each
Himself and not another, but my heart
Aches all at once for Thebes and me and thee.
Ye do not wake me slumbering and asleep:
But many tears doubt not that I have shed,
And threaded many a labyrinth of the mind.
And the one cure that I by searching found
I put to proof: for Creon, Menoeceus' son,
My own wife's brother, to the Delphic shrine 70
Of Phoebus I have sent, that he might ask
What act or speech of mine should save the state:
And counting o'er the days that he is gone
I marvel how he fares; for overlong

He tarries, past the time that should have served.
But when he comes, base should I be indeed,
Failing to do all that the god requires.

Priest. 'Tis seasonably spoken, and ev'n now
I hear it said that Creon hither comes.

Oed. Brightly he looks: O King Apollo, grant, 80
Bright fortune, fraught with safety, he may bring!

Priest. Glad news, no doubt, he brings: else had he not
With wealth of fruitful laurel decked his brows.

Oed. Soon we shall know. 'Tis not too far to speak.
Son of Menoeceus and my kinsman, prince,
What answer from the god dost thou report?

Cre. Good: all our sufferings, if it chance aright,
May turn to our advantage, as I think.

Oed. What says the god? Hearing thy present speech,
I neither hope, nor fear before the time. 90

Cre. If thou wilt hear while these are standing by,
Thou shalt: I am ready, or else to go within.

Oed. Speak in the ears of all: since more for these
Than for my own life is the grief I bear.

Cre. All that the god hath spoken thou shalt hear.
A plain command Apollo lays on us;
Pollution, harboured in the land, we must
Drive hence, nor harbour irremediably.

Oed. Yea, with what cleansing? How is our plight relieved?

Cre. Some one's to banish, or for blood that's shed 100
Blood must atone : such guilt disturbs our state.

Oed. Of what man spake the god, so foully slain?

Cre. Laïus, O king, was ruler of the land
Aforetime, ere the sceptre fell to thee.

Oed. I know his fame : himself I never saw.

Cre. His death requires our vengeance, and to do
Swift execution on his murderers.

Oed. But where are they? Where shall we look to trace
The faded record of an ancient crime?

Cre. In this land, so he said. Who seek may find: 110
The careless searcher makes the baffled search.

Oed. In city or in field—or was't abroad
That Laïus encountered with this death?

Cre. Bound, as he said, for Delphi, from his home
He fared, but to his home came not again.

Oed. Was there no messenger—companion, none—
Who saw, and might have told, if one had asked?

Cre. All died save one, who, flying, crazed with fear,
Of all he saw knew but one thing to tell.

Oed. Out then with that! One thing may find out many, 120
If but a little we take heart to hope.

Cre. Robbers, he said, met with the king and slew him,
Not single-handed, but a company.

Oed. How had a robber so presumed, unless
Traitors from Thebes had lined him with their gold?
  Cre. So we surmised: but, Laïus being dead,
No one was there to help us in our grief.
  Oed. What grief withheld you, not to learn the
    truth—
The royal house struck down by such a blow?
  Cre. The subtle-singing Sphinx compelled our
    thoughts   130
Back from the vague doubt to the instant need.
  Oed. I will begin again, and find out all.
Phoebus has well fulfilled his part, thou thine,
Spending this trouble for the dead man's sake:
Claim then and find in me no vain ally,
Helping at once this city and the god.
Not on behalf of friends of no account,
But for my own sake, shall I purge this guilt.
For who slew him, by such another blow
Belike may choose to be revenged on me.   140
So then in helping him I save myself.
But quickly, children, from this altar-foot
Rise ye, and take these suppliant boughs away:
And some one summon hither the Theban folk;
Nought will I leave undone. All hangs on this—
Weal, with the help of heaven, or woe to Thebes.
  Priest. Children, let us be gone: for to obtain
Ev'n what this man announces, came we hither.

Come, who didst send these oracles, Apollo,
To save and heal us of our sickness, thou! 150
   Chor. Sweet-sounding answer of Zeus, what art thou,
      that comest from Pytho,   [*Strophe* 1.
To glorious Thebes from the golden shrine?
Low at thy feet I am laid, with my heart in a flutter of
    fear,
Delian, Healer Apollo!
Filled full of wonder and dread,
What stern requirement thou wilt enact for us,
What word of doom, or new or old,
Come with revolving seasons back—
O tell us, daughter of golden Hope,
Immortal Voice!   [*Antistrophe* 1.
Daughter of Zeus, thee first I invoke, immortal Athene;
Our city's champion, thy sister, next,   160
Artemis high o'er the Agora's circle in glory enthroned,
Thee too, Far-shooter, Apollo!
Threefold averters of doom,
O now from heav'n come forth to deliver us,
If ever, when hung o'er our heads
Menace of woe, at your behest
The flaming ruin was rolled away,
Visit us now!
Unnumbered woes, alas, are mine to bear: [*Strophe* 2.
I see the sickness sweep our ranks along,
Nor weapon hath my thought,   170

That can its breath avert:
For neither of the goodly earth
Prosper the springing fruits,
Nor women from the lamentable pangs
Of childbirth rise again:
But one upon another shalt thou see
Like flocks of feather'd birds,
Swifter than fire that no man tames,
Swept onward to the shore,
Far west, of Pluto and the night.
Unnumbered dead! a city perishing! [*Antistrophe* 2.
For children unregarded in the streets
Lie, tainting the air with death,   180
Unwept: and gentle wives,
And grey-haired mothers, pressing round,
Their sad petitions pour,
Where the great altar lifted o'er the crowd
Stands like a seaward cliff:
And high and clear with flutes in solemn dirge
The wailing voices blend :—
O golden goddess, child of Zeus,
Have pity and send us Help,
Fair-visaged Help, with eyes benign.
And this fierce Ares, who,   [*Strophe* 3.
Not now with brazen shields,   190
But with the blasting of his fiery breath,
Wakes worse than din of battle in our midst,

I pray that he, far from my country's shores,
Backward at headlong speed may turn and flee,
Either to Amphitrite's western bower
Under the great salt sea,
Or those inhospitable tides that rave
On rock-bound shores of Thrace:
For, what the ravin'd night at last lets go,
Day makes of this his prey:
But, O our Father, Zeus,   200
Lord of the lightning's flaming might,
Slay with thy bolt the dreaded foe.
Lyceius, lord of light,   [*Antistrophe* 3.
Showered from thy golden string
Fain would I see thy shafts invincible
Fly forth, each shaft a champion winged with help,
And see in either hand of Artemis
The splendour of a torch that flames afar,
Wherewith the Lycian hills she ranges o'er:
And, lustrous as the juice
Of thine own vines, named of this Theban land, 210
Bacchus, I cry to thee—
Crowned with a golden diadem, and girt
With shouting Maenads round,
Come to our rescue now,
With blazing pinebrand all aglow,
Against the god whom gods disown.

   Oed. Thou askest: as thou askest, if thou wilt

Be serviceable and hearken to my words,
Help thou shalt have and respite of thine ills—
Words I shall speak, a stranger to the tale,
A stranger to the deed: else had I tracked it,   220
And not gone far, ere I had found some clue.
But I was then no citizen of Thebes;
Now therefore, Thebans, hear me, all of you.
Whoever among you knows by what man's hand
Died Laïus the son of Labdacus,
I bid him speak to me, and tell me all:
Speak though he fears, and clear us of the guilt,
Yea, and accuse himself: for he shall suffer
Nought worse than to depart out of the land
Unscathed: or, if he knows the murderer   230
Some stranger come to Thebes, yet let him speak:
I will reward and give him thanks to boot.
But, if ye hide this thing, and one, afraid
For his own sake or friend's sake, slights my words,
How then concludes my purpose, ye shall hear.
I charge all dwellers in this land, whereof
Sceptre and sovereignty are mine, to yield
That man, whoe'er he be, nor speech nor shelter:
No man must pray or sacrifice with him,
Or of the lustral water let him share: 240
To him all doors be barred, whose presence breeds
In Thebes pollution: as the oracle,
From Delphi newly brought, reveals to me.

So stands my purpose: to the god such help
I dedicate and to the murdered man:
And for the murderer, whether alone
He hides his guilt or has accomplices,
May he unblest wear out his guilty life!
And for myself I pray, my hearth and home
With my consent if ever he should share,   250
This doom I doomed for others fall on me!
And all these things I charge you to perform,
For my sake, and the god, and for this land,
Blighted and banned and ruined as ye see.
For even if this thing were not from heaven,
Ye should not thus have left such guilt unpurged,
The murder of your noblest and a king,
But sought the slayer: and now, because on me
There hath devolved succession to his throne,
And to his couch withal and fruitful wife,   260
From whom had sprung, had not his offspring failed,
A common race of children, his and mine—
But on his head this sudden mischief leapt—
Therefore, as son for father, I will fight
For him, and nothing spare, and shrink from nought,
Seeking the murderer of your king, whose sire
Was Labdacus, as Polydorus his,
From Cadmus sprung, son of Agenor old:
And, who'll not help in this, I pray the gods
Neither to yield them harvest of their fields,   270

Nor children of their wives, but let them perish,
Slain by this present plague or worse than this:
But you the rest, good Thebans all, who cleave
To my consent, be Justice your ally,
And all the gods befriend you evermore.

   Chor. King, as thy curse constrains me, I will speak—
I neither did the deed, nor can declare
The doer. Phoebus, he alone, who laid
This quest on us, could name the guilty one.

   Oed. True, but to wrest a secret from the gods,   280
Against their will, passes all power of men.

   Chor. Yet, if not this, there is a second-best.

   Oed. Second or third-best, speak: withhold it not.

   Chor. Teiresias with Phoebus, seer with seer,
I know more than all men like-gifted: Ask
Of him, O king, and thou shalt learn the truth.

   Oed. This also, friends, I have not left undone.
I sent two messengers, when Creon spoke:
Long since I marvel that he is not here.

   Chor. Enough: mere dull stale talk, no doubt, all else.   290

   Oed. What talk mean you? I question every hint.

   Chor. By travellers we heard the king was slain.

   Oed. And I: but gone from sight is he who saw it.

   Chor. Yet, if he knows what fear is, rest assured
He'll not endure, hearing thy grievous curse.

   Oed. From deeds who shrinks not, him no words
      affright.

Chor. There's one who shall convict him : hither led
Comes even now the seer, the man inspired,
Whose eyes, of all men's most, behold the truth.

   Oed. Teiresias, master-seer, who understandest   300
All mysteries and all knowledge, things in heaven
And things on earth, thou seëst not but knowest
What plague afflicts our state : whereof we find
No champion and no saviour, sage, but thee.
For Phoebus, if indeed the messengers
Told thee not, to our sending sent reply,
No riddance of this sickness should we have,
Until the murderers of Laïus
Were found and slain, or banished from the land.
Now therefore grudge neither thine auguries,   310
Nor any divinations that thou hast,
But save thyself and city, and save me,
And make us clean from all blood-guiltiness.
On thee we hang : and for a man to help
With all he has and can, is noblest toil.

   Teir. Alas, how sore a burden is the knowledge
That profits not the knower. This I knew,
But had forgotten : else had I not come hither.

   Oed. Why with thy looks so downcast art thou come ?

   Teir. Let me go hence : most easily will be   320
Performed my part and thine, if thou consent.

   Oed. 'Twere treason and ingratitude to Thebes,
Thy mother, thus to lock from her thy counsel.

Teir. Nay, for thy speech, I see, toward no good end
Is making; and I would not likewise err.

Oed. By heaven, if aught thou knowest, all we here
Thy suppliants pray, turn not thy face from us.

Teir. Ay, for ye all know nought: Urge me no more,
Lest *my* tale prove—an evil tale for *thee.*

Oed. How? dost thou know and wilt not tell, but rather   330
Betray thy people and destroy thy town?

Teir. I'll neither grieve myself nor thee. In vain
Thou dost importune me: my lips are sealed.

Oed. What, miscreant—for the patience of a stone
Thou'dst anger—not a word thou'lt speak, but keep
Thy stubborn and impracticable mood?

Teir. Thou dost reprove my temper, but thine own,
Lodged in thy breast, thou seest not, blaming me.

Oed. Who could refrain his anger, hearing now
Such words, wherewith thou dost dishonour Thebes?   340

Teir. Too soon the blow will fall, howe'er I hide it.

Oed. What blow will fall, I should be warned by thee.

Teir. I'll speak no more. Now bluster, if thou wilt:
The fiercest of thine anger let me feel.

Oed. This shall my anger do: what I perceive,
I'll speak. For know that now I understand,
Thou didst contrive, nay thou hast done, this deed—
All save to deal the blow: and, couldst thou see

Then surely I had said 'twas wholly thine.

Teir. Is't come to this? I charge thee to obey
Thine own commandment, and from this day forth 350
Speak neither to this people nor to me:
Thou art unclean: for *thee* we are accursed.

Oed. Such words, unblenching, blurtest thou at me?
How dost thou deem thou shalt escape for this?

Teir. Nay, I am safe. 'Tis true; and truth is strong.

Oed. Truth taught by whom? Not surely by thine art.

Teir. By thee: my lips, unwilling, thou hast opened.

Oed. What saidst thou? Speak again: I'll mark thee better.

Teir. Was my speech dark? or say'st thou this to prove me? 360

Oed. Perchance I understood not: speak again.

Teir. Him, of whose death thou askest, thou didst slay.

Oed. Not twice, unpunished, shall thy tongue offend.

Teir. More wilt thou hear, to be incensed the more?

Oed. Say what thou wilt: 'twill be but wasted breath.

Teir. Consorting with thy nearest, to thy shame,
Thou knowest not, nor seest what plight is thine.

Oed. Shalt thou say this, and triumph to the end?

Teir. If there is any potency in truth.

Oed. There is, except for thee. For thee there's none, 370

B

Blind as thou art, in ears and mind and eyes.

Teir. I pity thee, flinging the taunts, which soon
There's no one here will spare to fling at thee.

Oed. One lifelong night's thy portion; so that me
Thou canst not harm, nor any man who sees.

Teir. 'Tis not appointed thee by me to fall:
Sufficient is Apollo—he will do it.

Oed. By thee, or Creon, was this plot contrived?

Teir. Nay, Creon harms thee not: thou harm'st thyself.

Oed. O wealth and kingly state and sovereign art, 380
All art excelling, of our high-placed life—
What jealousy ye have in store for us;
When for this sceptre's sake, which Thebes to me
Intrusted—a free gift, by me unsought—
Creon, from first to last the faithful friend,
Seeks to unthrone me, springing unawares,
And has suborned a cunning sorcerer,
A cheating juggler, one who for his gains
Has eyes to see, but in his art is blind.
For, tell me, sirrah, when wast thou true prophet? 390
Why, when the chanting hound was at your doors,
Didst thou not save thy people by a word?
And yet to read such riddle was no task
For common men, but asked a prophet's skill:
But thou wast found with no such lore by birds
Instructed or by gods inspired:—then came

I, who knew nothing, Oedipus, and freed you,
Taught not by birds, but by my mind's sure guess;
Whom now thou wouldst thrust out, in hope to stand
By the right hand of Creon on his throne. 400
Methinks ye both shall rue your precious plot
Of cleansing thus the land: thou'rt old, I think—
Else hadst thou learnt—plagued with thine own inven-
 tions.

Chor. In anger spoken to our conjecture seem
Both this man's words, O Oedipus, and thine.
But other need is ours, to ponder well,
What heaven decrees, how best we may perform.

Teir. Though thou'rt a king, an equal right I claim
To give thee word for word: I too may speak—
No slave to thee—but slave to Loxias; 410
Not needing therefore, for a patron, Creon.
Blind thou didst call me, taunting me; I tell thee,
Thou seest and seest not what plight is thine,
Nor where thy home is, nor with whom 'tis shared.
Knowest thou whence thou art? and thou hast been
Foe to thy friends, unknowing, alive and dead;
And from this land of mother and of sire
The twofold curse shall drive thee with fierce feet,
Seeing with thine eyes, light now, but darkness then:
And then, responsive to thine outcries wild, 420
What haven, what Kithaeron will not ring,
Those nuptials known, that fatal harbour-home,

Wherein thy bark was moored, fair winds to help?
And many another grief hast thou to learn,
Both to thyself made equal and thy children.
Now upon Creon and these words of mine
Heap insults if thou wilt. There waits for no man
More swift and sure perdition than for thee.

   Oed. These things from him can I endure to hear?
Hence to destruction! hence and tarry not,   430
But void these doors, and from my sight be gone!

   Teir. I had not come, but thou didst summon me.

   Oed. I knew not that thou wouldst speak foolishness,
Else had I made small haste to bring thee hither.

   Teir. Let it be so: I am a fool for thee—
Wise enough for the father who begat thee.

   Oed. What father?—Stay: tell me, whose son am I?

   Teir. This day shall both beget thee and destroy.

   Oed. Thou dark'nest counsel still with riddling words.

   Teir. In reading riddles famous is thy skill.   440

   Oed. Ay—find what makes me great and sneer at that!

   Teir. This same success however has undone thee.

   Oed. But, if it saved the city, what care I?

   Teir. 'Tis time that I were gone. Boy, lead me hence.

   Oed. So let him lead. A hindrance and offence
Thou art, being present: gone, thou'lt plague no more.

   Teir. But first I'll speak my errand, unafraid,

Out to thy face: thy frown can nowise slay.
Hear then: this man, whom thou with threats requirest,
And makest inquisition for the blood 450
Of Laïus slain, he is amongst us here,
Lodged in our midst, an alien, as we deemed—
Now to be proved true Theban with the best—
No glad surprise: for blind, who now boasts sight,
Who now has wealth, a beggar, staff in hand,
To a strange land shall he grope forth his way.
Then shall he of the children round his hearth
Brother be proved and sire; both son and husband
Of her who bare him; having usurped the couch
O' the father whom he slew. Get thee within, 460
And meditate these things: if they prove false,
Say then my prophet's skill has taught me nothing.

 Chor. What man is he,   [*Strophe* 1.
Whom the prophetic Delphian cliff denounces,
With blood-stained hands
Doer of deeds inexpiable, nameless?
Now, now let him flee with feet
Than storm-footed steeds more swift
Far, far from the sunlight.
For with the fire of his lightnings leaps on him,
Armed, the Avenger, the Son of the Highest: 470
And the Fates, the relentless,
Track him, not to be baffled.
 For, late revealed,   [*Antistrophe* 1.

Forth from the snow-capt summits of Parnassus
Flashed there a Voice,
'Seek ye the sinner! from his hiding drag him!'
For through the wild woodland ways,
O'er rocks, and in mountain caves,
He roams, as a bull might,
Restless, joyless, far from his fellows,
Shunning the oracles pealed from earth's centre,   480
But for ever he hears them,
Deathless, hovering round him.
Sorely, most sorely, is my mind perplexed,   [*Strophe* 2.
By the wise augur's word:
I cannot yet believe, nor dare deny—
I know not what to say.
'Twixt hope and fear I hover doubtfully:
The present and the future—both are dark.
What quarrel had the son of Polybus
With Laïus or his house,   490
I neither heard before, nor now have learnt
Aught that should make me challenge to the proof
The general praise of Oedipus the king,
For Laïus moved with zeal,
And his mysterious end.
Wise are the gods: Apollo knows, and Zeus,   [*Antist.* 2.
What things are done on earth:
But what know I? and prophets are but men,
And, if this seer's voice   500

Be more than mine, there is no man who knows.
Yet one man's wit another's may surpass.
Still, let them talk, I will not say ' 'Tis so,'
Until I see the proof.
Once in our sight he met the wingèd Pest;
We saw him wise, we proved him sweet to Thebes:
And of this guilt my thoughts   510
Shall not condemn him now.

    Cre. Friends and my townsmen, hither, having heard
With what hard words King Oedipus assails me,
I come, impatient. For, in this distress
If aught in word or deed importing harm
He thinks that he has suffered at my hand,
I have no pleasure to prolong my days,
Laden with this reproach. No single loss
The danger of such charge imports to me,   520
But loss of all, if base by Thebes, and base
By thee and by my friends, I shall be called.

    Chor. Belike this accusation rather came,
Forced from his lips by anger, than believed.

    Cre. What proof had he, that, what the prophet spoke,
He falsely spoke, induced by my suggestion?

    Chor. This charge was made: what prompted it, I know not.

    Cre. With steadfast eyes and mind unfaltering

Against me was this accusation launched?

Chor. I know not: what kings do, I do not see. 530
But from the palace look you where he comes.

Oed. Sirrah, how cam'st thou hither? Hast thou such
A face of boldness, to confront me here,
Being, as well appears, my murderer,
And of my sovereign place convicted thief?
I prithee, say, what cowardice having seen
Or folly in me, hast thou devised this deed?
Its stealthy coming-on didst thou suppose
I should not mark, nor, if I marked, withstand?
Foolish I rather deem thy rash attempt, 540
Unhelped by numbers or by friends, to snatch
At power, that friends and wealth alone can win.

Cre. King, be advised. As thou hast said thy say,
Hear me say mine, and having heard consider.

Oed. Thou hast more skill to speak than I to hear
Thee, having found thee bitter and unkind.

Cre. Even of this hear first what I shall say.

Oed. This, that thou art no traitor, tell me not.

Cre. If mere self-will, divorced from reason, seems
A precious thing to thee, thou art deceived. 550

Oed. If wronging thus a kinsman thou dost think
Thou'lt 'scape the reckoning, thou art deceived.

Cre. That this is justly said, I do confess:

But tell me what's the wrong that thou hast suffered?

Oed. Didst thou advise or no, that I should send
Some one to bring this reverend man, the prophet?

Cre. The counsel that I gave, I'd give again.

Oed. Say now what time hath passed since Laïus—

Cre. Since he did what? I know not what thou askest.

Oed. Vanished from hence, slain by a murderous blow? 560

Cre. The time grows old: 'tis many years agone.

Oed. And did this prophet then profess his art?

Cre. Wise was he then as now, honoured no less.

Oed. And made he any mention then of me?

Cre. Whilst I was standing by to hear him, none.

Oed. But did ye not inquire who slew your king?

Cre. We asked, as we were bound: but asked in vain.

Oed. Why did not this wise prophet help you then?

Cre. I know not: things beyond me, I let be.

Oed. But this thou knowest; and, if thou'rt wise, wilt own. 570

Cre. What is it? what I know, I'll not deny.

Oed. That, had he not conspired with thee, the blood
Of Laïus to my charge he had not laid.

Cre. What he hath said, thou knowest: but I claim
To question thee, as thou hast questioned me.

Oed. Ask on: thou wilt not fix this guilt on me.

Cre. What then? Hast thou my sister to thy wife?
Oed. What thou hast asked, I may not well deny.
Cre. Reigns she with thee, the partner of thy power? 579
Oed. Her will is mine: nought is withheld from her.
Cre. Equalled with you twain am not I, the third?
Oed. How false a friend thou art, appears in this.
Cre. Not so, if to thyself thou'dst put my case.
Consider first—who, thinkest thou, would choose
To be a king with dreams of evil cheer,
When he might sleep secure, and reign no less?
Think not, I am so much ambition's fool,
I'd rather be a king than do like one—
So would not I, nor any prudent man.
Now without fear I have all things from thee; 590
But, were I king, I might not please myself.
How should I crave the name of king, who have
The power and kingliness without the pain?
I am not yet so senseless, to misprise
An honourable lot that costs me nought.
Now all men greet me, I am friends with all,
And those who'd speak with thee, call me aside;
'Tis the sure way to prosper in their suit:
And dost thou think I'd change my place for thine?
I needs must be a fool to be a traitor. 600
But neither of such treachery am I fain,
Nor to another's plots would I consent.

For proof—get thee to Delphi first, and ask,
Did I report the oracle aright:
This too—if thou dost find that with the seer
In aught I have conspired, pronounce my death,
Not with one voice but two, both thine and mine.
But on mere vague surmise condemn me not.
Unjust alike are random trust and blame,
To reckon false men true, or true men false :   610
And one had better lose, what he loves best,
His life, than throw away a faithful friend.
In time this lesson thou shalt surely learn :
For time alone can show the honest man,
But in a single day a knave is known.

Chor. One who walked warily, O king, might own,
He argued well : swift judgments are not sure.

Oed. When secret foes are sudden in attack,
Swiftly to meet them must my plans be laid.
If I sit still and wait, the moment's gone—   620
His plans have prospered, mine are frustrated.

Cre. What wilt thou do then? Wilt thou banish
    me?

Oed. Not banishment, but death, shall be thy doom.

Cre. When men have seen, and gauged, a tyrant's
    spite?

Oed. Wilt thou defy me, and dispute my will?

Cre. I see thy judgment errs.

Oed.   I guard my own.

Cre. Have I no rights as well?
Oed. Thou art a traitor.
Cre. If thou'rt mistaken?
Oed. Yet I must be king.
Cre. Not if thou rul'st unjustly.
Oed. Hear him, Thebes!
Cre. I have a voice in Thebes, as well as thou. 630
Chor. Princes, forbear: for hither in good time
Comes forth the queen, Jocasta, from the house:
The feud that is between you, she may heal.

Joc. What means this senseless din of warring tongues?
Unhappy men, have ye no shame, to voice
Your private wrongs, when Thebes is sick to death?
Go thou within, and, Creon, get thee home,
Make no more mountains of your molehill griefs.

Cre. Sister, this man, thy husband, Oedipus,
Claims to propound to me a bitter choice— 640
To be driv'n from my country, or to die.

Oed. 'Tis true: for I have found him, good my queen,
Contriving with base arts against my life.

Cre. May I not thrive, but be accurst, and perish,
If I have done aught that thou dost pretend!

Joc. O by the gods, believe him, Oedipus,
Revering both this oath which he has sworn,
And me, and all this friendly company.

Chor. Hear us, O king, we entreat,

With goodwill, and a prudent mind. 650
  Oed. In what, then, shall I yield to you?
  Chor. Have thou regard to this man,
Who never before was foolish, and now
In the strength of his oath is strong.
  Oed. Know ye, for what ye ask?
  Chor.   I know.
  Oed.   Say, what?
  Chor. The friend, who binds his conscience with an
      oath,
On bare suspicion tax not nor disgrace.
  Oed. But, when ye ask me this, be well assured
That death or banishment ye ask for me.
  Chor. By Helios, no—chief of the hosts of heaven! 660
Godless and friendless, if I wish thee ill,
To deepest depths of ruin let me fall!
But, seeing all the city perishing,
My spirit fails within me, if indeed
New ills to former ills your strife shall add.
  Oed. Well—let him go: and let me die outright,
Or else be thrust dishonoured from the land. 670
Thy mournful pleading moves me: therefore thee,
Not him, I pity; him my hate shall follow.
  Cre. Ungraciously thou yieldest: but for this
Thou wilt be sorry when the fit is past.
'Tis just, such tempers most should plague themselves.
  Oed. Wilt thou not hold thy peace and go?

Cre.   I go,
Stranger'd by thee, but trusted by my friends.
    Chor. Lady, why tarriest thou,
To shut the doors upon thy lord?
    Joc. Not till ye tell me what has chanced.   680
    Chor. Words have been angrily spoken,
Suspicious, impatient, ignorant words,
Unjust—but they carry a sting.
    Joc. From both did they proceed?
    Chor.   Yes.
    Joc.   What was spoken?
    Chor. Thebes has enough to bear: where the strife
        rests,
There let it end; and let no more be said.
    Oed. See, with thy friendliness what thou hast done,
My will unbent, and blunted my resolve.
    Chor. King, I have said it and will say it again—   690
Ill-counselling nor for wise counsels apt
Should I be proved, if thee I now renounce,
Who with a straight course home didst safely bring
The storm-tossed vessel of my people's hope—
And now again conduct us, if thou canst!
    Joc. I pray thee, king, hide not from me the cause,
That to such fierce displeasure thou art moved.   699
    Oed. Yea, for I honour thee, queen, more than these—
What Creon hath planned against me, thou shalt hear.
    Joc. Thy ground of quarrel let me clearly know.

Oed. By me he says that Laïus was slain.

Joc. As knowing it of himself, or from another?

Oed. A lying prophet he has set to say it;
Nor speaks one word that may commit himself.

Joc. Why, think no more then of what troubles thee.
Listen to me; I tell thee, there is not
Any such thing as prophecy on earth.
And, what I speak, I'll shortly prove it true. 710
There came to Laïus once an oracle,
I say not from the god, but from his servants,
That fate would bring to pass that he should die
Slain by his son, whom I should bear to him.
But Laïus, in a place where three roads meet,
As rumour went, robbers and strangers slew:
And from the child's birth ere three days had passed,
Binding his feet with cords, by hands of others
On the lone mountain-side his father flung him.
So failed Apollo's word that he should slay 720
His father, and that Laïus (the fate
He feared so much) should by his son be slain.
So prophets order the affairs of men;
Whom heed not thou: for, knowledge that the god
Seeks to impart, he will himself reveal.

Oed. Bewilderment, O lady, fills my soul,
Hearing thy word, and troubles all my thoughts.

Joc. What sudden doubt hath so surprised thy mind?

Oed. Methought I heard thee say that in a place

Where three roads met was Laïus overthrown. 730

Joc. 'Twas rumoured so, and so is still believed.

Oed. Where is the spot, where this disaster chanced?

Joc. The land is Phocian, and the branching roads
From Delphi and from Daulis thither lead.

Oed. And how long is it since these things were done?

Joc. A little ere we hailed thee king of Thebes—
So long ago, came tidings of the deed.

Oed. O Zeus, what is thy will concerning me?

Joc. What is it that so moves thee, Oedipus? 739

Oed. Ask me not yet: but tell me first, how looked
This Laïus—how far was his manhood spent?

Joc. Tall, and his hair a little mixed with grey,
And in his looks not all unlike to thee.

Oed. Ah me unhappy! a grievous curse, not knowing,
Upon myself it seems that I have laid.

Joc. What dost thou say? O king, I fear thy face.

Oed. I much misdoubt the seer indeed can see.
But tell me one thing more, and I shall know.

Joc. I fear, but what thou askest I will tell.

Oed. How went he—with a slender company, 750
Or with a goodly following, like a king?

Joc. Five men were all that followed him, and one
A herald: and one chariot bore the king.

Oed. It is enough: there is no doubt. But, lady,
What man was he who told this tale in Thebes?

Joc. A servant, who alone escaped alive.

Oed. About the palace now may he be found?

Joc. Not so: for when, come thence, he saw thee throned
King in the room of Laïus who was dead, 759
He touched my hand, and prayed that I would send him
Into the fields, that he might tend the flocks,
As far from sight of Thebes as he could go;
And so he went: he was an honest slave,
And greater boon than this had well deserved.

Oed. Let him come hither again without delay.

Joc. He can be called. But what wouldst thou with him?

Oed. More than I should, I fear that I myself
Have uttered, and would speak with him of this.

Joc. The man shall come. But have not I a right
To learn, O king, what so disquiets thee? 770

Oed. What dark forebodings weigh upon my soul,
I will not hide from thee. Who if not thou
Should share the knowledge of the path I tread?
Polybus, king of Corinth, was my father,
My mother Dorian Merope. No peer
Had I in Corinth, till upon a day
An incident befell, worthy indeed
Of wonder, but not worth the heed I paid it.
For at a feast a man, heated with wine,
Called me a foundling, not my father's son. 780
And I, indignant, till that day had passed

Hardly endured, and on the next I taxed
My parents face to face; and they, incensed
Against the slanderer, brooked not that reproach.
So was I satisfied by them, and yet
The rumour grew, and stung me night and day,
Till I without my parents' knowledge came
To Delphi. But in vain: Apollo deigned
No answer to the question that I asked:
But what a tale instead, as from his lips,
I heard—of woe and horror and despair!   790
That I was doomed to marry with my mother,
And show the world a sight intolerable,
The children of that union; and to be
The murderer of the father who begat me.
And hearing this I fled—fled through the night—
Away from Corinth, never to return—
Shaping my course by starlight—to a land
Where I should never see my life fulfil
The shameful presage of that dreaded doom.
So came I to the very place whereat
I hear thee say the king, thy lord, was slain.
Queen, I will tell thee all. When, journeying,   800
I drew near to the meeting of the ways,
There did a herald meet me, and a man
Rode in a colt-drawn chariot, as thou sayest.
They met me face to face: and from the path
Servant and master both essayed to force me.

Then I in wrath struck at the charioteer,
Who turned me back: but, when the old man saw it,
Waiting until I passed, with double goad
Full on the head he smote me from above.
Heavily he paid for it.   For in a minute   810
The good staff in my hand dealt such a blow,
Backward from the mid-car he reeled and fell.
I slew them every one.   But, if this stranger
Was any kinsman of the king that's dead,
Who is more miserable than I this day?
What man could be more hated by the gods?
Whom, citizen or stranger, no one must
Receive under his roof, or speak to me,
But thrust me from his doors.   And it was I,
No other, who laid this curse upon myself.   820
And these foul hands, that did the murder, stain
The bed o' the murdered man.   Am I not vile—
Unclean, from head to foot? who must pass hence
Exiled, and passing not reseek my home
Not tread my native soil, or fear that curst
Incestuous marriage, and to slay my sire,
Polybus—from whom I sprang, who reared my youth.
Should not one justly tax the heavens with spite,
That rained down such afflictions on my head?
Let me not live, ye high and holy gods,   830
Not live to see that day, but pass away
From sight of all men first, and not behold

The blot of evil, blackening all my life!

Chor. O king, this troubles us indeed: but, till
Thou hear'st from him who saw, hope for the best.

Oed. Why, so much hope in truth is mine, to wait
The shepherd's coming: this, and only this.

Joc. And should he come—what makes thine eagerness?

Oed. I'll tell thee: if his tale agrees with thine,
Then I am free; there's nought for me to fear. 840

Joc. What in my story squared not with thy deed?

Oed. Thou saidst he spake of robbers—of a band,
Who slew the king. If the same number still
He shall report, it was not I who slew him.
One man is not mistaken for a host.
But let him speak of one sole traveller—
That turns the scale: plainly the deed was mine.

Joc. Doubt not, he told the tale as I have said,
And what he spoke he cannot now reject,
For all the city heard, not I alone. 850
But should he swerve aught from his former speech,
Yet nowise, king, the death of Laïus
Shall he show true to promise, whom the god
Foredoomed to die, slain by his babe and mine.
Yet never did that child, the hapless boy,
Slay him—but died himself before his sire;
That never again should I take pains to look
This way or that, for fear of prophecy.

Oed. I hold with thee in that. But yet send one
To bid the hind come hither: omit not this. 860
  Joc. I'll send with speed. But go we now within:
For I will nothing do but what thou wouldst.
  Chor. O may my constant feet not fail, [*Strophe* 1.
Walking in paths of righteousness,
Sinless in word and deed—
True to those eternal laws
That scale for ever the high steep
Of heaven's pure ether, whence they sprang:
For only in Olympus is their home,
Nor mortal wisdom gave them birth,
And, howsoe'er men may forget,
They will not sleep; 870
For the might of the god within them grows not old.
Rooted in pride, the tyrant grows; [*Antistrophe* 1.
But pride that with its own too-much
Is rashly surfeited,
Heeding not the prudent mean,
Down the inevitable gulf
From its high pinnacle is hurled,
Where use of feet or foothold there is none.
But, O kind gods, the noble strength,
That struggles for the state's behoof,
Unbend not yet: 880
In the gods have I put my trust—I will not fear.
But whoso walks disdainfully, [*Strophe* 2.

In act or word,
And fears not Justice, nor reveres
The thronèd gods,
Him let misfortune slay
For his ill-starred wantoning,
Should he heap unrighteous gains,
Nor from unhallowed paths withhold his feet,   890
Or reach rash hands to pluck forbidden fruit.
Who shall do this, and boast
That yet his soul is proof
Against the arrows of offended Heaven?
If honour crowns such deeds as these,
Not song, but silence, then for me!
To Earth's dread centre, unprofaned   [*Antistrophe* 2.
By mortal touch,
No more with awe will I repair,
Nor Abae's shrine,   900
Nor the Olympian plain,
If the truth stands not confessed,
Pointed at by all the world.
O Zeus supreme, if rightly thou art called—
Lord over all—let not these things escape
Thee and thy timeless sway!
For now men set at nought
Apollo's word, and cry 'Behold, it fails!'
His praise is darkened with a doubt;
And faith is sapped, and Heaven defied.   910

Joc. Elders of Thebes, 'twas borne upon my mind,
Shrines of the gods to visit, and to bring
These garlands and this incense in my hands.
The soul of Oedipus is idly stirred
With manifold misgivings; and, whereas
Wise men conclude things present from things past,
Him the last speaker sways—who speaks of fear.
Now therefore, since my counsel nought avails,
To thee, Lyceian Apollo, who art most nigh,
With these entreaties suppliant I am come, 920
That thou wouldst cleanse and make us free from guilt.
For now our hearts wax faint, beholding him,
The pilot of our ship, distraught with fear.

Mess. Friends, might I of your courtesy inquire
Where is the house of Oedipus the king?
Or, better, where is he—if this ye know?

Chor. These are his doors, O friend, and he within;
And this his wife, the mother of his children.

Mess. Blessings on her, and blessings on her house
For ever—being a perfect wife to him! 930

Joc. I wish thee back thy wishes: for no less
Deserves thy courteous speech. But wherefore, friend,
Art thou come hither—with what news to tell?

Mess. Good news, queen, to thy house, and to thy
    lord.

Joc. What news? And by whose sending art thou
    come?

Mess. I come from Corinth. Tidings I shall tell—
Joyful past doubt, yet haply sorrowful.
    Joc. What tidings—sweet and bitter in a breath?
    Mess. The people of the Isthmian land are purposed—
So there 'twas said—to have him for their king.   940
    Joc. How? Doth not the aged Polybus still reign?
    Mess. Not he: for death has laid him in the tomb.
    Joc. What sayest thou? Polybus, old man, is dead?
    Mess. Let me not live, if I have spoken falsely.
    Joc. Lose not a moment, sirrah; to thy lord
Go, tell this news. O oracles of the gods,
Where are ye now? Fearing to slay this man
Did Oedipus flee from his home—who now
In nature's course, not by his act, is dead.
    Oed. O dearest presence of my wife Jocasta,   950
Why hast thou called me hither from the house?
    Joc. Hear this man's news; hear, and perceive, to what
The boasted oracles of the gods are come.
    Oed. Who is the man? what tidings does he bring?
    Joc. From Corinth he reports that Polybus,
Thy father, lives no longer, but is dead.
    Oed. How, sirrah? From thine own lips let me hear it.
    Mess. If first thou'dst have the certainty of this
Doubt not, but know, that Polybus is dead.

Oed. Visited by sickness, or by treason slain? 960
Mess. The lives of old men hang upon a thread.
Oed. Poor soul, 'twas sickness, then, that took him off?
Mess. That, and the length of years which weighed him down.
Oed. Alas, why then, O queen, should men regard
The Delphian hearth prophetic, or the birds
That scream i' the air; by whose direction I
Was to have slain my father—but he is dead
And in his grave, and I remain, whose hand
No sword came near; unless for love of me
He pined away—and so I caused his death:— 970
But certainly this prophecy at least
Is with the dead man buried, out of mind.
Joc. Said I not from the first this would be so?
Oed. Ay, so thou didst: but me my fears misled.
Joc. Bid now thy fears farewell: despond no more.
Oed. My mother's couch how can I cease to fear?
Joc. Why should men fear, who see that chance rules all,
And forecast of the future there is none?
Careless to live, as best one can, is best.
And this unnatural union fear not thou: 980
For many a man ere now, aghast, has dreamed
Of coupling with a mother. But who sets
At naught such fancies, bears life's burden best.

Oed. All this indeed were well and wisely spoken,
Did not my mother live: but, while she lives,
How true soe'er thy words, I needs must fear.
  Joc. Is not thy father's death new sight to thee?
  Oed. Ay, *there* I see: yet dread the living mother.
  Mess. What woman is it of whom ye are afraid?
  Oed. The wife of Polybus, Merope, old man.   990
  Mess. And what see ye in her that tends to fear?
  Oed. A dreadful prophecy the god has uttered.
  Mess. May it be spoken? Or must no man know it?
  Oed. Nay, thou shalt hear. To marry with my mother—
This doom hath Loxias pronounced for me,
And with these hands to shed my father's blood.
And therefore far from Corinth many a day
My life was passed: and this was well—and yet
Into their parents' eyes men love to look.
  Mess. Was this the fear that banished thee from
      thence?   1000
  Oed. This—and my father's murderer not to be.
  Mess. What hinders then, that, as I came thy friend,
I from this fear, king, should deliver thee?
  Oed. I should not prove a niggard of my thanks.
  Mess. Indeed to this end chiefly did I come,
That I might profit by thy coming home.
  Oed. Beneath my parents' roof I may not come.
  Mess. 'Tis plain, my son, thou know'st not what thou
      doest.

Oed. What meanest thou, old man? I prithee, speak.
Mess. If for this cause thou dost avoid thy home. 1010
Oed. Yea, for I fear lest the god's word come true.
Mess. Pollution from thy parents dost thou fear?
Oed. This ever—this, old man, makes me afraid.
Mess. Then dost thou know thou startest at a shadow?
Oed. How, if these were my parents, I their son?
Mess. Because no kin was Polybus to thee.
Oed. What dost thou tell me? was he not my father?
Mess. As much—no more than I who speak to thee.
Oed. Thou'rt nought to me—how then my father's equal?
Mess. Neither from his loins didst thou spring, nor mine. 1020
Oed. How did he let me then be called his son?
Mess. From my hands he received thee as a gift.
Oed. And yet a foundling he so greatly loved?
Mess. Persuaded by his former childlessness.
Oed. Was I thine own, or purchased with thy gold?
Mess. Among Kithaeron's wooded folds I found thee.
Oed. What errand led thee to the mountain ways?
Mess. The sheep upon the mountain were my charge.
Oed. Wast thou a vagrant and a hireling shepherd?
Mess. But on that day, my son, I rescued thee. 1030
Oed. In what distress, forsaken, didst thou find me?

Mess. Thy bruisèd feet may testify of this.

Oed. Ha, thou hast harped upon an ancient grief!

Mess. I loosed thy feet, pierced through and bound with cords.

Oed. O dread memorial of my childhood's shame!

Mess. So that from this misfortune thou wast named.

Oed. By father or mother was this done? O say!

Mess. Not I, but he who gave thee, should know this.

Oed. Thou didst receive me, then, and didst not find me? 1039

Mess. Nay, from another shepherd's hands I had thee.

Oed. Who was he? Dost thou know how to describe him?

Mess. He fed the sheep of Laïus, as I heard.

Oed. Of him who was aforetime king of Thebes?

Mess. Ay, that was he: his feeder this man was.

Oed. Is the man still alive, that I may see him?

Mess. That should be best known to your Theban folk.

Oed. Is any one among the standers-by
Who knows about this hind, of whom he speaks—
Has seen him, in the city or the fields?
Speak out: the time has come to find the truth.   1050

Chor. I think he is none other than the man
Whose presence from the fields thou didst desire:
But the queen best can tell if this be so.

Oed. Lady, thou mindest him, whom we erewhile

Bade summon hither? Spake this man of him?

Joc. What skills of whom he spake? Heed not his talk:
Vainly it were remembered: let it pass.

Oed. This cannot be, that having found this clue
I should not bring my parentage to light.

Joc. As thou dost love thy life, inquire no more— 1060
I charge thee by the gods: my grief's enough.

Oed. Nay, never fear; for, though three mothers back
Should stamp me thrice a slave, thou shalt not blush.

Joc. Yet be advised, I pray thee, and forbear.

Oed. I'll not consent not to learn all the truth.

Joc. Ah, yet in prudence I advise the best.

Oed. Too long thou dost torment me with this best.

Joc. O may'st thou never know what man thou art!

Oed. Will some one go and bring the shepherd hither?
And let this woman of rich kinsmen boast. 1070

Joc. Woe to thee, miserable! no other word
Have I for thee—now or for evermore! [*She goes out.*

Chor. What sudden frenzy, Oedipus, of grief
Swept hence the queen? To mischief, much I fear,
Her passion, from this silence, will break forth.

Oed. Break forth to what it will—yet I will choose
To trace, though mean, the sources of my blood.
Perchance this woman, more than women proud,
Of my ignoble lineage is ashamed.

But I am not dishonoured, since I deem 1080
Myself a child of Fortune, ever kind.
She truly is my mother, and the months,
Her children too, have made me small and great.
This, which I am, I cannot cease to be,
That I should fear the secret of my birth.

   Chor. If with my human wit   [*Strophe.*
The future I can read—
Olympus, hear me swear,
That of Kithaeron, all the moonlit night,
When next the moon's at full,
Our praises shall not fail— 1090
Of Oedipus compatriot true,
And nurse, and mother proved:
Nor shall the mountain miss
Due meed of dance and song
For kindness rendered to our lord the king.
O Phoebus, hear our cry,
And let our prayer with thee acceptance find!

Thy mother, O fair son—   [*Antistrophe.*
Some mountain nymph was she,
In fadeless beauty clad,
Whom Pan upon the mountain saw and loved? 1100
Or her to his embrace
Did Loxias woo and win?
For well our pastoral lawns he loves:
Or else Kyllene's lord,

Or Bacchus, who delights
The mountain-peaks to haunt—
Did some fair nymph o' the Heliconian train
(His playmates best-beloved)
Leave on the hills his babe for him to find?

Oed. If I may make conjecture, friends, of one 1110
Whose face I never saw, here comes methinks
The shepherd of our quest. For, full of years,
Chimes with this man the measure of his age:
Besides, my servants lead him, whom I know—
My own: yet may my knowledge be surpassed
Perchance by thine, who hast this shepherd seen.

Chor. I know him, doubtless. No more trusty fellow
Had Laïus for a herdsman, sire, than he.

Oed. Thee, sir, who art from Corinth, first I ask,
Is this the man?

Mess.   This, whom thine eyes behold. 1120

Oed. Now, aged sir, for thee: look hither and speak
To what I ask. Didst thou serve Laïus?

Serv. Not bought, but of his household born and bred.

Oed. Minding what task—to what employment bound?

Serv. Most of my time I followed with the flocks.

Oed. And whereabouts didst thou thy shepherding?

Serv. Now 'twas Kithaeron, now some neighbour hill.

Oed. Hadst thou with this man any dealings there?

Serv. What made he there? Of what man dost thou
    ask?

Oed. Who stands before thee: hast thou met him
   ever? 1130
Serv. I cannot on the instant call to mind.
Mess. No marvel, sire, if he forgets: but soon
Clearly he shall remember. Well I know,
He knows the time when on Kithaeron's slopes
He fed two flocks together; while with one,
From springtide till Arcturus, year by year,
Three times, each time six months, I was his neighbour:
Then, for the winter, home we drove our sheep,
He to the folds of Laïus, I to mine:
Sounds this like truth, or have I dreamed it all? 1140
Serv. No dream, but truth, though it is long since then.
Mess. A child thou gavest me—dost thou remember?
A tender babe, to nurse him for my own.
Serv. What wouldst thou have? Why dost thou ask
   me this?
Mess. The child became a man: look where he
   stands!
Serv. Hence to perdition—go; and cease thy prate!
Oed. Ah, do not chide, old man, his speaking: thine
Of such reproof stands more in need than his.
Serv. Most gracious sire, wherein do I offend?
Oed. Not speaking of the child of whom he asks. 1150
Serv. This trail is false: he speaks he knows not what.
Oed. In kindness thou'lt not speak: perforce thou
   shalt.

Serv. Me, who am old, I pray thee, do not harm!

Oed. Let some one bind me, quick, this fellow's arms.

Serv. Alas, for what? What more wouldst thou be told?

Oed. Thou gavest him this child of whom he asks?

Serv. Would I had died that day! but so I did.

Oed. Thou'lt come to this, not speaking all the truth.

Serv. Much more, if I shall speak, I am undone.

Oed. This man, it seems, will palter with us yet.   1160

Serv. What paltering? Said I not, I gave the child?

Oed. Whose was the babe? another's or thine own?

Serv. Nay, none of mine: one gave him to my hands.

Oed. Which of these Thebans gave—where dwelt the man?

Serv. No more: by heaven, O king, ask me no more.

Oed. Thou art undone, if I must ask again.

Serv. Born in the house of Laïus was the child.

Oed. And of the king's blood was he, or a slave?

Serv. Now, now, ah me, the fatal word's to speak.

Oed. Fatal for me to hear: but I must hear it.   1170

Serv. His child 'twas called indeed: but one within, Thy queen, can best attest if this was so.

Oed. She gave thee, then, the babe?

Serv.   My lord, she did.

Oed. And wherefore did she so?

D

Serv.   That it might die.
Oed. O cruel mother!
Serv.   Dire prophecies she feared.
Oed. What were they?
Serv.   That the child should slay his sire.
Oed. How then gav'st thou the child to this old man?
Serv. For pity, O master: to another land
Thinking that he would bear it, whence he came.
O woful life, ill-saved! For, if thou art   1180
What this man says, thou art most miserable.
    Oed. Out and alas! so all at last comes true!
Here let me look my last upon the sun,
That sees me father'd, mother'd, wived amiss,
And, whom I should not, sees that I have slain.
    Chor. O generations of the race of men,   [*Strophe* 1.
How all as if ye were not I account
This human life ye live.
For which, O which of you may hope to win
Of bliss a larger share,   1190
Than just enough to seem,
Then from that seeming to decline?
I, with thy fate for proof,
Thine, thine, O hapless Oedipus,
May deem no mortal blest:
Who as a master-bowman cleft the mark,   [*Antistr.* 1.
And all-admired prosperity he won—

O Zeus, and is this he?—
Against that maiden with her vulture claws,
And subtle songs of doom,
He rose, a tower of strength,   1200
And slew her, and our lives redeemed:
We hailed him then our king,
Our worship at his feet we laid:
This mighty Thebes he ruled.

                                                  [*Strophe* 2.

Now what name sounds more lamentable than his?
Or who, in life's reverse,
With fierce calamity hath dwelt,
And anguish, like to this?
Where is his glory now,
Whom, entering rash that chamber, son with sire,
The same wide harbour hath received?   1211
How could, how could, O hapless Oedipus,
The furrows of thy father's field
So long in silence bear with thee?

                                            [*Antistrophe* 2.

But now all-seeing Time hath found and doomed
This thine unconscious sin—
In guilty union linked with one,
Thy mother, and thy wife.
O son of Laïus, thee
I would that never, never I had seen!
No measure of my grief I know,

Nor how my cries to stint. For, sooth to tell,   1220
Thou didst my life renew, and now
Because of thee my days are dark.

  Mess. O ye most honoured ever of this land,
What deeds your ears, your eyes, what grief your souls
Shall know, if for the race of Labdacus
Ye from your hearts are careful as of old.
Not Ister's flood, nor Phasis, as I think,
With pure ablution could make clean this house—
Such guilt it hides—and other guilt full soon,
Willing and not unwilling, shall disclose: 1230
Worst grief of all, when men afflict themselves.

  Chor. That which we knew before lacked not to be
Most lamentable; what hast thou more to tell?

  Mess. Word soonest told and soonest heard is this—
The godlike presence of the queen is dead.

  Chor. Unhappy lady, what cause had she to die?

  Mess. Her own rash act: the worst of what was done
Thou canst not know, not having it to see,
But yet, far as my memory may serve,
The tale of her undoing thou shalt hear.   1240
Soon as in that fierce mood she came inside
The porch of the house, straight to her nuptial couch
She hied, with all the strength of both her hands
Rending her hair, and violently she made
The doors upon herself, and called aloud
On Laïus, her dead lord, and made her moan

Of that her ancient childbed, whence he gat
A son that slew himself—and died and left
That mother to that son, quick-wombed to bear
Offspring accursed: O hateful marriage-bed,
Twice fruitful, whence to her, ill-starred, there sprang
Husband from husband, children from her child! 1250
So much I know, but know not how she died:
For in there burst, with outcries loud, the king,
And filled my sight: her end I might not see.
But him my eyes still followed where he roamed,
Now here, now there, craving of us a sword,
And where to find that wife, no wife indeed,
Mother and wife in one, a field twice-tilled,
That bore himself for fruit, and fruit to him.
So as he raved, some god directed him—
No man at least, of us who watched him there:
And with a dreadful cry he leapt against 1260
The folded doors, as one had led the way,
And from their sockets burst the bending bolts,
And entered. Hanging there—the queen we saw
Tight in the death-grip of a pendent cord.
With one dread voice of horror at that sight
He loosed the hanging noose, and on the ground
Laid down the piteous corse: and then we saw
A dreadful sight: for, tearing from her robe
The golden clasp that pinned its folds aright,
He smote and stabbed the circles of his eyes, 1270

Exclaiming, that on him they should not look,
What things he suffered and what things he did;
Nor see henceforth whom not to see behoved—
See and mistake those whom he craved to know.
Such burden chanting, he full many a time
With lifted hand struck at his eyes: and both
Their bleeding orbs rained forth unceasingly
Great drops of oozing gore that drenched his beard,
Two pelting showers together of dark red hail.
Such sudden doom, not single, his and hers,   1280
On both, by act of both, hath broken forth.
Gone is the former bliss, which, while it was,
Was bliss indeed: a day, and all is changed,
Wailing and woe are here, and death, and shame,
And all are here, all evils that are named.

 Chor. From grief, poor soul, what respite finds he now?

 Mess. Loudly he bids unbolt the doors, and let
All eyes in Thebes look on the parricide,
Who with his mother—unhallowed deeds he names
Nameless for me!—then from the land he will   1290
Banish himself, nor here abide the curse
Himself invoked. But strength he lacks, and one
To lead him: his affliction else is more
Than he can bear. Look for thyself. I hear
The bolts undraw. A sight thou shalt behold,
Should wring compassion even from his foes.

Chor. O woful plight for men to see,
Most woful sight that ever I have seen!
What madness, O unhappy king,
Possessed thee? On thine ill-starred life,   1300
A leap beyond all measure of how far,
What god hath leapt?
I cannot bear to look on thee,
Albeit of many things I fain would ask,
Of many things my ears, my eyes inform:
Such shuddering takes hold of me.

   Oed. Alas, alas unhappy that I am!
Whither I wend, I know not; and my voice
To the four winds of heaven is idly borne.   1310
Whereunto hath this fierce fate leapt on me?

   Chor. To horror, neither to be heard nor seen.

   Oed. O thou thick cloud of darkness,
That on my life hast settled,
Abominable, unutterable,
Indomitable,
By pitiless winds swept hitherward on me;
Alas!
And yet again, alas, and woe is me!
Such maddening pain
Of those sharp daggers at my eyes,
Blent with remembrance of my misery,
Pierces my inmost soul.

   Chor. No marvel if, in such extremity,

Thy grief is twofold, as thy suffering is.   1320
    Oed. O my good friend,
I am not then forsaken yet of thee?
O constant friend, who of thy love for me
Yet weariest not though I am blind!—Ah me!
Ah woe is me!
Spite of this darkness, yet I know thee well,
Hearing thy voice: a friend hath no disguise.
    Chor. O rash and overbold, how didst thou dare
Mar thus thy sight? What god stirred thee to this?
    Oed. Apollo, O my friends,
Apollo on my life
This evil doom, this evil doom hath laid;   1330
But no hand dealt,
No hand save mine alone, the grievous blow:
For what to me did eyes avail,
Who seeing had no pleasant sight to see?
    Chor. Even as thou sayest, so it was.
    Oed. What should my eyes behold,
Or heart desire, or ears
Take pleasure any more
Of human speech, O friends, to hear:
Convey me hence as quickly as ye may,   1340
Hence, O my friends, from all men's sight,
Me, most pernicious—me,
Of mortals most accurst,
And hated by the gods of all men most.

Chor. Would God that I had never seen thy face,
In wisdom as in fortune all unblest!
　Oed. Perish the man who found me
On the wild mountain-side,
And from the cruel cords that bound my feet　　　1350
Loosed me, and rescued me, and saved from death,
A kindness most unkind:
For then should I have died,
Not lived, to grieve my friends and vex myself.
　Chor. My wish in this consents to thine.
　Oed. So had I not my father slain,
And not been called by all the world
Husband of her from whom I sprang:
Now I am godless—son of an impious race—　　　1360
Wedded, O miserable, with her from whom I sprang.
All misery that misery exceeds
Hath Oedipus obtained.
　Chor. I know not how to say thou hast counselled
　　　well:
Better thou hadst not been than blind to live.
　Oed. That I have done what was not best to do,
Instruct me not, nor counsel any more.　　　1370
I know not with what eyes I should have met
My father face to face in the halls of death,
Or that my wretched mother—having done
Wrongs worse than hanging both to him and her.
But was the sight of children then so dear,

For me to see them, born as they were born?
Nay, to my eyes no welcome sight were they,
Nor yet this city, nor these towers of Thebes,
Nor sacred shrines o' the gods, wherefrom I wretched
Who once most nobly lived of all in Thebes   1380
Debarred myself, myself charging all men
To drive me forth, the impious one, by heaven
Proclaimed unclean—and son of Laïus.
How, having brought home to myself such guilt,
With steadfast eyes this people could I face?
Nay but, the fount of hearing in mine ears
Could I have choked withal, I had not spared
This miserable body to seal up,
That sight nor sound had reached me: could my soul
So dwell, fenced round from evil, that were bliss.   1390
Why did Kithaeron nurse me? Why not rather
Take me and slay me there, never to show
The shuddering world the secret of my birth?
O Polybus, O Corinth, and O home
That once I deemed my sire's, what festering sore
Lurked underneath your love that showed so fair!
Vile of a vile race I am found the son.
O triple ways, and dark mysterious dell,
Where 'neath the copse the three roads straitly met,
O ye that from my hands drank deep my blood,   1400
My father's that I shed, do ye remember
What deed ye saw me do, ere hither I came,

And did what deeds again? O marriage-bed
My bed of birth, that bore me, and again
By that self seed requickened gave to view
The father, brother, son, one blood with her,
That bride, both wife and mother: O horrid sight
Of deeds most shameful that on earth are done!
But, since of things ill done 'tis ill to speak,
Now by the gods make haste and hale me forth 1410
And hide me hence, or slay, or in the deep
Fling me where ye shall see me never more.
Shrink not to touch me, wretched that I am:
Fear nothing, but consent. For this my load
Of sorrow none may bear but I alone.

  Chor. Lo timely to thine asking, even now,
To do and to advise, comes Creon—he,
Who single in thy stead protects the land.

  Oed. Ah me, what speech to him shall I address?
What plea shall now suffice me? for to him 1420
All that I said before is found unjust.

  Cre. I am not come to mock thee, Oedipus,
Nor to reproach thee with the former wrong.
But ye—grown reckless that the sons of men
Should see such sight unblest, yet to the beam,
All-quickening, of the Sun-god fear to show,
Unveiled, a man impure, whom earth rejects,
And rain that drops from heaven, and holy light.
Into the house conduct him speedily.

Most right it is, the evils of their kin   1430
Kinsmen should see and hear, and none but they.

   Oed. By heaven, for thou hast plucked my fears away,
With nobleness requiting me most vile,
Grant, for thy sake, not mine, the boon I crave.

   Cre. With what request dost thou importune me?

   Oed. Make haste to banish me out of this land,
Where none shall see me, none shall speak to me.

   Cre. Surely ere now I had done this, but first
I wished to learn the pleasure of the god.   1439

   Oed. One voice we heard from him, to let me perish,
The parricide, the impious that I am.

   Cre. It was reported so: but in this need
'Twere best we should learn further what to do.

   Oed. Will ye inquire for one so miserable?

   Cre. 'Tis time that even thou shouldst trust the gods.

   Oed. Thou therefore do my bidding, and consent:—
Bury indeed the woman in the house
According to thy pleasure: 'tis thy right,
For she is thine: but doom not me alive
Here in my father's city to abide: 1450
Out on the mountain yonder let me dwell,
Kithaeron called, and mine, that living tomb
My parents gave me once to be my own:
So shall their murderous will at last be done.
And yet I know no sickness and no harm
Could touch me then: else had I not been saved

Out of that death, but to fulfil my doom.
So be that doom fulfilled, whate'er it be.
But for my children, Creon—for the boys
No need that thou shouldst care: for they are men, 1460
And cannot starve, wherever they may be—
But of my daughters twain, poor helpless maids,
Whose place at board was ever at my side,
One board for me and them, one fare for both,
And nothing that I touched they might not share—
Care thou for them: and let me, if I may,
Touch them but once, and weep, and bid farewell.
Grant this, O prince,
Out of thy noble heart. For, might I touch them,
My own, as when I saw them, they would seem.— 1470
What do I say?
O heaven, do I not hear my darlings somewhere
Weeping, and Creon has had pity on me,
And brought them here, my children, my beloved?
Is it not so?

Cre. I brought them here indeed, thee having seen
In former days delighted even as now.

Oed. O for this meeting be thou blest, and safe
In heaven's good keeping rest, more safe than I! 1479
Children, where are ye? Come hither and draw near,
To these fraternal hands, my hands that have
A goodly sight provided you to see,
Your father's eyes, dark now, that once were bright,

Since you I gat whence I myself was born,
Seeing and knowing not what now appears.
Children, I see you not, but weep for you,
Of your sad life's remainder when I think,
What life abhorred by men ye both shall lead.
Into what concourse or what festival
Of Thebans shall ye come, nor thence go home   1490
Blind with your tears, that festal sight unseen?
And, when at last for marriage ye are ripe,
Who will consent, O children, who will dare
Such scathing taunts to meet as then shall light
Both on my parents and on yours no less?
For what reproach is wanting? I, your father,
My father slew, and with the mother couched
From whom my life began; and, from the womb
That bare your sire, ye to your sire were born.
Such taunts shall ye endure. Who then will wed
    you?   1500
No man, my daughters, none; but certainly
Unwedded and unfruitful ye shall pine.
Son of Menoeceus, then—for thou art left
Sole father that they have—since parents both
They both have lost—O leave them not to wander
Begging their bread, unhusbanded, thy kin;
Let them not in misfortune rival me:
But pity them, seeing their tender years
Left destitute and friendless, but for thee.

Lay hand in mine; be noble, and consent. 1510
And you, my children, could ye mark my words,
Much had I counselled: now, pray this for me,
To live where chance will have me—but that you
A better than your father's life may find.

    Cre. Thou hast had enough of weeping: now within the house begone.

    Oed. I must do, though hard, thy bidding.

    Cre.   All things are, in season, best.

    Oed. On what terms I go, thou knowest?

    Cre.   Let me hear, then I shall know.

    Oed. From the land I must be banished.

    Cre.   With the god thy asking rests.

    Oed. Am I not of gods most hated?

    Cre.   Therefore thou shalt have thy wish.

    Oed. Is it promised?   1520

    Cre. I have said it: what I say shall be performed.

    Oed. 'Tis enough; now hence conduct me.

    Cre.   Loose thy daughters, then, and go.

    Oed. Do not take from me my children.

    Cre.   Something be content to yield:
More thou hast obtained already than thy life had well deserved.

    Chor. Look and learn, all Theban people, and this Oedipus behold,
This, that read the famous riddle, and we hailed him chief of men,

And his glory and his fortune was no Theban but
    admired—
Now upon his head the billows of disaster dire are
    poured.
Therefore, waiting still and watching for that final day of
    all,
On no mortal man the verdict 'He is happy' we pro-
    nounce,   1529
Till his goal of life he passes, clear of sorrow to the close.

OEDIPUS AT COLONUS

E

PERSONS.

Oedipus.
Theseus.
Creon.
Polyneices.
Athenian Stranger.
Messenger.
Antigone.
Ismene.
Chorus of Elders of Colonus.

Oedipus at Colonus

Oed. ANTIGONE, daughter of this old blind man,
Say to what land come we, what city of men?
Who to this houseless Oedipus will yield
The hospitable pittance of to-day?
Little indeed I crave, and, though men give
Ev'n less than little, yet so am I content.
Three teachers teach me patience—grief, and time,
Companion old—these, and a noble mind.
But now, child, look where I may sit me down:
Be it common ground or by some grove of gods—   10
Conduct me, set me there; so might we learn,
Whither we are come.   Strangers of denizens
We needs must ask, and as we hear must act.

Ant. O father Oedipus, toil-worn, far hence
I see indeed the city fenced with towers;
But, doubt not, holy ground is this, thick-set
With olive, laurel, and vine, in whose deep shade
The frequent nightingales make melody.
Here, on this unhewn slab, sit down and rest:
Far hast thou journeyed for an old man's strength.   20

Oed. Here set me then—with heed, the sightless one.

Ant. That duty I have learned, if time can teach.

Oed. Canst thou yet tell me of our whereabouts?

Ant. 'Tis Athens yonder, but this place I know not.

Oed. So much we heard from every wayfarer.

Ant. Shall I go hence, ask how the spot is called?

Oed. If men may here inhabit, surely go.

Ant. Inhabitants there are. But go belike
I need not; for I see some one approach.

Oed. Bends he toward us his steps and his intent? 30

Ant. Already he draws nigh. Whate'er thou hast
Timely to speak, speak, for the man is here.

Oed. Friend, for I learn, from who hath sight for me
And for herself, thy coming—whose timely speech
May of thy knowledge help our ignorance——

Stra. Before thou questionest farther, from this seat
Rise, get thee gone: for here no foot may tread.

Oed. What is the place? what god possesses it?

Stra. Untouched, unlodged in. For the goddesses,
Earth's and the Night's dread daughters, here abide. 40

Oed. Say by what awful name are they invoked?

Stra. Our people call them the Eumenides,
All-seeing: other names elsewhere they love.

Oed. So greet they graciously their suppliant,

As this land's sanctuary I quit no more!

Stra. What speech is this?

Oed. Speech that declares my state.

Stra. Nay, nor I dare not raise thee hence, myself—
But seek our city's warrant, how to act.

Oed. Nay, I implore thee, stranger, scorn me not,
Poor wanderer as I am—but tell me this. 50

Stra. Speak, and of me thou shalt not suffer scorn.

Oed. How call ye then this place wherein we stand?

Stra. Attend, and what's my knowledge shall be thine.
This ground indeed is sacred all, possessed
By great Poseidon, and by the god fire-fraught,
Titan Prometheus; but where thy feet are set
Men call brass-paven threshold of the land,
Coign-rock of Athens; and the neighbour fields
Boast for their prince the hero of the steed,
Colonus there, behold him; by whose name, 60
The one good name for all, his folk are called.
Thou hast it now, our hamlet's lore—unsung
Of poet, treasured in its people's love.

Oed. The place, then, hath a people of its own?

Stra. A people, truly, named after the god.

Oed. Ruled by a prince, or by the general voice?

Stra. The king o' the city is our ruler too.

Oed. Who wields such potency of voice and hand?

Stra. King Theseus, in his father Aegeus' room.

Oed. Would some one go from hence, to bring him
    hither? 70
Stra. Charged to what end to bid or urge him come?
Oed. Poor service done, to reap a rich reward.
Stra. How can a blind man do him any good?
Oed. Words I shall speak, nowise bereft of sight.
Stra. Heed, friend, meantime, my counsel:—since
    indeed
Noble thou seemest, setting thy fate aside:—
Here, where I found thee, still remain; the while,
Not in the city, but to our neighbours here,
I tell thy tale. They shall pronounce for thee
Leave to remain, or bid thee hence retire. 80
Oed. Say, hath the stranger left us, child, and gone?
Ant. Gone, father; so that thou mayest speak thy
    mind
Out freely, none to hear thy speech but I.
Oed. O dreadful Forms august, whose sanctuary,
This land's first refuge, rests these wearied limbs—
Have no illwill to Phoebus and to me—
Phoebus, who prophesied of all that grief,
But this my rest after long years foretold—
Such land my goal, where I should win at last
Of awful Powers a hospitable seat; 90
There of this weary life to make an end,
There bring a blessing where I found a home—
But to who sent, who drave me forth, a curse.

Yea, and hereof he promised sign should be,
Earthquake, or thunder-sound, or fire of Zeus.
Now then I know, this way that I have come,
It must be that an omen clear from you
Unto this grove hath led me. For not else
Into your presence first my feet had chanced—
Encountering, I who taste no wine, with you
To whom no cup is poured—nor found for seat   100
This solemn boulder-block, by axe unwrought.
Be it, O goddesses, as Apollo spake—
Grant that ev'n now my life may pass, have end—
Unless ye deem lifelong too short a while,
More than all men to have been thrall to grief.
Come ye, sweet daughters of primeval Night,
Come, city of all cities most renowned,
Athens, by mightiest Pallas claimed her own,
Pity this, once a man, once Oedipus,
Poor phantom now—wreck of mine ancient self!   110

   Ant. No more, for to espy thy resting-place
Come hither certain elders, bowed with age.

   Oed. Nay, I am mute; and thou, lead from the way,
Hide me within the grove here, till I learn
Out of their speech their purpose. Learning that,
We shall proceed with caution to our end.

   Chor. Look, then. What was he? Where lurks he
      now?   [*Strophe.*
This bold, this unabashed intruder— [*They search for him.*

Flown hence and gone, ye see; gone whither? 120
Make quest for him, look for him,
On all sides search and seek!
Some wandering fellow, doubt it not,
Strange to the place: not else had he dared
Invade this unfrequented grove,
Where the resistless Maidens dwell,
Whose names we dare not utter,
Whose presence pass with eyes averted, 130
Speechlessly, wordlessly, breathing only
The voiceless breath of a reverent thought—
So we: but now, we hear, hath come
Some impious one who knows no fear:
For whom I look, the precinct through,
But look in vain, discovering not
Where all the while he hides.

   Oed. I, whom ye seek, am here: for you
I see with ears, as the proverb is.   [*He discovers himself.*
   Chor. Alas! 140
Out, horrid sight and horrid sound!
   Oed. Lawless, I charge ye, deem me not!
   Chor. Zeus shield us, what can the old man be?
   Oed. You shall not, guardians of this state,
Admiring, rank my fortunes high.
Ye see me what I am, whose steps
Are guided by another's sight,
Whose strength on weakness leans for help.

Chor. Ah me, for pity! What! blind beside? 150
                                                     [*Antistrophe.*
Quite gone, thy sight? 'Tis easy guessing,
Thy length of days is length of sorrow.
These curses, with leave of mine,
Thou shalt not add thereto.
Trespass enough; be warned, nor plunge
Deep in yon silent heart of the glade,
Whose grass-lipped basin's woodland pool
Fills with the confluence downward-drawn
Of streamlets softly flowing— 160
Their peace, all-hapless one, disturb not,
Dare not to enter, come forth, come hither! . . .
Too wide a distance divides our speech.
O toil-worn wanderer, hear'st thou me?
But, hast thou any word to speak
And seek advice, from hallowed ground
Hither remove, where all may tread—
Here speak; or else refrain.

    Oed. Daughter, I know not what to think. 170
    Ant. Father, this people's will is ours:
To yield with no ill grace were best.
    Oed. Lend, then, thy hand.
    Ant.   In thine 'tis placed.
    Oed. Ye for my safety, friends, are bound:
I come, relying on your faith.
    Chor. Rest yonder; none of us, old man,

Will drag thee thence against thy will.

Oed. What, further? [*Strophe.*

Chor. A little further still. [*He comes out.*

Oed. And still?

Chor. Conduct him, maiden:
Still onward lead him; thou canst see.

Ant. Follow me, father, follow hither,
With poor blind feet, the way I lead.

. . . .

Chor. An alien in an alien land,
Thou'rt bold amiss; be bold to yield—
Hate where this people cherish hate,
And honour what they love.

Oed. Conduct me, child,
Where, safe in paths of piety,
Unchidden we may hear and speak:
To struggle with our fate were vain.

Chor. There stay thy steps, nor stray beyond
Yon platform of confronting rock.

Oed. Thus far? [*Antistrophe.*

Chor. I have said, no further go.

Oed. But sit?

Chor. Ay, on the stone's edge
Sit, sideways bending, stooping low.

Ant. My office, father: slowly, gently—
But first thy foot adjust to mine.

Oed. Ah, woe is me!

Ant. Then forward on my loving arm   200
Lean thou thy weight of years.

Oed. O frenzied, fatal work!

Chor. Now that thy boldness somewhat yields,
Declare to us thy parentage:
Who art thou, miserably led?
What country is thy home?

Oed. O strangers, city have I none:
But spare, O spare me this.

Chor. What have we done, that we should spare?

Oed. Forbear, forbear, to ask my name;   210
Let me alone and ask no more.

Chor. What now?

Oed.   My birth, ah horror!

Chor.   Reveal it.

Oed. How shall I answer them, O my daughter?

Chor. Tell us, O stranger, what sire begat thee?

Oed. Ah, child, tell me, what must I do?

Ant. Speak; for escape is none, or evasion.

Oed. Yes, I will speak what I may not hide.

Chor. Long ye delay: come, tell us quickly.

Oed. Have ye heard of a son of Laïus . . .

Chor.   Ah!   220

Oed. Heir of the house of Labdacus . . .

Chor.   Shield us!

Oed. Miserable Oedipus?

Chor.   *Thou art he?*

Oed. Fear not to hear me tell my tale.

                      [*They drown his voice with clamour.*

Oed. Unlucky that I am!

                            [*The tumult continues.*

Oed. Daughter, what think you they intend?

Chor. Out of the land—avoid! begone!

Oed. Your promise how will ye redeem?

Chor. Heaven is just, nor exacts from the wronged one
Requital for wrongs he requiteth: and guile,   230
When for guile it is rendered again, like for like,
To the giver gives back, for his own, not a boon,
But a bane. From thy resting-place rise and begone,
And my land and its shelter forego, at thy speediest,
Lest of thy guilt on us
Heavier yet be imposed the burthen.

   Ant. O strangers, yet be merciful:
And though ye suffer not
My old blind father, hearing fame
Of how unwittingly he sinned—   240
Yet upon me, the unfortunate, strangers, have pity—
     regard me, I pray—
Who for my father alone your compassion
Entreat—yes, entreat—not with eyes that are blind
In your eyes gazing full—standing here to be seen,
As your daughters might plead with you—all, that this
     man

May get pity.   Nay, for as gods we wretched
Lean on you, helpless beside.   But oh, grant us the
    boon, ye who now bid despair;
Yea, by your children, your own, whom ye love—   250
All that moves, that constrains you—the gods whom ye
    fear—
For in vain shall ye look for such strength in mortality,
Strong, if a god shall lead—
Strong to be free, and escape his leading.
   Chor. Daughter of Oedipus, of this be sure—
We pity your misfortunes, thine and his :
But, reverencing the gods, we may not speak
Another word than that which we have spoken.
   Oed. Of praise then, and of honourable report
What profit, squandered on the barren air?
Have I not heard, your Athens fears the gods   260
Indeed—and strangers, outcast and distressed,
That she alone can save, alone protect?
But now to me what succour? raised by you,
A suppliant, from these rocks, by you cast forth,
Because my name affrights you ; since myself
Ye do not fear—no, nor my deeds—deeds truly
To suffering than to doing more akin,
Might I recount my parents' part in them—
Theirs, for whose sake ye shun me.   This I know
Full surely.   Nay, but where's the guilt i' the grain   270
Of me, who struck the striker? when, had I known

What deed I did, not even this were guilt—
But I not knowing rushed blindfold on my doom.
Not so did they; aware, they sought my life.
Now therefore by the gods I charge you, friends,
Even as ye lifted me, so succour me;
And, having withal such reverence of the gods,
Set not your gods at nought; but rather think
Their eyes behold on earth the righteous man,
And of the impious make account, nor ever   280
Was mortal yet unholy, and escaped.
With whom at one, stoop to no impious deed,
Nor hide the light of Athens, their beloved.
Your faith is plighted to the suppliant here:
Defend me and deliver—scorn me not,
Because uncômely ye behold my form.
A holy man, reverent, I come; and bring
Advantage to this people.   When he comes
Whose will is law, lord of the land, your king,
Ye shall hear all and understand; but now,   290
Until he come, forbear, and keep your faith.

   Chor. Much need, old man, have we to pause and
       fear,
Such thoughts hast thou suggested, shaped in words
Of no light import.   Therefore be it so;
The rulers of the land—they shall decide.

   Oed. But where, O strangers, is your lord the king?
   Chor. From the city of his fathers, where he dwells,

One who sent me, is gone to seek and send him.
 Oed. Think ye that for a blind man he will care,
And so regard me, hither himself to come?   300
 Chor. Doubt not of that, when he shall hear thy name.
 Oed. But who will go and bear him this report?
 Chor. 'Tis far to go: but rumour in the air
Flies thick, the talk of travellers; hearing which
Fear not but he will come. Much noised, thy name,
Old man, all ears hath entered: roused by that
From sloth, from slumber, quickly will he haste.
 Oed. So coming, may he bless the state he rules,
And me. Kind to themselves are all good men.   309
 Ant. Zeus, what is this? What shall I say or think?
 Oed. What see you, child, Antigone?
 Ant.   I see
Come riding on a swift Aetnaean colt
Toward us a maiden, but her face is hid
By a Thessalian hat that shades the sun.
What shall I say?
Is it, or is it not? Am I deceived?
It is, and is not, and I know not which.
Alas, I cannot tell.
Yes, it is she. See with what joyful eyes
She greets me, coming. Now no doubt, it is   320
Ismene's self, no other, plain to see.
 Oed. How say you, daughter?
 Ant.   That I see thy child,

My sister : soon her voice shall make her known.

 Ism. O father and O sister, names to me
Linked in a double dearness—hardly found,
How hardly now I see you for my grief!

 Oed. Child, art thou come?

 Ism.   Father, thy woful plight!

 Oed. My child, come back?

 Ism.   Come, many a weary mile.

 Oed. Daughter, give me thy hand.

 Ism.   A hand to each.

 Oed. O children—sisters!

 Ism.   O unhappy life!   330

 Oed. Mine, and this maid's?

 Ism.   Ill-fated, mine no less.

 Oed. What brings thee, child?

 Ism.   Father, my care of thee.

 Oed. To see me?

 Ism.   Tidings, too, myself to bear—
With the one faithful servant that I have.

 Oed. Young are thy brothers : where at need were
   they?

 Ism. They work their work. A sorry tale to tell!

 Oed. O altogether, in the hearts of them,
Conformed to ways of Egypt, and in life!
For there all day the men within the house
Sit at the loom, and let their womankind   340
Outside slave ever for the daily bread.

So, daughters, ye—while they to whom belonged
These toils, girl-like, shut doors and keep the house—
Ye in their stead with toil are ministrant
To my affliction. One, from when she grew
Past childhood's nursing to a woman's strength,
Hath ever shared my wandering grievous life,
Prop of my aged steps, full oft astray
Barefoot and fasting in wild woodland ways,
And oft with rain, and oft with fierce noon-heat,   350
Poor soul, distressed, yet for the life at home
Repines not, might but I have bread to eat.
And thou, my daughter, barest to me before,
Asking no Theban leave, all that the god
Foretold concerning me;—and staunch and true
Wast thou in the peril, when they banished me:—
And now again what tidings hast thou brought,
Ismene? What occasion sped thee hither?
Since not for nought thou comest, that I know
Full well, but bringing some new fear to me.   360

 Ism. Father, my toil and trouble by the way,
Seeking thy place of sojourn and abode,
Let pass unsaid. Why should I twice be grieved,
Recounting now all that I suffered then?
What storm about thy two unhappy sons
Now gathers—I am come to tell thee this.
For at the first rivals they were, to cede
The throne to Creon, nor pollute the state,

Fearing the memories of the ancient curse,
About thy miserable house that clung: 370
But then some god and their infatuate hearts
Pricked them, to seize, O fools thrice miserable,
Rivals in guilt, the kingdom and the crown.
And now thy younger son, the headstrong boy,
The elder, Polyneices, of his throne
Hath dispossessed and banished from the land.
And rumour now is rife that he is gone,
Exiled, to Argos in the vale, and finds
Alliance there in marriage, gathers head;
And boasts that Argos in the fall of Thebes 380
Shall triumph straight, or lift her to the skies.
No tale of idle words, father, is this,
But dreadful fact; nor can I see the end,
When heaven will have compassion on thy griefs.

Oed. Wast thou so fond indeed, to hope the gods
Would yet take thought for my deliverance?

Ism. Such hope the latest oracle inspired.

Oed. Yea, in what sort? What hath the god foretold?

Ism. That unto thee one day the folk of Thebes,
Living or dead, shall look, to work their weal. 390

Oed. Who could get good from such an one as I?

Ism. 'Tis said that on thy help depends their strength.

Oed. Am I a man, now, when my years are spent?

Ism. The gods, who erst would slay, uplift thee now.

Oed. 'Tis ill uplifting old, who young fell down.

Ism. Moreover, know that Creon for this cause
Will seek thee—soon, and at no distant day.

Oed. With purpose what to do? Explain thy speech.

Ism. To make thee dwell not far from Thebes, within
Their power, without the confines of the land.   400

Oed. Laid at their gates, how can I profit them?

Ism. They rue thy burial, if it chance amiss.

Oed. Why, that were clear without an oracle.

Ism. Therefore they fain would set thee hard at hand,
Not leave thee where thou'rt master of thyself.

Oed. What, will they cover me with Theban dust?

Ism. Thou hast shed kindred blood: they may not
   so.

Oed. Masters of me, then, they shall never be.

Ism. Hereof shall grow matter for Thebes to rue.

Oed. In what far-off conjuncture of events?   410

Ism. Of thy displeasure, when at thy tomb they stand.

Oed. Whence hast thou, daughter, this intelligence?

Ism. So said the envoys from the Delphic hearth.

Oed. Of me this also hath the god foretold?

Ism. If they speak true, who came from him to
   Thebes.

Oed. Hath either of my sons heard this report?

Ism. Yea, both alike, and know that this is so.

Oed. Yet, knowing this, did they, unnatural both,
Set sovereignty before their love of me?

Ism. Such news, most grievous to mine ears, I bring. 420
Oed. But may the gods of this predestined strife
Quench not the heat, and would that it were mine
To rule the issue of the fatal fray,
Whereto they now set hand and lift the spear:
For neither should who now is lord and king
Continue, neither he who hath gone forth
Return again—false sons, who, when their sire
From hearth and home thus shamefully was thrust,
Forbade not, nor avenged it, but unhoused
They let me go, my exile heard proclaimed. 430
Say you, it was my wish—'twas fitly done—
The state then granted me the boon I asked?
I tell you, no: that first, that dreadful day,
My heart so hot within me, when most sweet
Had been to die and to be stoned with stones,
No friend was found to give me my desire.
But then, when time had mellowed all that grief,
And my remorse had erred, I knew, in wild
Self-judgment for the sins that I had sinned—
Why, then it pleased the state to banish me, 440
Too late, unwilling; and the twain my sons,
Sons with the power, lacked yet the will, to help
Their father—whom a little word had saved;
Homeless I wandered forth to beg my bread.
And whilst to these, according to their strength,
Weak maidens both, I owe my wants supplied,

This land's safe shelter, and their filial care,
Those sacrificed their father for a throne,
To wield the sceptre and usurp the realm.
Friend and ally they shall not find in me, 450
Nor shall it profit them to have reigned in Thebes,
Full well I know, hearing the prophecies
This maiden brings, and pondering with myself
The things that Phoebus promised long ago.
Now therefore let them send to seek for me
Creon, and who beside in Thebes is great:
For if it be your pleasure, O my friends,
With these majestic Guardians of the place,
To save me—for your city ye shall win
A strong deliverer, and confound my foes. 460

Chor. Worthy compassion, Oedipus, ye are,
Thou and thy daughters; but, to this regard
Since our deliverance to be wrought by thee
Is added, best advice I have be thine.

Oed. All that thy friendship counsels, I will do.

Chor. Make then atonement to the Powers, who first
Received thee, and whose grove thy foot profaned.

Oed. How shall I make atonement? Teach me, friends.

Chor. Draw first and bring, handling with holy hands,
Sacred libations from the fountain's source. 470

Oed. The draught unmixed when I have brought, what then?

Chor. Then there are bowls, fair-wrought of skilful hands,
Whose edge and twin symmetric handles crown. . . .
Oed. With crowns of leafage, or of wool, or what?
Chor. Wool of an eanling lamb and newly clipt.
Oed. Good; and thereafter how conclude the rite?
Chor. Pour forth libations, fronting to the dawn.
Oed. From the urns ye spake of, shall I pour them forth?
Chor. A threefold stream: filled to the brim, the last.
Oed. Wherewith shall it be filled? this teach me too. 480
Chor. Water and honey; but of wine no drop.
Oed. And when the sunless earth hath drunk of this?
Chor. Set in it sprays of olive, three times nine,
From both thy hands, and pray these prayers the while.
Oed. Ay, let me hear the prayers: this most imports.
Chor. That, as we call them gracious, so they will
Their suppliant graciously receive and save—
Thyself, or else some other in thy stead,
Pray, under breath, not lifting up thy voice;
Then go, nor look behind thee. Do thou this, 490
And boldly I will dare to stand thy friend;
But, this undone, I am afraid for thee.
Oed. Children, have ye heard these denizens of the place?
Ant. We heard, and wait thy bidding what to do.
Oed. I cannot go, for lack of strength indeed

And lack of sight—two evils, old and blind:
Go, one of you, and do as they require.
This rite, methinks, ten thousand should not pay
Better than one—one kindly heart and true.
But do the thing with speed, and leave me not   500
Untended: all too weak my strength would be
To walk alone, without some hand to lead.

   Ism. I will perform the rite; but, ere I go,
Where I must seek the spot, I fain would learn.

   Chor. Beyond this grove, O maiden. There, if aught
Thou needest more, dwells one, who will explain.

   Ism. So to my task: meanwhile, Antigone,
Guard thou our father, here. For parents done,
Of toilsome service we forget the toil.

   Chor. The ancient grief from its lair, O stranger,
     I fear to arouse,   [*Strophe.*   510
But yet I fain would hear. . . .

   Oed. What wouldst thou hear?

   Chor. Of thine encounter, how it fell,
With sorrow, pitiful, past redress.

   Oed. Nay, kind and hospitable men,
Strip not of silence this my shame.

   Chor. Nay, for rumour is rife and ceases not,
I would hear from thy lips the tale aright.

   Oed. Ah, woe is me!

   Chor.   Ah, yet be content, I pray thee.

Oed. Alas, alas!

Chor. Grant my desire, as I grant thee thine. 520

Oed. Suffering was mine to endure, O strangers, God
knoweth, was mine, [*Antistrophe.*
Doing I knew not what.

Chor. But tell us how?

Oed. Bound by the state, all unaware,
With cursèd nuptials, a fatal bride.

Chor. And was the couch, men call (O name
Of shame) thy mother's, filled by thee?

Oed. Every word, O my friends, is sharp like death
In mine ears: but in truth these are my own. . . . 530

Chor. What wilt thou say?

Oed. Two daughters, two curses rather. . . .

Chor. What do I hear?

Oed. Sprung from the womb that conceived their sire.
[*Strophe* 2.

Chor. What, these thy children were indeed . . . ?

Oed. Yea, were own sisters of their sire.

Chor. Alas!

Oed.   Alas indeed—
Dire visitation of unmeasured ills!

Chor. Thou hast suffered. . . .

Oed. What I have suffered, how shall I forget?

Chor. Thou hast wrought. . . .

Oed.   Nay, nothing wrought.

Chor.   What then?

Oed. Say rather, I received from Thebes
A gift—O never to receive
Such prize as this, to break my heart, 540
I helped her at her need!   [*Antistrophe* 2.

Chor. Yet tell me—hapless, didst thou slay. . . .
Oed. What now? what is it thou wouldst learn?
Chor. Thy sire?
Oed.   Ah, there again—
A second thrust! distress upon distress.
Chor. Thy father!
Oed. I slew my father; yet was not the deed . . .
Chor. O speak!
Oed.   Without excuse.
Chor.   How then?
Oed. Nay, ye shall hear: for caught, surprised,
I struck, I dealt that fatal blow:
The law acquits me of the guilt—
I struck I knew not whom.

Chor. Lo where the son of Aegeus, at thy call,
Obedient to the summons, hither comes. 550

Thes. Hearing from many in the former time
That violence done upon thy bleeding eyes,
I know thee, son of Laïus: and my knowledge
Signs I have gathered by the way confirm.
For both thy garb and that disfeatured face
Proclaim thee who thou art: and pitying thee,
Unhappy Oedipus, I fain would ask

With what petition to the state and me
Thou comest—thou and this thy sad companion.
Answer me : thou hadst need to tell a case   560
Dreadful indeed, whence I should stand aloof,
Knowing that I an alien passed my youth,
As thou ; and, no man more, in alien lands
Endured the frequent peril of my life :
Now therefore from a stranger, as thou art,
I cannot turn aside, refusing help.
I also am a man ; and may not count,
No more than thou, to-morrow for my own.

   Oed. Theseus, thy courtesy asks brief response,
Of tedious speech dispensing me the need.   570
For, who I am, already thou hast said,
Son of what sire, citizen of what land,
Nor more remains save only that, wherein
I need thy help, I say, and make an end.

   Thes. This and no more it is, I wait to hear.

   Oed. I come to offer thee this wretched body,—
No goodly gift indeed to outward view,
But more than beauty is the gain it brings.

   Thes. What manner of gain imports this vaunted gift ?

   Oed. Hereafter shalt thou know, but hardly now.   580

   Thes. But when shall be disclosed the benefit ?

   Oed. When I am dead, and thou hast buried me.

   Thes. Life's latest boon thou cravest : all between
Thou either hast forgotten or despised.

Oed. All other boons to me are summed in this.
Thes. In little room the favour is contained.
Oed. Look to it well; not small shall be the peril.
Thes. By reason of thy children, or from whom?
Oed. They would compel me—to convey me thither.
Thes. Consent then, or thine exile is thy fault. 590
Oed. When I myself consented, they forbade.
Thes. O foolish, in misfortune to be proud.
Oed. Hear first and then admonish: now, forbear.
Thes. Say on: for I will judge before I speak.
Oed. Wrong heaped on wrong, Theseus, I have endured.
Thes. Of the old affliction of thy birth thou'lt speak?
Oed. Nay, for of that all Hellas tells the tale.
Thes. What, passing human sufferance, hast thou suffered?
Oed. Thus stands my case—by my own flesh and blood
Exiled for ever from my native land, 600
A parricide, never to be restored.
Thes. How should they claim thee then, to live apart?
Oed. The warning of the god enforces them.
Thes. What peril hath the oracle foreshown?
Oed. Defeat they needs must suffer, in this land.
Thes. Whence should grow enmity 'twixt me and them?
Oed. O son of Aegeus, friend, to gods alone

Comes neither age nor death to make an end:
All-conquering time confounds all else that is.
Strength of the earth decays, and strength of man,   610
And faith grows faint and dies, and doubt is born;
And the same spirit never of friend and friend,
Or state with state, abides unchangingly.
For, soon or late, comes there a time to all,
When sweet grows bitter, and again is dear;
And, though to-day fair weather bodes no storm
'Twixt Thebes and thee, yet countless nights and days
Time in his countless course engendereth,
Wherein they shall, upon some trivial cause,
Fling to the winds of war this plighted peace,   620
Even there, above my grave, where laid on sleep
My clay, death-cold, shall drink their warm life-blood—
If Zeus be Zeus, and Phoebus still his prophet.
But, for I shrink fate's secrets to disclose,
Here let me end where I began; keep thou
Thy faith, thou shalt not say that in this place
To Oedipus thou gavest room to dwell
For nought, unless the gods will play me false.

  Chor. O king, these words before and like to these
We heard him promise that this land should prove.   630

  Thes. How shall I then reject the proffered love
Of such an one, to whom, ally and friend,
A place beside our hearth belongs by right;
And now he comes, a suppliant to the gods,

Nor pays light tribute to this land and me.
Such claims command my reverence, nor to slight
His friendship, but receive him for our guest.
And if his pleasure be to sojourn here,
On thee I charge his safety; if to go
With me—choose, Oedipus, of this and that, 640
According to thy will: thy will is mine.

Oed. All men of liberal soul may Zeus reward!

Thes. What is thy pleasure? Wilt thou go with me?

Oed. So, if I might, I would. But in this place—

Thes. What in this place shall be? I thwart thee not.

Oed. Here they who cast me forth shall feel my might.

Thes. So should thy presence prove great boon to us.

Oed. Only hold fast thy word, to make it good.

Thes. Fear not for me: thou shalt not be betrayed.

Oed. I will not bind thine honour with an oath. 650

Thes. It should not serve thee better than my word.

Oed. What wilt thou do?

Thes.   What fear disquiets thee?

Oed. Men will come hither. . . .

Thes.   Trust our friends for that.

Oed. Beware lest leaving me. . . .

Thes.   I know my part.

Oed. My fears are urgent. . . .

Thes.   Fear my heart knows none.

Oed. Thou know'st not how they threaten.

Thes.   But I know

No man shall drag thee hence in my despite.
Oh many threats full many a braggart word
Have hotly threatened—but the passion cools,
And reason reigns, the bubble threats are gone! 660
And they, however bold to speak great words,
Shall find, I know, or ere they steal thee hence,
Wide seas and boisterous are first to cross.
Enough—if Phoebus sent thee, though my will
Were not to help, small need thou hast to fear;
But now I know, ev'n though I be not nigh,
My name shall guard thee, safe from all misuse.

 Chor. To the land of the steed, O stranger,

           [*Strophe* 1.

To the goodliest homes upon earth thou comest—
White-cliffed Colonus, this, 670
Loud with the melody piercing sweet
Of nightingales that most delight
Its deep green glades to haunt—
Lovers old of the ivy sheen
And the myriad-berried thick-leaved bower
Of the grove of the god, no foot profanes,
Sunproof, nor vexed by wind,
Whatever storms may blow;
Where Dionysus, wandering still, enrapt,
Waits on the heavenly maids, his nurses once. 680
And the clustering fair narcissus   [*Antistrophe* 1.
Eve by eve out of heaven the fresh dew drinketh—

Meet for the mighty brows,
Erst at Eleusis its florets graced—
And bright the crocus springs like gold:
Nor fail the sleepless founts,
Whence, Cephisus, thy streams are fed;
But they flow, and the quick-conceiving plains
Of the bountiful-bosomed earth are glad,
Undwindling, day by day,   690
Of thine untainted shower:
Nor hath such haunt displeased the Muses' choir,
Nor Aphrodite of the golden rein.
A marvel now,   [*Strophe* 2.
Of Asian soil I have not heard,
Nor that its like in the great Dorian home,
Island of Pelops, ever sprang—
A tree grows here, self-sown, inviolate—
A tree, the terror of all hostile spears,
And o'er the land its boughs are spread—   700
That grey-leaved olive's parent-shade,
Which never chieftain, young or old,
Although he smite, shall bring to nought:
So guards it Morian Zeus with sleepless watch,
And the grey-eyed Athene loves it well.
Another praise   [*Antistrophe* 2.
Of this our mother and our home,
Boon of the mighty god, her proudest boast,
Best praise of all, I have to sing—   710

Land of fair steeds, fair foals, and fairest sea.
For, son of Cronos, lord Poseidon, thou
Didst at such height of boasting set
Our streets for which was shaped by thee
The bit that heals the horse's rage:
And the oar-blade wings its wondrous way,
Sped by stout arms, and bounding o'er the wave—
The Nereïds' hundred feet no faster flee.

Ant. O land whose praises in our ears are loud, 720
These glowing words the time hath come to prove.

Oed. Daughter, what peril?

Ant. Peril near at hand:
Creon, not unattended, hither comes.

Oed. O good old men, if now ye fail me not,
The goal of my deliverance is in sight.

Chor. Doubt not thy safety. What though I be old?
The strength at least of Athens time hath spared.

Cre. Good friends and noble citizens of this land,
I see within the eyes of all of you
Some fear of my intrusion, fresh portrayed; 730
But shun me not, nor blame with hasty speech:
For hither, charged with words, not deeds, I come,
I who am old, and know that ye are strong,
Ye and your city—in Hellas stronger none.
But I, thus old and weak, was sent to bring
This man by mild persuasion back to Thebes—
Not sent by one man's sending, but by all,

All with one voice insistent, since to me
To mourn a kinsman's sufferings most belonged.
Then, Oedipus, unhappy one, consent, 740
With me return.   All Thebes cries out for thee—
Just claimants all—but none so just as I,
My right, unless I be of men most base,
The right of deepest pity for thy wrongs,
Beholding thus thy piteous alien plight,
Alien and homeless, and thy scanty fare,
And this one woman's arm that props thee, who—
Alas, I had not thought she could have fallen
Unto this depth of misery that I see,
The hapless one, thee and thy poor blind eyes 750
In beggared state still tending—maiden yet,
Who should be wife, the first rough hand may snatch.
Ah me, and must I cast, on thee and me
And all our race, intolerable shame?
Nay, for one may not hide what seeks the light,
Hide thou the shame, O by our fathers' gods—
Yea, hear me, Oedipus—consent—return
To thine own city and thy father's home,
With loving speech to Athens, as is fit,
But Thebes, thine ancient nurse, claims reverent deeds. 760

  Oed. All shameless, and all reckless whence thou weavest
The fine fair mask of honourable words,
What vain attempt is this, a second time

To trap me—in the snare, would gall me most?
For at the first, when, with my proper griefs
O'erburthened, all my prayer was 'Banish me,'
Thy will was not as mine to grant me this;
But, when I had my fill of fierce remorse,
And now my comfort was to live at home,
That was thy time to thrust me from the doors— 770
This bond of kinship was forgotten then:
And now, no sooner hast thou seen this state
And people entertain me for a friend,
Thou'dst pluck me hence with cruel courtesies. '
Such love enforced, I count it no more kind
Than if to thine entreaty one were deaf—
'He could not give,' 'he had no mind to help'—
But, when thy soul was sated of thy wish,
Lo, he should proffer then the graceless grace:
Were't not a barren pleasure thou shouldst taste? 780
Yet are thy gifts to me no more than thus,
Fair in the sound, but in the substance nought.
Nay, these shall hear, how I will prove thee base.
Thou'lt bear me hence, not to conduct me home,
But outdoors pension me, that so thy town
Her reckoning with this land may 'scape unscathed.
Another way I read your fortunes: there,
Lodged in your midst, my curse, for evermore;
And, for the heritage of those my sons,
Room in my land enough, wherein to die. 790

Shall Thebes not own my wisdom passing thine?
Yea, wiser far, by truer teachers taught,
By Phoebus, and his father, Zeus supreme.
But thou com'st here with counterfeit fair speech,
With glozing tongue sharp-edged; but all thy talk
Shall win thee more of mischief than of good.
Yet, for I know thou'rt warned in vain, begone,
And leave me here to dwell; for not amiss,
Howe'er amiss, I dwell, contented so.

   Cre. Who loses in our parley, thinkest thou?   800
Foils me thy fence, or hast thou foiled thyself?

   Oed. If neither me, nor these who hear us both,
Thou canst persuade, I have what I desire.

   Cre. Poor soul, grown grey, but none the more grown
        wise,
That liv'st to blot with shame the name of age!

   Oed. Thy tongue bites shrewdly; but I have not seen
The honest man, all themes made eloquent.

   Cre. The many words not always cleave the mark.

   Oed. Thine are so few, and all exact of aim!

   Cre. Nay, not to one whose wit is such as thine.   810

   Oed. Begone—for I will speak for these—nor here
With prowling siege beset my destined home.

   Cre. Judge these 'twixt thee and me: but for the words
Thou answerest thy friends with, when thou'rt ta'en—

   Oed. Who takes me, and defies such friends as these?

   Cre. Nay, short of this, I shall afflict thy soul.

Oed. 'Tis threatened well: but where's the deed to match?

Cre. Of thy two daughters one's my prisoner,
Packed hence already: and this one follows her.

Oed. O heaven!

Cre. Louder thou'lt call on heaven soon. 820

Oed. Thou hast my child?

Cre. And this child soon shall have.

Oed. O friends, what will ye? Now forsake me not,
But drive this impious fellow from the land.

Chor. Sirrah, with haste depart: unrighteous deeds
Thou both hast done before, and now wouldst do.

Cre. Good now, bestir; if she will go, 'tis well—
If not, unwilling hence she must be borne.

Ant. Ah, wretched, whither shall I flee? what help
Seek, or of gods or men?

Chor. What wouldst thou, sirrah?

Cre. She is my own: this man I shall not touch. 830

Oed. O for the king to help!

Chor. The deed's unjust.

Cre. 'Tis just.

Chor. How just?

Cre. I carry hence my own.

Oed. Great city, help!

Chor. What wilt thou? Release her,
Or prove thy strength with us.

Cre. Stand back there.

Chor. But first then relinquish thy purpose.
Cre. 'Tis war with Thebes, if ye lay hands on me.
Oed. Is it not come to pass as I foretold?
Chor. Unhand the maiden—quick!
Cre. Command thy slaves.
Chor. Loose her, I say.
Cre. I say, she must along. 840
Chor. What ho, a rescue! Neighbours, help!
My city is despoiled, is robbed.
Friends, to the rescue haste.
Ant. O friends, I am too weak; they drag me hence.
Oed. Where art thou, daughter?
Ant. Torn from thee away.
Oed. Reach hither, child, thy hands.
Ant. My hands are fast.
Cre. Away with her!
Oed. O miserable me!
Cre. Good, so this pair of crutches shall not prop
Thy steps again: but since thou hast a mind
To overbear thy country and thy friends 850
(Whose bidding, though a prince, I have performed),
Why, have thy way. So shalt thou know, too late,
That to thyself no friend's part hast thou played,
Now, or before, self-willed in friends' despite,
Slave still of passion, that hath wrecked thy life.
Chor. Sirrah, stand there.
Cre. Lay not thine hands on me.

Chor. Give back thy captives, else thou shalt not go.

Cre. Be warned, or Thebes shall wrest a costlier prize:
For not these women only will I seize.

Chor. Whither wilt thou turn?

Cre.   I will bear hence this man.   860

Chor. Bold words are these.

Cre.   No longer words, but deeds—
Unless your king himself shall hinder me.

Oed. O shameless voice! wilt thou lay hands on me?

Cre. Hold thou thy peace.

Oed.   Ye guardian Powers o' the place,
Yet one prayer more before the silence falls!
O thou most base, who, when my eyes were out,
These poor remains of sight hast plucked away—
May Helios hear me, who from heaven sees all—
Hear and reward thee, thee and all thy race,
With such old age as mine, afflicted so.   870

Cre. People of this land, see ye how I am used?

Oed. They see us both, and seeing note that I
Thy violent deeds have but repaid with words.

Cre. My rage I'll curb no more: though I'm alone
And slow with age, I'll bear thee hence by force.

Oed. O piteous plight!

Chor. Bold art thou, O stranger,
If this thou think'st to do.

Cre. I'll do it.

Chor. This city I'll hold then no city.
Cre. In the just cause the small o'erthrows the great.
Oed. Hear ye what words he speaks?
Chor. But make them good Zeus knows he shall not. 880
Cre. Zeus may know, not thou.
Chor. Insolence!
Cre. Insolence that ye must brook.
Chor. O rulers of the land, and all
Ye people, haste, O haste to help—
Ere these the frontier pass.
Thes. Say what mean ye by this clamour? what's the matter? what the fear,
Called me from the smoking altars of the sea-god's temple there,
Whom Colonus hails her patron? Speak, and let me know the truth,
What's the cause impelled me hither, faster than my feet desired. 890
Oed. O friend, for by thy voice I know thee now,
This man, this hour, hath done me foul despite.
Thes. How art thou wronged? Who hath molested thee?
Oed. This Creon, whom thou seëst, hath torn from me
My daughters both, the two that were my all.
Thes. What sayest thou?
Oed. I say what I have suffered.

Thes. Let some one of my servants haste and go
To yonder altars, and compel the folk,
Footmen and horsemen all, with loosened rein
To leave the sacrifice and post to where, 900
Threading the hills, the two main roads converge,
Before the captives pass, and I become
Food for this stranger's mirth, despoiled by force.
Go, do my bidding quick.   But for this man,
Came I in wrath to meet him, as I might,
He had not gone out of my hand unscathed.
But now, the laws that he himself brought hither,
These and no other will I mete to him.
Out of this land thou shalt not budge, until
Brought back these maidens stand before my face.   910
For thou hast dealt unworthily of me,
And hast disgraced thy people and thy birth,
Who, coming to a land where men are just,
And law determines every cause, didst spurn
With boisterous foot my town's authority,
To plunder at thy pleasure and to snatch;
Deeming or void of men or manned with slaves
This city, and me its king a thing of nought.
Not by thy Theban nurture art thou base :
Thebes is no mother of unrighteous sons, 920
Nor think that she would praise thee, did she know,
Me thou hadst spoiled and spoiled the gods, nor held
From men distressed, their suppliants, thy hand.

And I, had I set foot within thy state,
Not though my claim were of all claims most just,
Had dared, without the king, or who was lord,
To wrest or plunder, but had better known
What mien became a stranger in the land.
But thou hast shamed, that better things deserved,
Thine own good city—and, in vain grown old,   930
Fulness of years hath left thee void of sense.
Now then I say, that which I said before,
Let some one bring me quick the maidens here,
Unless within our borders thou wouldst dwell
By force, not choice, an alien; thou art warned—
And, what my tongue affirms, my mind intends.

    Chor. Seëst thou thy plight, O stranger? by thy birth
Deemed honest, but thy deeds have proved thee base.

    Cre. Not counting void of valour or of wit
Thy city, son of Aegeus, as thou sayest,   940
I did this deed, but deeming not its folk
Such passion for my kinswomen would feel,
To undertake for them in my despite.
And that a parricide, a man unclean
They'd not receive, I knew, nor one to whom
Of son and mother clave the guilty love.
For in their land, I knew, such wisdom sat,
Throned on their Ares' hill, that not allows
This town to harbour wanderers such as this:
Whom trusting, I was bold to snatch this prey.   950

Yet had I spared to do it, but he poured
On me and all my race a bitter curse,
So stung me, that I dared requite him thus.
For anger knows not other old age, except
To die: the dead, not any pain can touch.
Now therefore work thy will; for, though my cause
Be just, yet stand I here forlorn of friends,
Of small account; but, howsoever small,
I'll do my part to give thee deeds for deeds.

 Oed. O bold and unabashed, where thinkest thou   960
Thine insults fall, on my grey hairs or thine?
Who pratest thus of incest and of blood,
All the dark tale of horror that I bore,
Unwilling: so the gods ordained, belike
Upon my race wreaking some ancient grudge—
Since, of my own, reproach me if thou canst
With any sin, whereof I paid the price
In sinning thus against myself and mine.
For tell me, if an oracle from heaven
Foretold my father's death, slain by his son,   970
How justly then is this reproach to me,
Whom neither mother had conceived, nor sire
Begotten, shaped not yet within the womb?
And if, so born to sorrow as I was,
I met my father—met, and struck and slew,
Discerning not the person nor the deed,
How shalt thou fairly blame the blindfold blow?

But of my mother, sister to thee, rash man,
Hast thou no shame to force me to avouch,
As needs I must, that union? how refrain, 980
When thine unhallowed speech hath thus transgressed?
My mother—yes, my mother—woe is me,
Who bare me, and, not knowing who knew not her,
To me bare children—to herself disgrace.
But this one thing I know, thy will consents
To slander her and me, but never mine
To wed her—nay, nor now to speak these things.
But neither in this marriage shall men call
Me guilty—nor that murder of my sire,
Wherewith thy bitter taunts upbraid me still. 990
For answer this one question that I ask.
Thou'rt just: stood one before thee, here and now,
To slay thee, say, wouldst ask the murderer
'Art thou my father?' or reckon with him straight?
I think, as life is dear to thee, thou'dst pay
The aggressor back, nor reason of the right.
Yet into such an evil strait came I,
Driven by the gods; nor would my father's spirit,
Come back to life, methinks, gainsay me this.
Unjust thou art—thou who hast deemed it well, 1000
Things named and nameless, all to blurt alike,
Before these men heaping such taunts on me.
Well, too, to flatter with thy tongue the king,
And this well-settled order of the state;

But thou hast forgotten of many praises one,
That, of all lands that know to serve the gods
With holy worship, none with this may vie,
Whence thou hast stolen—old, and a suppliant,
Laid hands on me, and borne my daughters hence.
Therefore, importunate, with instant prayer, 1010
I do entreat these goddesses to come
My friends and my deliverers, that thou
May'st learn what manner of men defend this town.

Chor. The man is innocent, O king : consumed
By misery—worthier therefore of our help.

Thes. Enough of words : the robbers with their prey
Are fleet—and we, the plundered, stand amazed.

Cre. What is thy will ? how serve the sightless one ?

Thes. Lead thou the way ; I'll keep thee company ;
The road lies there—so, if hard by thou hast 1020
These children hid, thou shalt thyself produce them ;
But, if their captors flee, we may sit still :
There are who chase them—whom, out of this land,
They shall not boast to heaven they have escaped.
Lead, then : and know that grappling thou art grappled,
In thine own pit by good hap fallen : as when
Kept fraud possession of its ill-got gains ?
Nor put thy trust in friends : for surely thou
Not friendless nor unfurnished hast put on
This brazen front, that would outface us here ; 1030
But, some one trusting, didst attempt this deed.

This must be looked to, nor through my neglect
One man prove stronger than a cityful.
Doth this move thee, or seems it all as vain
Now, 'twixt my lips, as when the plot was hatched?

 Cre. Thee here I shall not blame, say what thou wilt:
At home, we too shall know what things to do.

 Thes. Threaten, but go: and, Oedipus, remain
Untroubled here, trusting my word for this,
That, if I live so long, I shall not rest   1040
Until thy children are thine own again.

 Oed. My blessing, Theseus, on thy noble mind,
And this so loyal care in our behalf.

 Chor. Oh might I be, where soon   [*Strophe* 1.
The foemen's ranks at bay
Shall mix the brazen clangour of the fight,
Or on the Pythian cliffs,
Or by the torchlit strand,
Where nurse those Powers august their awful rites
For mortal men, upon whose tongue   1050
The ministrant Eumolpidae
Have laid the pressure of their golden key:
For there methinks shall Theseus wake the war,
And with the captive sister maidens twain
Close, with a shout of victory:
There shall they turn and fight—   1060
Or farther to the west   [*Antistrophe* 1.
Beyond the snowy peak,

Past Oea's pastures fair, perchance they flee,
Either on horses borne
Or racing chariots swift.
But vain their flight: stout champions hath this place,
And mighty men call Theseus king.
For flashes every rein like flame,
And every rider on his steed's stretched neck
Flings loose the bridle-gear, and gallops hard—.   1070
Knights, who the Virgin-Knight Athene serve,
And this land's patron, Rhea's son,
The ruler of the sea.

Are they about it now,   [*Strophe* 2.
Or do they breathe before they fight?
I know not, but my mind
Presageth me that soon
The spoiler shall give back
The maiden sorely tried, sorely by kinsmen vexed.
To-day, to-day, some great thing Zeus shall do:
I prophesy the triumph of the right.   1080
Oh that I were a dove, that I might wing the wind
With pinion swift and strong,
And from some airy pinnacle of cloud
Content mine eyes with gazing on the fray!

Zeus, who beholdest all,   [*Antistrophe* 2.
Whom all in earth and heaven obey,
Give ear unto my prayer,
That, with victorious might,

The guardians of this land
Upon the goodly prize may spring, and make an end—
And hear me, Pallas, Athene, Virgin dread: 1090
And thou, Apollo, lover of the chase,
And thou, his sister, huntress-maid, that followest up
The dappled fleet-foot stag—
Oh hear me both, and come, a double strength,
To help this land and people at their need.
O wanderer, our guest, thou shalt not call
Thy watchman a false prophet; for I see,
Escorted hither, thy daughters near at hand.

 Oed. Oh where? what sayest thou?

 Ant.   O father mine,
I would some god would give thee sight to see 1100
This noble man, who hath brought us back to thee.

 Oed. O child, are ye come back?

 Ant.   Yea, for these hands
Of Theseus saved us, and his friendly troop.

 Oed. Come near and stand beside me, let my arms
Fold whom they never thought to clasp again.

 Ant. Have thy desire: we crave what we bestow.

 Oed. Where then, where are ye?

 Ant.   Close beside thee here.

 Oed. O dearest saplings from this parent stem!

 Ant. A father loves his own, whate'er it be.

 Oed. Props I have leaned on.

 Ant.   Luckless we and thou. 1110

Oed. I hold ye, dear ones; nor were ill content
So now to die, with you beside me both.
So let an arm of each on either hand
Press close and prop me, children, so that I
May rest from wandering, weary and alone.
And tell me briefly how the deed was done:
Brief speech for tender maidens shall suffice.

Ant. This man, O father, saved us; ask of him.
So briefly I shall speak and thou shalt hear.

Oed. Marvel not, friend, these dear ones lost and found
Made me forget myself in eager speech.
Full well I know that all from thee proceeds
This joy I have to see their face again.
For thou, no other man, didst rescue them.
May heaven all my will perform for thee,
And for thy land; since nowhere upon earth,
Save only here, I found god-fearing hearts,
And generous minds, and lips that could not lie.
I know what deeds with these poor thanks I pay.
All that I have's thy gift and only thine.
Reach hither thy hand, O king, that I may touch it,
And kiss thy face, unless I am too bold.
Nay, but what words are these? Shall I, poor wretch,
Desire that thou shouldst touch a man, in whom
What guilty stain's not deep ingrained? Not I:
Nay, nor thou shalt not. Only they can bear

This load with me, who know it for their own.
Untouched—I bid thee hail; and be thou still
True friend to me, as to this hour thou art.

Thes. Small marvel, truly, if thy glad surprise
Poured itself forth and overflowed in speech—   1140
And first to these, not heeding me the while.
Nought's to forgive: such slight is none to me.
For not in high-flown speeches but in deeds
I'd have the splendour of my life appear.
Thou hast the proof. Have I now sworn to thee
And not performed? For here thy daughters stand
Living, and all unscathed of all those threats.
And how the fight was won, what need that I
Should idly boast? Some day they'll tell thee all.
But now let thy conjecture second mine,   1150
What means this rumour, met me by the way,
Soon told indeed, but worth thy pondering.
There's nought so small, merits a man's contempt.

Oed. What rumour, son of Aegeus? let me hear:
I know not yet whereat thy question aims.

Thes. 'Tis said some man, no countryman of thine,
But kinsman, prostrate in some suppliant wise,
Hath clasped Poseidon's altar, where erewhile
I left the sacrifice to succour thee.

Oed. Yea, of what land? and wherefore suppliant?   1160

Thes. I know not, save that, as they say, brief speech
And nowise burthensome he craves with thee.

H

Oed. Yet suppliant? 'tis no trifle that he seeks.
Thes. He asks, they say, to come, confer with thee,
Then go, and of his coming take no harm.
Oed. Who can he be that sits and thus entreats?
Thes. Bethink thee, hast thou at Argos any kin,
Who might desire this favour at thy hands?
Oed. O good my friend, no more!
Thes. What ails thee, say.
Oed. Require it not.
Thes. Require not what? explain. 1170
Oed. I know, for these have told me, who he is.
Thes. Who can he be, of me to merit blame?
Oed. My son, O king, that hated one, whose speech
Of all men's most would vex my ears to hear.
Thes. How? canst thou not hear and not do, if that
Mislikes thee? Is it so bitter a thing, to hear?
Oed. My son's voice, king, to me sounds hatefully:
'Pray thee, constrain me not to yield this thing.
Thes. Bethink thee, doth not his suppliant state constrain?
Look thou forget not, but of the god beware. 1180
Ant. My father, hear the counsel of a child.
Suffer this man, in this that he desires,
Give to his soul, and to the god, content:
And yield to us, to let our brother come.
He may not pluck thee from thy steadfast mind,

Or force consent to words unprofitable:
What harm to hear him speak? Hear then and judge:
Let speech declare if deeds be purposed well.
Is he not thine—thy son? whom, no, not even
Of all ill sons most impious though he be,   1190
May'st thou, my father, with ill deeds requite.
Oh let him—other men, with thankless sons,
And spirits hot as thine, are of their mood
Exorcised by the wisdom of a friend—
So thou, look from the present to the past,
Think of thy parents and the former grief,
And, pondering this, I know thou wilt confess,
Anger that's evil hath an evil end;
Since no slight argument herein is thine,
The lifelong losing of thy blinded eyes.   1200
Yield thou to us. Insistence ill beseems
Our just petition; ill beseems that thou,
Receiving, knowest not how to render good.

  Oed. A grievous pleasure, child, ye wring from me—
Ye with your pleading. But be it as ye will
Only, if come he must, friend, have a care,
No violent hands upon my life be laid.

  Thes. I have no mind, old man, to hear again,
Once heard, thy terrors. Braggart I am none:
Know thyself safe, if any god saves me.   1210

  Chor. Beyond the common lot who lusts to live, [*Str.*
Nor sets a limit to desire,

Of me no doubtful word shall win—
A fool, in love with foolishness.
Since long life hath in store for him to know
Full many things drawn nearer unto grief,
And gone from sight all pleasant things that were;
Till, fallen on overmuch
Fulfilment of desire,
One only friend he sees can help—   1220
Friend, who shall come when dawns at last
The day that knows not bridal song
Nor lyre nor dance, that fatal day
Whose equal doom all we abide—
Shall come, kind Death, and make an end!
Not to be born is past disputing best: [*Antistrophe.*
And, after this, his lot transcends,
Who, seen on earth for briefest while,
Thither returns from whence he came.
For, with its fluttering follies all aswarm,   1230
Who needs, while youth abides, go far afield
To heap vexation? What's the missing plague?
Slaughters are here, and strife,
Factions, and wars, and spite.
And still life's crowning ill's to bear—
Last scene of all, of all condemned,
Unfriended, uncompanioned Age,
When strength is gone, but grief remains,
And every evil that is named—

Evil of evil, grief of grief.
As now this man, not wretched I alone—　　[*Epode.*
Lo, like some promontory northward set,　　　1240
Wave-buffeted by all fierce winds that rave—
So buffet him, nor cease,
Poured on his helpless head,
All shattering billows of outrageous fate,
Some from the setting sun,
And from the rising some,
Some with the mid-noon beam,
Some from the starry shimmerings of the night.

　Ant. Lo where toward us the stranger, as I think,—
Nay, none but he, my father—from his eyes　　1250
Full flood of tears outpouring, hither comes.

　Oed. Say, who?

　Ant.　　The same that from the first our thoughts
Conjectured, Polyneices—stands beside thee.

　Pol. Ah me, what shall I say? shall I lament
First for myself, O sisters, or for him,
This old man, this my father, whom I see?
Whom, exiled, in a strange land here with you
I find, clad in such garb, whose foulness mars,
Inveterate, unlovely, like a blight,
The time-worn flesh it cleaves to; and his locks　　1260
Wild on the breeze from sightless temples stream;
And fare with garb seems all too well to suit—
This that, to stay the hunger-pinch, he bears.

O agony of knowledge known too late!
Vilest of men I stand, thy plight for proof,
Self-witnessed: ask not others what I am.
Ah yet, for Mercy by the side of Zeus
Sits throned for judgment ever—shall she not
By thee find place, my father? Give me leave
To mend my fault; I cannot make it worse. 1270
Still silent?
Speak to me, father: turn not away thy face!
Answerest thou me nothing? shall I go,
Scorned, with no word—thine anger silent too?
O ye, my sisters, daughters of this man,
Perchance ye shall be able to unlock
These most obdurate, unrelenting lips—
Let him not thus with scorn dismiss me hence,
Poseidon's suppliant, answered not at all. 1279

   Ant. Thyself, unhappy, say, what wouldst thou here?
Stint not thy speaking; pleasant words to hear,
Indignant words, or words compassionate—
Speak on—till speech from silence wring response.

   Pol. Yes, I will speak: thou dost instruct me well.
Thus then, entreating first Poseidon's self
To aid me, from whose altar came I hither
Raised by the ruler of this land, with leave
To speak and hear, and scatheless to depart:—
Whose promise, strangers, rests with you, and these
My sisters and my father, to make good. 1290

Wherefore I came, now, father, thou shalt hear.
Exiled and outcast from my home am I,
For that I urged, being of elder birth,
My title to possess thy kingly seat.
Therefore did Eteocles thrust me forth,
His elder, nor with reasons vanquished me,
Nor challenged me to trial of deeds and strength,
But stole the heart o' the city. Mark me—first,
I say that thine Erinys hath done this:
Next, hearken what from prophets I have learned.   1300
For, when to Dorian Argos I had come,
And had Adrastus' daughter to my wife,
Swore oath to help me, of the Apian land,
All foremost names and honourablest in war—
That, gathering, I with them, the sevenfold host
'Gainst Thebes, I fighting for the right should fall,
Or dispossess the doers of the wrong.
But now, these things being so, why came I here?
With supplication and with prayer to thee,
Both for myself, O father, and my friends—   1310
The seven spears that gathering even now
With seven armies gird the Theban plain:
Swift-speared Amphiaraüs, best of all
In battle, best to read the flights of birds;
And the Aetolian son of Aeneus second,
Tydeus: and Argive Eteoclus third:
The fourth was by his father Talaus sent,

Hippomedon; and Capaneus, the fifth,
Vows that with fire Thebes-city he will rase;
Arcadian Parthenopaeus rushes sixth,   1320
Named of his mother, virgin-famed till he
Was born—of Atalanta trusty son;
Last, I thy son (or, if not thine, but child
Of mere mishap, yet named at least of thee)
From Argos lead 'gainst Thebes a fearless band.
Father, all these entreat thee—for the love
Thou hast of these thy daughters and thy life—
Let not thy stubborn anger come between
And screen my brother from my swift revenge—
Brother, that stripped and thrust me from my home. 1330
For, unto whom, if oracles speak true,
Thou shalt be friend, the victory is his.
Then, by our fountains and our fathers' gods,
Father, I charge thee, hear me and relent.
Beggared am I and exiled, exiled thou;
And on the smiles of others thou and I
Live, courtiers both, like fortune having found.
And there the while—O torture—in our home
He kings it in his pride, and flouts us both.
But, let thy purpose second mine, it costs   1340
Small toil or time to bruise such pride to dust.
So shall I bring thee home, at home to dwell,
And home return myself, and cast him forth.
Such triumph I may boast, if thou consent;

Without thee, life's not mine, to call my own.
   Chor. For his sake, Oedipus, who brought him hither,
Answering what things are meet, so send him hence.
   Oed. Had it not chanced the keeper of your land,
King Theseus, friends, had brought him to this place,
And for him claimed that he should hear my mind,   1350
Scarcely this voice had sounded in his ears.
Now, graced he shall depart and answered, so,
It shall not add much comfort to his life :—
Thy life, most base, that, sceptred and enthroned,
Sitting where now in Thebes thy brother sits,
Me, thine own father, didst banish from the land,
And mad'st me citiless and to wear this garb,
That moves thy tears, beholding, now thou'rt come,
With me, into the self-same evil plight.
Ay, well for thee to weep, but I must bear   1360
This—whatso life is mine, remembering thee
My murderer; for thou didst acquaint my days
With grief, and cast me forth and banish me
To beg from door to door my daily bread :
And, for thy part, but that my daughters were
My nurses, surely now I had not been:
Now, these have nursed me, these have saved my life,
These maidens—men, not maidens, for their help :
But ye, called sons, are no true sons of mine.
Therefore the god regards thee—nowise yet   1370
As soon he shall, if Thebes-ward now thy hosts

Are moving. Never shall ye call fair Thebes
Your city. Red with brother's blood shall glow
Thy hands and his; together shall ye fall.
Forth from my lips aforetime went the curse,
And now I call it, 'Curse, come fight for me'—
That ye may know a father should be honoured,
And scorn no more, though he be blind, who got
Such sons. For these my daughters did not so.
Then prate not of thine altars and thy thrones;   1380
From both thou'rt banned, if Justice as of old
Interprets still the ancient laws of Zeus.
Go hence, abhorred, beyond all baseness base,
Unfather'd: and for blessing this my curse
Go with thee—neither with thy spears to storm
The city of thy kin, nor Argos-vale
Revisit, but there with fratricidal hand
Slay who hath banished thee, and by him be slain.
I curse thee with these curses, and I bid
The hated gloom of Tartarus receive
And yield thee heritage of homes far hence.   1390
And ye, dread goddesses, and Ares, help,
That hast of furious hate fulfilled their hearts!
Go, bear my answer hence, and tell it out
To every Theban, and thine own good friends—
To those stout champions say, that Oedipus
Such goodly gifts unto his sons dispensed.

 Chor. Polyneices, of thy goings heretofore

Small joy I give thee; and now with haste go hence.

Pol. Ah me, my coming, and my hopes o'erthrown!
And ah, my friends! to what a journey's end   1400
Fared we from Argos forth, woe worth the day—
Such end, ·I dare not even speak and show
My friends, to turn them back the way they came;
But silent I must go to meet my doom.
Yet, daughters of this father, sisters mine,
That hear my father curse me to my face,
O sisters, ye, have pity—if the curse
Fall, and to you be given safe return
To Thebes and home, dishonour me not then—
With all due rites of burial see me laid.   1410
So shall the praise, of daughters ministrant,
That now ye have, get other praise beside,
Nor meaner, for such service done to me.

Ant. I pray thee, Polyneices, hear me speak.

Pol. What wouldst thou, sister, dear Antigone?

Ant. Make haste to bid thy host to Argos back;
Wreak not destruction on thyself and Thebes.

Pol. I may not hear thee. How again could I
Lead on those armies, once had seen me blench?

Ant. Why needs thy wrath be kindled any more?   1420
What gain to thee, thy city in the dust?

Pol. Shame now to me, that I the elder-born
Am banished by my brother and defied.

Ant. A swift fulfilment then his word shall win,

Who dooms you each the other's murderer.

Pol. His word's his wish: no yielding is for me.

Ant. Nay then what help? But who dares follow thee,
Hearing what fate thy father hath foretold?

Pol. Ill words I'll not report. Wise generals
Announce the better tidings, hide the worse.   1430

Ant. Boy, art thou then resolved to go thy way?

Pol. Resolved, beyond withholding. Drear and dark
Shall be, I know, this road that I must fare:
My father and his Furies so have willed.
Be your path happier—so ye mind, in death,
My asking; since in life no more ye may.
Now loose me—and farewell. For nevermore
Shall ye behold me living.

Ant.   Woe is me!

Pol. Weep not for me.

Ant.   Who, brother, would not mourn
Thy headlong haste into the jaws of death?   1440

Pol. If I must die, I will.

Ant.   Nay, hearken yet.

Pol. Nought that I should not.

Ant.   Wretched then am I,
If I must lose thee!

Pol.   Fortune sees to that—
Whether thou shalt or no. But for you twain,
Gods grant me this, no evil hap to you:
For, that ye have deserved none, all men see.

Chor. Lo how from new occasion trouble new [*Strophe.*
And new entanglement of evil grows—
And whom to blame? This sightless stranger still?
Or Fate's inevitable stroke? 1450
This rather: for I cannot tell
Of aught that Heaven in vain hath willed.
All time, all time, be witness else—
Time that is charged with other work to-day,
But shall to-morrow build what now lies low.
List to the thunder! Shield us, Zeus!
  Oed. O children, would that some one—some one
    near—
Would go to bring the noble Theseus hither.
  Ant. What business, father, hast thou with the king?
  Oed. Hence now to Hades summons me this winged
Zeus-voice of thunder. Tarry not, but send. 1461
  Chor. Again, with louder noise, the air is rent— [*Antistr.*
Uproar, that from the hand of Zeus is hurled,
Unutterable. Fear through all my blood
Runs freezing, to my startled hair.
My spirit shrinks: again, again,
The lightning flames across the sky.
What follows in its fiery wake?
Ah me, I fear; for not indeed for nought,
But boding some mischance, these portents blaze. 1470
O great dread sky! O sovereign Zeus!
  Oed. Children. the end is come of all my days;

The god fulfils his word; retreat is none.

 Ant. How knowest thou? or what sign hast of this?

 Oed. I know it well. But quickly let them go.
And call me here the ruler of this land.

 Chor. Again the ear-besieging   [*Strophe.*
Soul-piercing rattle of the storm!
Ye gods, have pity, pity on us,
If on our mother land   1480
Frown thus your sunless skies.
O righteous be the feet,
Whose ways encounter mine;
Nor let me see a man accurst,
Lest I partake with him
Reward not fraught with gain—
Lord Zeus, I cry to thee!

 Oed. Is the man near? O children, shall he find
Me living, ordering still my thoughts aright?

 Ant. What certitude wouldst thou thy thought should
  hold?

 Oed. To pay the debt I owe them, and make good
That promise, when he gave me my desire.   1490

 Chor. O son, come forth, come hither: [*Antistrophe.*
Or, at the cliff's edge, where the cliff
Curves, and Poseidon's altars smoke
Seaward, if haply there
Thou sacrificest—come!
Thy guest, this stranger, deems

Thy town and friends and thou,
For help ye gave him at his need,
Have at his hands deserved
Like measure to receive.
King, pause not, hither haste! 1499

Thes. How now? what clamour raise ye all at once—
Distinct your voices, and the stranger's clear?
Lightning from Zeus appals ye, or the sharp
Scourge of the driving hail-shower? Nought's beyond
Conjecture, when the god brews storm like this.

Oed. Desired, O king, thou comest; and some god
Gives thee good fortune, in that thou art come.

Thes. What new thing, son of Laïus, is to tell?

Oed. My life determines here. Nor would I die
A promise-breaker to thy town and thee. 1509

Thes. Wherein rests thy belief that thou shalt die?

Oed. The gods themselves are heralds of their will,
Nor of the signs predestined fails there aught.

Thes. What signs, old man? How are these things
    revealed?

Oed. By this unceasing thunder, peal on peal—
With bolt on bolt, flashed from the almighty hand.

Thes. It is enough: prophet of many things,
True prophet, I have found thee: speak thy will.

Oed. My words, O son of Aegeus, shall endure,
To stead thy city—nor with age wax faint.
'Tis time that I should lead thee—I, no hand 1520

My steps to lead—thither, where I must die.
But secret be the spot from all men else,
What thicket hides it, and what region holds;
That, more than many shields, and borrowed spear
Of neighbours, help unfailing may be thine.
And thou shalt learn, come thither, thou alone,
Such things—accurst be he that utters them:
To no one of thy people may I tell
Their purport, nor my children, whom I love.   1529
Locked in thy breast, still keep them: and when thy life
Draws to its close, repeat them but to one,
Thy chiefest; he to his heir, and he to his—
So shall the Dragon's brood not harm thy home,
This city. But a people, myriad-voiced,
Lightly, in fairest-ordered state, breaks forth
To licence. For the seeing gods see late,
When men turn madmen and forget to fear.
Be that, O son of Aegeus, far from thee.
Enough; I teach thee, by thine own heart taught:
Now, for the god is instant, calling me,   1540
Seek we the place, brood not, nor question more.
Come, children, follow, for our parts are changed;
Behold, your father leads you, whom ye led.
Follow, and touch me not, but let me find,
Myself, the holy place, the destined tomb,
Where in this land this body must be laid.
Onward, still onward, follow: this way lead

Attendant Hermes and the Queen of Shades.
O darkened light, light that wast sometime mine,
This body of mine shall feel thee never more.　　1550
For now I go, go hence to hide, where all
Is dark, my life's departing.　Friend beloved,
·Upon thy servants and this land and thee
All blessings light; and, when ye most are blessed,
Remember me, whose death your bliss secured.

　Chor. If to the Invisible Goddess, and to thee,　[*Str.*
King of the kingdoms of the night,
To fall down and to worship and to pray
Be not unmeet for me,
O dread dark lord Aidoneus, grant me this,　　1560
That by no troublesome and no grievous death
This stranger to the Stygian halls may win,
And those vast fields at last of the under-world,
Whose universal glooms enfold
The nations of the dead.
So after all his evil days,
So evil and so many and so thwart,
The gods shall right him, for the gods are just,
With honour at the last.
O under earth great Goddesses, and thou　[*Antistrophe.*
Indomitable and monstrous Form,
That at the pillared shining doors, men say,　　1570
Keepest thy kennelled couch,
And from the cavern's jaws thy gnarring noise

I

Sounds, and the fame is constant, that thine eyes
Fail not from watching at the gate of Death—
Grant me, great son of Tartarus and Ge,
Clear of the dreadful hound's approach
The stranger's path may lie—
That sunless path whereby he hastes
Down to thy shadowy-peopled fields, O Death—
Yea, for I cry to thee, lord of the night
Whose sleep no morning breaks.

   Mess. Sirs, and my townsmen, summed in a word, my tale
Concludes in this, that Oedipus is dead: 1580
But of the manner needs more breath to tell,
Nor was it in the acting all so brief.

   Chor. Dead, hapless one, is he?

   Mess.   Doubt not, but know,
What life, lifelong, was his, is his no more.

   Chor. Had the gods pity? Passed he with no pain?

   Mess. Ay, there thou hast it; marvel now at this.
Hence how he went, thou knowest, for thou wast here
Beholding—guided by no friendly hand,
Followed by us instead, himself the guide.
But when to that sheer threshold he had come,   1590
Paven with brass and rooted in the rock,
Of the divided ways he chose him one,
And nigh the urn that keeps the memory

How Theseus with Peirithoüs plighted faith,
'Twixt that he stood and the Thorician scaur,
Midmost the hollow pear-tree and the tomb,
Rock-hewn ; then sate him down, and loosed his soiled
Apparel, and called his children, and bade them bring
Water for washing from some fountain near
And for libation. They to yonder height,
Hill of Demeter who clothes the fields with green,   1600
Hied them, and brought the bidding of their sire,
With swift despatch, and washed and did on him
Fair raiment, as the manner is to do.
But when of doing he had all content,
And nought that he desired was left undone,
Came thunder underground, and at the sound
The maidens shuddered, and at their father's knees
Fell weeping, nor refrained, but beat their breasts
And with their lamentations filled the air.
But, when he heard that sudden bitter cry,   1610
He folded them within his arms, and said,
"O daughters, ye are left fatherless this day:
For all my life falls from me ; never more
Shall ye be troubled with your care of me.
Children, I know how hard it was ; and yet
One little word, I know, pays all the pain.
There is not any one who loves you so
As this man loved you, orphaned of whose love
This day and all your days henceforth shall be."

So locked together in a last embrace,   1620
They sobbed and wept, all three. But when at last
Their tears were spent, and no cry more outbrake,
But they stood silent, on the silence fell
A voice of one who summoned, and its sound
Stiffened with sudden fear the hair of all
Who heard: for the god called, and called again,
"Oedipus, Oedipus, why tarriest thou
With these so long? 'tis time that we were gone."
And when he knew the summons of the god,
He bade the king, Theseus, come nigher to him,   1630
And when he came besought him, "O my friend,
Give to these children, and children, ye to him,
Right hands, the ancient pledge; and promise thou,
Thou'lt not forsake them willingly, and wilt do
All that thou doest, wisely, for their good."
Then he, the noble man, with no weak tears,
Promised, and sealed the promise with an oath.
So Theseus sware, and Oedipus thereat
Felt for his daughters with his sightless hands,
And found, and said, "O children, get ye gone,   1640
With noble hearts and patient; nor desire
To see the things ye may not, nor to hear.
Make haste to go: the things that shall be done
No man but Theseus it concerns to know."
Such words he spake, and we obeyed his speech,
All we that heard, and stinting not our tears

Forth with the maidens followed; but went not far,
Or ere we turned to look, and looked, and saw
The man was gone, no Oedipus was there;
Only the king, holding athwart his brow   1650
A hand that screened his eyes, as to shut out
Some dreadful and intolerable sight.
And then, for one brief minute and no more,
We saw him make obeisance, all at once,
Both to the earth and to the gods in heaven.
But by what manner of death died Oedipus,
No man can tell, but Theseus, he alone.
For it was not any firebolt, swift from heaven,
Despatched him, no, nor a whirlwind from the sea
Rose in a minute and caught him from our sight;   1660
But either the gods took him, or the earth
Was kind, and opened for him her cavernous jaws.
For nowise lamentably he passed, nor slain
By sickness, pitiably—a marvel, how—
Whose like was never.   Idle is my talk?
Who lists may think so; him I'll not regard.
   Chor. Where are the maidens and their company?
   Mess. Not they far hence: hither not doubtfully
Voice of their weeping heralds their approach.
   Ant. Alas, not now, ah not for us— [*Strophe* 1.   1670
Daughters we of a strain accurst—
To weep and to refrain:
We, upon whom erewhile was laid

Constant the weight of our father's sorrow,
And what we have seen at the last and suffered,
None may conjecture, save we who tell.

Chor. How is't with you?

Ant. Ah, friends, this baffles thought.

Chor. Gone is he?

Ant. As thou wouldst go, if thou couldst choose.
How else, whom not in battle [*Strophe* 2.
Death met, nor on the sea, 1680
But with invisible hand the viewless fields
Clutched him, and dragged him down?
Alas, but on our sight hath fallen
A darkness as of death.
Nay, for in far-off lands unknown,
Or homeless on the tossing wave,
Our life's intolerable plight
How shall our hearts endure?
I know not. Hades, shedder of blood, 1689
Me also, young with the old, daughter with father, slay,
Wretched. Not life any more, but death for me!

Chor. O ye two noble daughters,
Heaven's gracious will chide not,
Nor with rash heat your hearts inflame:
Not blamably ye fare.

Ant. How precious now seems pain before— [*Ant.* 1.
Dear, the pang that we least desired—
When him we still embraced.

Father, we love thee, love thee yet;   1700
Wrapt in the gloom of the grave for ever—
But old we have loved thee, and dead remember;
We are thy daughters; our love endures.
    Chor. He fared. . . .
    Ant.   Fared, even as his soul desired.
    Chor. Say, how?
    Ant.   In alien land, the land he chose,
Died he: and hath thereunder   [*Antistrophe* 2.
His dark deep bed alway,
Nor leaves not grief behind, to weep his loss.
For still these eyes of mine,
Father, run over with tears for thee;   1710
Nor know I how to ease
Of its dull ache my desolate heart.
Ah me, in alien land to die
Thou hadst desired; but so, for me,
Lonely thy death befell.
Out and alas, for me and for thee
Hereafter, sister beloved, destitute, helpless quite,
Thus of our father bereft, what lot remains?
    Chor. O children, blissful quittance
Of life's last hour was his.   1720
Cease your complaint: what mortal lives,
Impregnable to grief?
    Ant. Back, sister, let us haste.
    Ism.   What thing to do?

Ant. Desire possesses me.
Ism. Of what?
Ant. To visit once the home. . . .
Ism. Say whose?
Ant. Where under ground, woe's me! our father rests.
Ism. How should this thing be granted? Dost thou not
Consider?
Ant. Ah, sister, chide me not for this. 1730
Ism. Then too bethink thee. . . .
Ant. What's my second fault?
Ism. Tomb he hath none, and no man saw his death.
Ant. Lead me to where he died, and slay me there.
Ism. Alas for poor Ismene then!
How, lonely, helpless, shall I pass
The sad remainder of my days?
Chor. Fear not, my daughters.
Ant. Whither shall I flee?
Chor. Fled is that fear and past.
Ant. How fled?
Chor. Harm cannot touch you now. 1740
Ant. I think. . . .
Chor. What idle doubt perplexes now thy heart?
Ant. How they will suffer us, returning home,
I know not.
Chor. But what then? Nor seek to know.

Ant. O heavy grief!
Chor. Not light thy load before.
Ant. Oh then past cure, but worst is now grown worse.
Chor. Upon a huge sea then your barks were launched!
Ant. Ah, Zeus, ah whither must we go?
Fate drives us onward still, to where
Fear in the distance darkly looms. 1750
Thes. Weep no more, children, for him
With whom in the tomb abides a blessing:
Grieve not, nor arraign the gods.
Ant. O son of Aegeus, grant us a boon.
Thes. Children, what crave ye that I should grant?
Ant. With our own eyes that we might look
On our father's tomb.
Thes. Anear that place no foot may tread.
Ant. King, lord of Athens, what word is this?
Thes. O children, so did thy father charge me, 1760
To let no mortal come nigh the spot,
No voice break silence there, about
The sacred grave wherein he rests.
And, if I did his bidding well,
He said that I should keep this land
Safe from all harm for aye.
I promised: and Heaven the promise heard,
And Horkos, all-hearing, sprung from Zeus.
Ant. Nay but, if he will have it so,
So let it be: but now to Thebes,

The ancient city, send us hence; 1770
If haply we may come between,
And, ere our brothers' blood be spilt,
Prevent the coming strife.

 Thes. Even this I will: and what beside,
That may to you be profitable,
Or to the dead man, late gone hence,
For pleasure, I shall not faint but do.

 Chor. But now leave off; now, now no more
Kindle with grieving grief:
This promise holds, whate'er betide. 1779

ANTIGONE

PERSONS.

Creon.
Haemon.
Teiresias.
Sentinel.
Messenger.
Second Messenger.
Eurydice.
Antigone.
Ismene.
Chorus of Theban Elders.

Antigone

Ant. O SISTER-LIFE, Ismene's, twin with mine,
Knowest thou of the burden of our race
Aught that from us yet living Zeus holds back?
Nay, for nought grievous and nought ruinous,
No shame and no dishonour, have I not seen
Poured on our hapless heads, both thine and mine.
And even now what edict hath the prince
Uttered, men say, to all this Theban folk?
Thou knowest it and hast heard? or 'scapes thy sense,
Aimed at thy friends, the mischief of thy foes? 10

Ism. To me of friends, Antigone, no word
Hath come, or sweet or bitter, since that we
Two sisters of two brothers were bereaved,
Both on a day slain by a twofold blow:
And, now that vanished is the Argive host
Ev'n with the night fled hence, I know no more,
If that I fare the better or the worse.

Ant. I knew full well, and therefore from the gates
O' the court I led thee hither, alone to hear.

Ism. There's trouble in thy looks: thy tidings tell. 20

Ant. Yea, hath not Creon, of our two brothers slain,

Honoured with burial one, disdained the other?
For Eteocles, they say, he in the earth
With all fair rites and ceremony hath laid,
Nor lacks he honour in the world below;
But the poor dust of Polyneices dead
Through Thebes, 'tis said, the edict has gone forth
That none may bury, none make moan for him,
But leave unwept, untombed, a dainty prize
For ravening birds that gloat upon their prey. 30
So hath our good lord Creon to thee and me
Published, men say, his pleasure—ay, to *me*—
And hither comes, to all who know it not
Its purport to make plain, nor deems the thing
Of slight account, but, whoso does this deed,
A public death by stoning is his doom.
Thou hast it now; and quickly shall be proved
If thou art noble, or base from noble strain.

 Ism. O rash of heart, if this indeed be so,
What help in me, to loosen or to bind? 40
 Ant. Consider, toil and pain if thou wilt share.
 Ism. On what adventure bound? What wouldst thou do?
 Ant. To lift his body, wilt thou join with me?
 Ism. Wouldst thou indeed rebel, and bury him?
 Ant. My brother I will bury, and thine no less,
Whether thou wilt or no: no traitress I.
 Ism. O all too bold—when Creon hath forbid?

Ant. My rights to hinder is no right of his.

Ism. Ah, sister, yet think how our father died,
Wrapt in what cloud of hate and ignominy 50
By his own sins, self-proved, and both his eyes
With suicidal hand himself he stabbed:
Then too his mother-wife, two names in one,
Fordid with twisted noose her woful life:
Last, our two brothers in one fatal day
Drew sword, O miserable, and each to each
Dealt mutual slaughter with unnatural hands:
And now shall we twain, who alone are left,
Fall like the rest, and worse—in spite of law,
And scorning kings, their edicts and their power? 60
Oh rather let us think, 'tis not for us,
Who are but women, to contend with men:
And the king's word is mighty, and to this,
And harsher words than this, we needs must bow.
Therefore will I, imploring of the dead
Forgiveness, that I yield but as I must,
Obey the king's commandment: for with things
Beyond our reach 'twere foolishness to meddle.

Ant. I'll neither urge thee, nor, if now thou'dst help
My doing, should I thank thee for thine aid. 70
Do thou after thy kind: thy choice is made:
I'll bury him; doing this, so let me die.
So with my loved one loved shall I abide,
My crime a deed most holy: for the dead

Longer have I to please than these on earth.
There I shall dwell for ever: be it thine
To have scorned what gods have hallowed, if thou
    wilt.

Ism. Nay, nothing do I scorn: but, how to break
My country's law—I am witless of the way.

Ant. Be this thy better part: I go to heap   80
The earth upon my brother, whom I love.

Ism. Alas, unhappy, how I fear for thee!

Ant. Fear not for me: guide thine own fate aright.

Ism. Yet breathe this purpose to no ear but mine:
Keep thou thy counsel well—and so will I.

Ant. Oh speak: for much more hatred thou wilt get,
Concealing, than proclaiming it to all.

Ism. This fever at thy heart by frost is fed.

Ant. But, whom I most should please, they most are
    pleased.

Ism. So wouldst thou: but thou canst not as thou
    wouldst.   90

Ant. Why, then, when strength shall fail me, I will
    cease.

Ism. Not to attempt the impossible is best.

Ant. Hated by me, and hated by the dead—
To him a hateful presence evermore—
Thou shouldst be, and thou shalt be, speaking thus.
But leave me, and the folly that is mine,
This worst to suffer—not the worst—since still

A worse remains, no noble death to die.

   Ism. Go if thou wilt: but going know thyself
Senseless, yet to thy friends a friend indeed.   99

   Chor. Lo, the sun upspringing!   [*Strophe* 1.
Fairest light we hail thee
Of all dawns that on Thebes the seven-gated
Ever broke! Eye of golden day!
Over Dirce's fount appearing,
Hence the Argive host white-shielded,
That in complete arms came hither,
Headlong homeward thou didst urge
Faster still with shaken rein.
At call of Polyneices, stirred   110
By bitter heat of wrangling claims,
Against our land they gathered, and they swooped
Down on us—like an eagle, screaming hoarse,
White-clad, with wings of snow—
With shields a many and with waving crests.
But above our dwellings,   [*Antistrophe* 1.
With his spears that thirsted
For our blood, at each gate's mouth of the seven
Gaping round, paused the foe—and went,
Ere his jaws with blood were sated,   120
Or our circling towers the torch-flame
Caught and kindled: so behind him
Raged intense the battle-din—
While for life the Serpent fought.

        K

For Zeus the tongue of vaunting pride
Hates with exceeding hate; he marked
That torrent army's onward flood, superb
With clank of gold, and with his brandished fire 130
Smote down who foremost climbed
To shout his triumph on our ramparts' heights.
Hurled from that height with swift reverse,   [*Strophe* 2.
The unpitying earth received him as he fell,
And quenched the brand he fain had flung,
And quelled the mad endeavour,
The frantic storm-gusts of his windy hate.
So fared it then with him;
Nor less elsewhere great Ares dealt
Against the foemen thunderous blows—
Our trace-horse on the right.   140
For seven chieftains at our seven gates
Met each his equal foe: and Zeus,
Who foiled their onset, claims from all his due,
The brazen arms, which on the field they left:
Save that infuriate pair,
Who, from one father and one mother sprung,
Against each other laid in rest
Their spears, victorious both,
And each by other share one equal death.
But now of Victory be glad: [*Antistrophe* 2.
She meets our gladness with an answering smile,
And Thebes, the many-charioted,

Hears far resound her praises:
Now then with war have done, and strife forget! 150
All temples of the gods
Fill we with song and night-long dance;
And, Theban Bacchus, this our mirth
Lead thou, and shake the earth!
But lo the ruler of this Theban land,
Son of Menoeceus, Creon comes,
Crowned by these new and strange events, he comes—
By will of heav'n our new-created king,
What counsel pondering?
Who by his sovereign will hath now convoked, 160
In solemn conference to meet,
The elders of the state;
Obedient to whose summons, we are here.

   Cre. Sirs, it hath pleased the gods to right again
Our Theban fortunes, by sore tempest tossed:
And by my messenger I summoned hither
You out of all the state; first, as I knew you
To the might o' the throne of Laïus loyal ever:
Also, when Oedipus upheld the state,
And when he perished, to their children still
Ye with a constant mind were faithful found:
Now they are gone: both on one fatal field 170
An equal guilt atoned with equal doom,
Slayers of each other, by each other slain:
And I am left, the nearest to their blood,

To wield alone the sceptre and the realm.
There is no way to know of any man
The spirit and the wisdom and the will,
Till he stands proved, ruler and lawgiver.
For who, with a whole city to direct,
Yet cleaves not to those counsels that are best,
But locks his lips in silence, being afraid, 180
I held and hold him ever of men most base:
And whoso greater than his country's cause
Esteems a friend, I count him nothing worth.
For, Zeus who seeth all be witness now,
Nor for the safety's sake would I keep silence,
And see the ruin on my country fall,
Nor would I deem an enemy to the state
Friend to myself; remembering still that she,
She only brings us safe; her deck we pace,
Unfoundered 'mid the storm, our friends and we. 190
So for the good of Thebes her laws I'll frame:
And such the proclamation I set forth,
Touching the sons of Oedipus, ev'n now—
Eteocles, who fighting for this land
In battle has fall'n, more valiant none than he,
To bury, and no funeral rite omit,
To brave men paid—their solace in the grave:
Not so his brother, Polyneices: he,
From exile back returning, utterly
With fire his country and his fathers' gods 200

Would fain have burnt, fain would with kinsmen's blood
Have slaked his thirst, or dragged us captive hence:
Therefore to all this city it is proclaimed
That none may bury, none make moan for him,
But leave him lying all ghastly where he fell,
Till fowls o' the air and dogs have picked his bones.
So am I purposed: not at least by me
Shall traitors be preferred to honest men:
But, whoso loves this city, him indeed
I shall not cease to honour, alive or dead. 210

   Chor. Creon, son of Menoeceus, 'tis thy pleasure
The friend and foe of Thebes so to requite:
And, whatso pleases thee, that same is law,
Both for our Theban dead and us who live.

   Cre. Look to it, then, my bidding is performed.

   Chor. Upon some younger man impose this burden.

   Cre. To watch the body, sentinels are set.

   Chor. What service more then wouldst thou lay on us?

   Cre. That ye resist whoever disobeys.

   Chor. Who is so senseless that desires to die? 220

   Cre. The penalty is death: yet hopes deceive,
And men wax foolish oft through greed of gain.

   Sent. That I come hither, king, nimble of foot,
And breathless with my haste, I'll not profess:
For many a doubtful halt upon the way,
And many a wheel to the right-about, I had,

Oft as my prating heart gave counsel, 'Fool,
What ails thee going into the lion's mouth?'
Then, 'Blockhead, wilt thou tarry? if Creon learns
This from another man, shalt thou not smart?' 230
So doubtfully I fared—much haste, scant speed—
And, if the way was short, 'twas long to me.
But to come hither to thee prevailed at last,
And, though the speech be nought, yet I will speak.
For I have come fast clutching at the hope
That nought's to suffer but what fate decrees.

   Cre. What is it that hath troubled thus thy mind?

   Sent. First for myself this let me say: the deed
I neither did, nor saw who was the doer,
And 'twere not just that I should suffer harm. 240

   Cre. Wisely, thyself in covert, at the mark
Thou aimest: some shrewd news, methinks, thou'lt tell.

   Sent. Danger to face, well may a man be cautious.

   Cre. Speak then, and go thy way, and make an end.

   Sent. Now I will speak. Some one ev'n now hath buried
The body and is gone; with thirsty dust
Sprinkling it o'er, and paying observance due.

   Cre. How? By what man was dared a deed so rash?

   Sent. I cannot tell. No mattock's stroke indeed,
Nor spade's upcast was there: hard was the ground, 250
Baked dry, unbroken: track of chariot-wheels
Was none, nor any sign who did this thing.

But he who kept the watch at earliest dawn
Showed to us all—a mystery, hard to clear.
Not buried was the dead man, but concealed,
With dust besprinkled, as for fear of sin:
And neither of dog, nor any beast of prey,
That came, that tore the body, found we trace.
Then bitter words we bandied to and fro,
Denouncing each the other; and soon to blows 260
Our strife had grown—was none would keep the peace—
For every one was guilty of the deed,
And none confessed, but all denied they knew.
And we were fain to handle red-hot iron,
Or walk through fire barefoot, or swear by heaven,
That neither had we done it, nor had shared
His secret with who planned it or who wrought.
So all in vain we questioned: and at last
One spake, and all who heard him, bowed by fear,
Bent to the earth their faces, knowing not 270
How to gainsay, nor doing what he said
How we might 'scape mischance. This deed to thee
He urged that we should show, and hide it not.
And his advice prevailed; and by the lot
To luckless me this privilege befell.
Unwilling and unwelcome is my errand,
A bearer of ill news, whom no man loves.

 Chor. O king, my thought hath counselled me long since,

Haply this deed is ordered by the gods.   279

    Cre. Cease, ere my wrath is kindled at thy speech,
Lest thou be found an old man and a fool.
Intolerably thou pratest of the gods,
That they to yonder dead man have respect.
Yea, for what service with exceeding honour
Sought they his burial, who came here to burn
Their pillared shrines and temple-offerings,
And of their land and of their laws make havoc?
Or seest thou that the gods allow the wicked?
Not so: but some impatient of my will
Among my people made a murmuring,   290
Shaking their heads in secret, to the yoke
With stubborn necks unbent, and hearts disloyal.
Full certainly I know that they with bribes
Have on these men prevailed to do this deed.
Of all the evils current in this world
Most mischievous is gold. This hath laid waste
Fair cities, and unpeopled homes of men:
Many an honest heart hath the false lure
Of gold seduced to walk in ways of shame;
And hence mankind are versed in villanies,   300
And of all godless acts have learnt the lore.
But, who took hire to execute this work,
Wrought to their own undoing at the last.
Since, if the dread of Zeus I still revere,
Be well assured—and what I speak I swear—

Unless the author of this burial
Ye find, and in my sight produce him here,
For you mere death shall not suffice, until
Gibbeted alive this outrage ye disclose,
That ye may know what gains are worth the winning, 310
And henceforth clutch the wiselier, having learnt
That to seek gain in all things is not well.
For from ill-gotten pelf the lives of men
Ruined than saved more often shall ye see.

  Sent. May I speak a word, or thus am I dismissed?
  Cre. Know'st thou not that ev'n now thy voice offends?
  Sent. Do I afflict thy hearing or thy heart?
  Cre. Where I am pained, it skills not to define.
  Sent. The doer grieves thy mind, but I thine ears.
  Cre. That thou wast born to chatter, 'tis too plain. 320
  Sent. And therefore not the doer of this deed.
  Cre. At thy life's cost thou didst it, bought with gold.
  Sent. Alas!
'Tis pity, men should judge, yet judge amiss.
  Cre. Talk you of 'judging' glibly as you may—
Who did this deed, I'll know, or ye shall own
That all your wondrous winnings end in loss.
  Sent. With all my heart I wish he may be found:
But found or no—for that's as fortune will—
I shall not show my face to you again.
Great cause I have to thank the gracious gods, 330
Saved past all hope and reckoning even now.

Chor. Many are the wonders of the world,   [*Strophe* 1.
And none so wonderful as Man.
Over the waters wan
His storm-vext bark he steers,
While the fierce billows break
Round his path, and o'er his head:
And the Earth-mother, first of gods,
The ageless, the indomitable,
With his ploughing to and fro   340
He wearieth, year by year:
In the deep furrow toil the patient mules.
The birds o' the air he snares and takes,   [*Antistrophe* 1.
All the light-hearted fluttering race:
And tribes of savage beasts,
And creatures of the deep,
Meshed in his woven toils,
Own the master-mind of man.
Free lives of upland and of wild
By human arts are curbed and tamed:
See the horse's shaggy neck   350
Submissive to the yoke—
And strength untired of mountain-roaming bulls.
Language withal he learnt,   [*Strophe* 2.
And Thought that as the wind is free,
And aptitudes of civic life:
Ill-lodged no more he lies,
His roof the sky, the earth his bed,

Screened now from piercing frost and pelting rain;
All-fertile in resource, resourceless never
Meets he the morrow; only death
He wants the skill to shun:
But many a fell disease the healer's art hath foiled.
So soaring far past hope, [*Antistrophe* 2.
The wise inventiveness of man
Finds diverse issues, good and ill:
If from their course he wrests
The firm foundations of the state,
Laws, and the justice he is sworn to keep,
High in the city, citiless I deem him,
Dealing with baseness: overbold,
May he my hearth avoid,
Nor let my thoughts with his, who does such deeds, agree!
What strange portentous sight is this,
I doubt my eyes, beholding? This—
How shall I gainsay what I know?—
This maiden *is*—Antigone!
Daughter of Oedipus,
Hapless child of a hapless sire,
What hast thou done? It cannot be
That thou hast transgressed the king's command—
That, taken in folly, *thee* they bring!

   Sent. This same is she that did the burial:
We caught her in the act. But where's the king?

   Chor. Back from the palace in good time he comes.

Cre. What chance is this, to which my steps are
    timed?

Sent. Nothing, sir king, should men swear not to do;
For second thoughts to first thoughts give the lie.
Hither, I made full sure, I scarce should come   390
Back, by your threats beruffled as I was.
Yet here, surprised by most unlooked-for joy,
That trifles all delights that e'er I knew,
I bring you—though my coming breaks my oath—
This maiden, whom, busied about the corpse,
We captured. This time were no lots to throw:
My own good fortune this, and none but mine.
Now therefore, king, take her yourself and try her,
And question as you will: but I have earned
Full clearance and acquittal of this coil.   400

Cre. Where, on what manner, was your captive taken?

Sent. Burying the man, we took her: all is told.

Cre. Art thou advised of this? Is it the truth?

Sent. I say I saw her burying the body,
That you forbade. Is that distinct and clear?

Cre. How was she seen, and taken in the act?

Sent. So it fell out. When I had gone from hence,
With thy loud threats yet sounding in my ears,
We swept off all the dust that hid the limbs,
And to the light stripped bare the clammy corpse,   410
And on the hill's brow sat, and faced the wind,
Choosing a spot clear of the body's stench.

Roundly we chid each other to the work;
'No sleeping at your post there' was our word.
So did we keep the watch, till in mid-heaven
The sun's bright-burning orb above us hung,
With fierce noon-heat: and now a sudden blast
Swept, and a storm of dust, that vexed the sky
And choked the plain, and all the leaves o' the trees   419
O' the plain were marred, and the wide heaven it filled:
We with shut eyes the heaven-sent plague endured.
And, when after long time its force was spent,
We saw this maiden, and a bitter cry
She poured, as of a wailing bird that sees
Her empty nest dismantled of its brood:
So she, when she espied the body bare,
Cried out and wept, and many a grievous curse
Upon their heads invoked by whom 'twas done.
And thirsty dust she sprinkled with her hands,
And lifted up an urn, fair-wrought of brass,   430
And with thrice-poured libations crowned the dead.
We saw it and we hasted, and at once,
All undismayed, our captive, hemmed her round,
And with the two offences charged her there,
Both first and last. Nothing did she deny,
But made me glad and sorry, owning all.
For to have slipped one's own neck from the noose
Is sweet, yet no one likes to get his friends
In trouble: but my nature is to make

All else of small account, so I am safe. 440
 Cre. Speak thou, who bendest on the earth thy gaze,
Are these things, which are witnessed, true or false?
 Ant. Not false, but true: that which he saw, he speaks.
 Cre. So, sirrah, thou art free; go where thou wilt,
Loosed from the burden of this heavy charge.
But tell me thou—and let thy speech be brief—
The edict hadst thou heard, which this forbade?
 Ant. I could not choose but hear what all men heard.
 Cre. And didst thou dare to disobey the law? 449
 Ant. Nowise from Zeus, methought, this edict came,
Nor Justice, that abides among the gods
In Hades, who ordained these laws for men.
Nor did I deem *thine* edicts of such force
That they, a mortal's bidding, should o'erride
Unwritten laws, eternal in the heavens.
Not of to-day or yesterday are these,
But live from everlasting, and from whence
They sprang, none knoweth. I would not, for the breach
Of these, through fear of any human pride,
To heaven atone. I knew that I must die: 460
How else? Without thine edict, that were so.
And if before my time, why, this were gain.
Compassed about with ills, who lives, as I,
Death, to such life as his, must needs be gain.

So is it to me to undergo this doom
No grief at all: but had I left my brother,
My mother's child, unburied where he lay,
Then I had grieved; but now this grieves me not.
Senseless I seem to thee, so doing? Belike
A senseless judgment finds me void of sense. 470

   Chor. How in the child the sternness of the sire
Shows stern, before the storm untaught to bend!

   Cre. Yet know full well that such o'er-stubborn wills
Are broken most of all, as sturdiest steel,
Of an untempered hardness, fresh from forge,
Most surely snapped and shivered should ye see.
Lo how a little curb has strength enough
To tame the restive horse: for to a slave
His masters give no licence to be proud.
Insult on insult heaped! Was't not enough 480
My promulgated laws to have transgressed,
But, having done it, face to face with me
She boasts of this and glories in the deed?
I surely am the woman, she the man,
If she defies my power, and I submit.
Be she my sister's child, or sprung from one
More near of blood than all my house to me,
Not so shall they escape my direst doom—
She and her sister: for I count her too
Guilty no less of having planned this work. 490
Go, call her hither: in the house I saw her

Raving ev'n now, nor mistress of her thoughts.
So oft the mind, revolving secret crime,
Makes premature disclosure of its guilt.
But this is hateful, when the guilty one,
Detected, thinks to glorify his fault.

 Ant. To kill me—wouldst thou more with me than this?

 Cre. This is enough: I do desire no more.

 Ant. Why dost thou then delay? I have no pleasure
To hear thee speak—have not and would not have: 500
Nor less distasteful is my speech to thee.
Yet how could I have won myself a praise
More honourable than this, of burying
My brother? This from every voice should win
Approval, might but fear men's lips unseal.
But kings are fortunate—not least in this,
That they may do and speak what things they will.

 Cre. All Thebes sees this with other eyes than thine.

 Ant. They see as I, but bate their breath to thee. 509

 Cre. And art thou not ashamed, from them to differ?

 Ant. To reverence a brother is not shameful.

 Cre. And was not he who died for Thebes thy brother?

 Ant. One mother bore us, and one sire begat.

 Cre. Yet, honouring both, thou dost dishonour him.

 Ant. He in the grave will not subscribe to this.

 Cre. How, if no less thou dost revere the guilty?

 Ant. 'Twas not his slave that perished, but his brother.

Cre. The enemy of this land: its champion, he.
Ant. Yet Death of due observance must not fail.
Cre. Just and unjust urge not an equal claim. 520
Ant. Perchance in Hades 'tis a holy deed.
Cre. Hatred, not ev'n in death, converts to love.
Ant. Not in your hates, but in your loves, I'd share.
Cre. Go to the shades, and, if thou'lt love, love there:
No woman, while I live, shall master me.
  Chor. See, from the palace comes Ismene—
Sisterly drops from her eyes down-shedding:
Clouded her brows droop, heavy with sorrow;
And the blood-red tinge of a burning blush
Covers her beautiful downcast face. 530
  Cre. Thou, who hast crept, a serpent in my home,
Draining my blood, unseen; and I knew not
Rearing two pests, to overset my throne;
Speak—wilt thou too confess that in this work
Thou hadst a hand, or swear thou didst not know?
  Ism. I'll say the deed was mine, if she consents:
My share of the blame I bear, and do not shrink.
  Ant. Justice forbids thy claim: neither didst thou
Agree, nor I admit thee to my counsels.
  Ism. I am not ashamed, in thine extremity, 540
To make myself companion of thy fate.
  Ant. Whose was the deed, know Hades and the dead:
I love not friends, who talk of friendliness.
  Ism. Sister, disdain me not, but let me pour

L

My blood with thine, an offering to the dead.

Ant. Leave me to die alone, nor claim the work
Thou wouldst not help. My death will be enough.

Ism. What joy have I to live, when thou art gone?

Ant. Ask Creon that: thou art of kin to him. 549

Ism. Why wilt thou grieve me with thy needless taunts?

Ant. If I mock thee, 'tis with a heavy heart.

Ism. What may I do to serve thee even now?

Ant. Look to thyself: I grudge thee not thy safety.

Ism. And may I not, unhappy, share thy death?

Ant. Thou didst make choice to live, but I to die.

Ism. Might I unsay my words, this were not so.

Ant. Wise seemed we—thou to these, and I to those.

Ism. But now our fault is equal, thine and mine.

Ant. Take heart to live: for so thou dost: but I—
Dead is my life long since—to help the dead. 560

Cre. One of these two, methinks, proves foolish now;
The other's folly with her life began.

Ism. Nay, for, O king, misfortunes of the wise
To madness turn the wisdom that they have.

Cre. 'Tis so with thee, choosing to share her guilt.

Ism. How should I live alone, without my sister?

Cre. Call her not thine: thou hast no sister now.

Ism. But wilt thou tear her from thy son's embrace?

Cre. Are there no women in the world but she?

Ism. Not as their faith was plighted, each to each. 570

Cre. An evil wife I like not for my son.

Ant. Haemon! beloved! hear not thy father's scorn.
Cre. Thou and thy love to me are wearisome.
Chor. Wilt thou indeed snatch from thy son his bride?
Cre. 'Tis death that will unloose their marriage-bond.
Chor. It seems thou art resolved that she must die?
Cre. Of that we are agreed.   Delay no more:
Ye, servants, lead them in.   For from this time
Women they needs must be, and range no more:
Since ev'n the bold may play the runaway, 580
When death he sees close-creeping on his life.
   Chor. Happy indeed is the life of the man who tastes not of trouble! [*Strophe* 1.
For when from the gods a house is shaken,
Fails nevermore the curse,
On most and on least of the race descending:
Like to a rolling wave,
By furious blasts from the Thraceward driven— 589
Out of the nethermost deeps, out of the fathomless gloom,
Casting up mire and blackness and storm-vext wrack of the sea—
And back, with a moan like thunder, from the cliffs the surf is hurled.
So from of old to the Labdacid race comes sorrow on sorrow: [*Antistrophe* 1.
And, ev'n as the dead, so fare the living:

Respite from ills is none,
Nor one generation redeems another—
All will some god bring low.
Now o'er the last root of the house, fate-stricken,
Woe for the light that had shined, woe for the lingering
      hope! 600
Smooth over all is lying the blood-stained dust they
      have spread—
Rash speech, and a frantic purpose, and the gods who
      reign below.
What human trespass, Zeus,   [*Strophe* 2.
May circumscribe thy power,
Which neither sleep o'ercomes,
That saps the strength of all things else,
Nor months that run their tireless course,
But thou for ever with an ageless sway
The dazzling splendour dost possess
Of thine Olympian home? 610
'Tis now as it hath ever been,
And still in years to come
The old order will not change:
Never from human life departs
The universal scourge of man,
His own presumptuous pride.
Hope wings her daring flight,   [*Antistrophe* 2.
By strong winds borne afar—
And some are blessed; and some

Are cheated of their vain desires,
That learn their folly all too late,
When in the fire they tread with scorchèd feet.
'Twas said of old—and time approves   620
The wisdom of the saw—
That, when in foolish ways, that end
In ruin, gods would lead
A mortal's mind astray,
Evil that man miscalls his good:
A brief while then he holds his course
By fatuous pride unscathed.
See, thy son Haemon comes hither, of all
Thy children the last.   Comes he lamenting
The doom of the maiden, his bride Antigone—
And the frustrated hope of his marriage?   630

 Cre. Soon we shall know, better than seers could say.
My son, in anger art thou come to me,
Hearing the sentence, not to be reversed,
Which on thy destined bride I have pronounced?
Or am I still thy friend, do what I may?

 Haem. Father, I am in thy hand: with thy wise
  counsels
Thou dost direct me; these I shall obey.
Not rightly should I deem of more account
The winning of a wife than thy good guidance.

 Cre. Be this thy dearest wish and next thy heart,
In all things to uphold thy father's will.   640

For to this end men crave to see grow up
Obedient children round them in their homes,
Both to requite their enemies with hate,
And render equal honour to their friends.
Whoso begets unprofitable children,
What shall be said of him, but that he gets
Grief for himself, loud laughter for his foes?
Never, my son, let for a woman's sake
Reason give way to sense, but know full well
Cold is the pleasure that he clasps, who woos   650
An evil woman to his board and bed.
What wounds so deeply as an evil friend?
Count then this maiden as thine enemy,
Loathe her, and give her leave, in that dark world
To which she goes, to marry with another.
For out of all the city since I found
Her only, and her openly, rebellious,
I shall not to the city break my word,
But she shall die.   Let her appeal to Zeus,
And sing the sanctity of kindred blood—
What then?   If in my own house I shall nurse
Rebellion, how shall strangers not rebel?   660
He who to his own kith and kin does right,
Will in the state deal righteously with all.
Of such a man I shall not fear to boast,
Well he can rule, and well he would obey,
And in the storm of battle at his post

Firm he would stand, a comrade staunch and true.
But praise from me that man shall never have,
Who either boldly thrusts aside the law
Or takes upon him to instruct his rulers,
Whom, by the state empowered, he should obey, 670
In little and in much, in right and wrong.
The worst of evils is to disobey.
Cities by this are ruined, homes of men
Made desolate by this; this in the battle
Breaks into headlong rout the wavering line;
The steadfast ranks, the many lives unhurt,
Are to obedience due. We must defend
The government and order of the state,
And not be governed by a wilful girl.
We'll yield our place up, if we must, to men;
To women that we stooped, shall not be said. 680

   Chor. Unless an old man's judgment is at fault,
These words of thine, we deem, are words of wisdom.

   Haem. Reason, my father, in the mind of man,
Noblest of all their gifts, the gods implant,
And how to find thy reasoning at fault,
I know not, and to learn I should be loth;
Yet for another it might not be amiss.
But I for thee am vigilant to mark
All that men say, or do, or find to blame.
Thy presence awes the simple citizen 690
From speaking words that shall not please thine ear,

But I hear what they whisper in the dark,
And how the city for this maid laments,
That of all women she the least deserving
Dies for most glorious deeds a death most cruel,
Who her own brother, fall'n among the slain,
Left not unburied there, to be devoured
By ravening dogs or any bird o' the air:—
'Should not her deed be blazoned all in gold?'
Upon the darkness still such whisper grows. 700
But I of all possessions that I have
Prize most, my father, thy prosperity.
Welldoing and fair fame of sire to son,
Of son to sire, is noblest ornament.
Cleave not, I pray thee, to this constant mind,
That what thou sayest, and nought beside, is truth.
For men who think that only they are wise,
None eloquent, right-minded none, but they,
Often, when searched, prove empty. 'Tis no shame,
Ev'n if a man be wise, that he should yet 710
Learn many things, and not hold out too stiffly.
Beside the torrent's course, of trees that bend
Each bough, thou seest, and every twig is safe;
Those that resist are by the roots uptorn.
And ships, that brace with stubborn hardihood
Their mainsheet to the gale, pursue their voyage
Keel-uppermost, their sailors' thwarts reversed.
Cease from thy wrath; be not inexorable:

For if despite my youth I too may think
My thought, I'll say that best it is by far   720
That men should be all-knowing if they may,
But if—as oft the scale inclines not so—
Why then, by good advice 'tis good to learn.

Chor. What in thy son's speech, king, is seasonable
'Tis fit thou shouldst receive : and thou in his :
For there is reason in the words of both.

Cre. Shall I, grown grey with age, be taught indeed—
And by this boy—to think what he thinks right?

Haem. Nothing that is not right : though I am young,
Consider not my years, but how I act.

Cre. Is this thine act—to honour the unruly?   730

Haem. Wrongdoers, dishonour—outrage, if thou wilt!

Cre. Hath not this maiden caught this malady?

Haem. The general voice of Thebes says no to that.

Cre. Shall Thebes prescribe to me how I must govern?

Haem. How all too young art thou in speaking thus!

Cre. Whose business is't but mine how Thebes is governed?

Haem. A city is none, that to one man belongs.

Cre. Is it not held, the city is the king's?

Haem. Finely thou'dst rule, alone, a land dispeopled! 739

Cre. It seems this boy will plead the woman's cause.

Haem. Woman art thou? my care is all for thee.

Cre. Shameless—is't right to wrangle with thy father?

Haem. I see that wrong for right thou dost mistake.
Cre. Do I mistake, to reverence my office?
Haem. What reverence, heaven's honours to contemn?
Cre. O hateful spirit, ruled by a woman's will!
Haem. To no base service shalt thou prove me bound.
Cre. Art thou not pleading all the time for her?
Haem. For thee and me, and for the gods below.
Cre. Thou shalt not marry her, this side the grave. 750
Haem. If she must die, she shall: but not alone.
Cre. Art grown so bold, thou dost fly out in threats?
Haem. What threats, to argue with a foolish purpose?
Cre. Thou'lt rue—unwise—thy wisdom spent on me.
Haem. Thou art my father; or wise I scarce had called thee.
Cre. Slave—to thy mistress babble, not to me.
Haem. Wouldst thou have all the talking for thine own?

Cre. Is't come to this? But, by Olympus yonder,
Know well, thou shalt be sorry for these taunts,
Wherewith thou dost upbraid me. Slaves, what ho!
Bring that abhorrence hither, that she may die, 760
Now, in her bridegroom's sight, whilst here he stands.

Haem. Neither in my sight—imagine no such thing—
Shall she be slain; nor shalt thou from this hour
Look with thine eyes upon my face again:
To friends who love thy madness I commit thee.

Chor. Suddenly, sire, in anger he is gone:

Young minds grow desperate, by grief distemper'd.
  Cre. More than a man let him conceive and do;
He shall not save these maidens from their doom.
  Chor. Both sisters art thou purposed to destroy?   770
  Cre. Not her whose hands sinned not; thou askest well.
  Chor. What of the other? how shall she be slain?
  Cre. By paths untrodden of men I will conduct her,
And shut her, living, in a vault, rock-hewn,
And there, with food, no more than shall suffice
To avert the guilt of murder from the city,
To Hades, the one god whom she reveres,
She, praying not to die, either shall have
Her asking, or shall learn, albeit too late,
That to revere the dead is fruitless toil.   780
  Chor. O Love, our conqueror, matchless in might,   [*Strophe.*
Thou prevailest, O Love, thou dividest the prey:
In damask cheeks of a maiden
Thy watch through the night is set.
Thou roamest over the sea;
On the hills, in the shepherds' huts, thou art;
Nor of deathless gods, nor of short-lived men,
From thy madness any escapeth.   790
Unjust, through thee, are the thoughts of the just,   [*Antistrophe.*
Thou dost bend them, O Love, to thy will, to thy spite.

Unkindly strife thou hast kindled,
This wrangling of son with sire.
For great laws, throned in the heart,
To the sway of a rival power give place,
To the love-light flashed from a fair bride's eyes:
In her triumph laughs Aphrodite. 800
Me, even now, me also,
Seeing these things, a sudden pity
Beyond all governance transports:
The fountains of my tears
I can refrain no more,
Seeing Antigone here to the bridal chamber
Come, to the all-receiving chamber of Death.

Ant. Friends and my countrymen, ye see me
Upon the last of all my ways
Set forth, the Sun-god's latest light
Beholding, now and never more:
But Death, who giveth sleep to all, 810
Yet living leads me hence
To the Acherontian shore,
Of marriage rites amerced,
And me no bridal song hath ever sung,
But Acheron will make of me his bride.

Chor. Therefore renowned, with praise of men,
To yonder vault o' the dead thou goest,
By no slow-wasting sickness stricken,
Nor doomed to fall with those who win

The wages of the swords they drew, 820
But, being to thyself a law,
Alone of mortals the dark road
To deathward, living, thou shalt tread.

   Ant. I heard of one, most piteous in her ending,
That stranger, child of Phrygian Tantalus,
On heights of Sipylus enclasped,
And ivy-like enchained,
By clinging tendrils of the branching rock,
Who day and night unceasingly
'Mid drizzle of rain and drift of snow
Slow-wasting in her place
Stands, as the tale is told, 830
Her lids surcharged with weeping, and her neck
And bosom drenched with falling of her tears :—
A fate most like to hers
Seals up with sleep these eyes of mine.

   Chor. She was a goddess, sprung from gods :
Mortals, of mortal birth, are we.
But for one dead to win with those
Who rank no lower than the gods—
In life and afterwards in death—
An equal lot, were much to hear.

   Ant. Ah, I am mocked ! Nay, by our fathers' gods,
Withhold thy taunts till I am gone— 840
Gone and evanished from thy sight.
O Thebes, my city !

O wealthy men of Thebes!
But *ye* will witness—yes, to you I turn—
O fount Dircaean, and this sacred grove
Of Thebè the fair-charioted,
By what stern law, and how of friends unwept,
To that strange grave I go,
The massy dungeon for my burial heaped.
O luckless wight, 850
Exiled from earth nor housed below,
Both by the living and the dead disowned!

   Chor. To furthest brink of boldness thou didst stray,
And stumbling there, at foot of Justice' throne,
Full heavily, my daughter, hast thou fallen:
Yet of thy father's fault belike
This suffering pays the price.

   Ant. Thou hast touched, ev'n there, my bitterest pang of all,
A thrice-told tale, my father's grief— 860
And all our grievous doom that clung
About the famed Labdacidae.
O that incestuous bed
Of horror, and my father's sin—
The hapless mother who bore him to the light,
By him enclasped—wherefrom I luckless sprang:
With whom, accurst, unwedded,
I must go hence to dwell.
O brother, a bride ill-starred

Who to thy couch didst win, 870
How, being dead, me living thou hast slain!

   Chor. Religion prompts the reverent deed:
But power, to whomso power belongs,
Must nowise be transgressed; and thee
A self-willed temper hath o'erthrown.

   Ant. Unwept and unfriended,
Cheered by no song Hymenaeal—
Lo, I am led, heavy-hearted,
This road that awaits me.
The sacred light-giving eye in heaven 880
Now no more must I see, unhappy:
But for my fate not a tear falls,
Not a friend makes moan.

   Cre. Know ye not, songs and weepings before death
That none would pretermit, were he allowed?
Hence with her, hence, and tarry not, but deep
In her tomb-prison, even as I have said,
Leave her alone, forsaken: to die, or else
Live, in that vault entombed, if so she will:
Since of this maiden's blood our hands are clean,
Only we ban her sojourn in the light. 890

   Ant. O tomb! O nuptial chamber! O house deep-
      delved
In earth, safe-guarded ever! To thee I come,
And to my kin in thee, who many an one
Are with Persephone, dead among the dead:

And last of all, most miserably by far,
I thither am going, ere my life's term be done.
But a good hope I cherish, that, come there,
My father's love will greet me, yea and thine,
My mother—and thy welcome, brother dear:
Since, when ye died, I with mine own hands laved 900
And dressed your limbs, and poured upon your graves
Libations; and like service done to thee
Hath brought me, Polyneices, now to this.
Yet well I honoured thee, the wise will say:
Since not for children's sake would I, their mother,
Nor for my husband, slain, and mouldering there,
Have travailed thus, doing despite to Thebes.
According to what law, do I speak this?
One husband slain, another might have been,
And children from another, losing these; 910
But, father and mother buried out of sight,
There can be born no brother any more.
Such was the law whereby I held thee first
In honour; but to Creon all mistaken,
O dear my brother, I seemed, and overbold—
And now, made captive thus, he leads me hence
No wife, no bride for ever—of marriage-joy
And nursery of children quite bereft:
So by my friends forsaken I depart,
Living, unhappy, to dim vaults of death. 920
Yet I transgressed—what ordinance of heaven?

Why to the gods, ill-fated, any more
Should I look up—whom call to succour—since
Impiety my piety is named?
But, if these things are pleasing to the gods,
I'll freely own I suffered for my fault;
If theirs the fault, who doomed me, may to them
No worse befall than they unjustly do!

 Chor. Stormily still o'er the soul of the maiden
The selfsame gusts of passion sweep.   930

 Cre. Therefore, I warn them, ruth for their lingering,
To those who lead her, this shall cause.

 Ant. Short shrift, swift death—ah! woe is me—
This speech portends.

 Cre. Lay to thy soul no flattering hope,
That unfulfilled this doom may be.

 Ant. O country of Thebes and my father's city,
And gods my progenitors,
Lo, how they lead me—now, and delay not.
O all ye princes of Thebes, behold me—   940
Of the race of your kings, me, sole surviving—
What things at the hands of what men I suffer,
For the fear of the gods I feared.

 Chor. Out of the sunlight so,   [*Strophe* 1.
In brass-bound prison-courts,
Were pent the limbs of Danaë,
And in a living tomb sealed up from sight;
Albeit, O daughter, she as thou

Came of a noble line,
And that life-quickening treasure of his golden rain 950
She had in charge from Zeus to keep.
O dread mysterious power of fate,
That neither wealth nor war can quell,
Nor walls shut out, nor ships escape,
Dark-fleeing o'er the foam!
And that Edonian king   [*Antistrophe* 1.
Was bound, the choleric son
Of Dryas, splenetive and hot,
Fast in the rock by Dionysus chained.
Such fierce and fevered issue streams
From madness at the height. 959
With splenetive rash speech what madness had assailed
The vengeful god, too late he learned.
To women-worshippers inspired
Their torchlit revels he forbade,
And flutings that the Muses loved
Had silenced with his scorn.
From the dark rock-portals of the divided sea   [*Strophe* 2.
Here go the cliffs of Bosporus, and there
The savage Thracian coast
Of Salmydessus, where the neighbour-worshipped God
Of Battle saw the blinding blow accurst, 970
Dealt by that fierce stepdame,
Darkling descend on both the sons
Of Phineus—on their sightless orbs

That plead for vengeance, stricken through and stabbed
By the sharp shuttle in her murderous hands.
Wasted with their sorrow, their mother's hapless fate

[*Antistrophe* 2.

They hapless wept, and in their mother's shame
Had part, as those base-born : 980
Yet she from the old Erechtheid blood her birth derived,
And in deep caverns of the hills was nursed,
Amid her father's storms,
Child of the North-wind—up the steep
Hillsides no bounding foal so fleet,
A daughter of the gods : but her, O child,
Fate's everlasting hands availed to reach.

Teir. Princes of Thebes, we come—one sight for both
Our common road descrying, as behoves
Blind men to find their way by help of others. 990
Cre. What tidings, old Teiresias, dost thou bring?
Teir. Hear then the prophet, and attend his speech.
Cre. Have I aforetime from thy wisdom swerved?
Teir. So, clear of shoals, thou pilotest the state.
Cre. The service thou hast rendered I attest.
Teir. Once more on razor's edge thy fortunes stand.
Cre. Hearing thy speech, I shudder : tell me more.
Teir. My art's prognostications hear and judge.
For in my ancient seat, to watch the birds
In that their general gathering-place, I sat, 1000
And heard an unintelligible noise,

A cry and clangour of birds, confused with rage;
And what fierce fray they waged with murderous claws,
I guessed too surely by the whirr of wings.
Scared by that sound, burnt-offerings I then
Essayed on blazing altars; but no flame
Leapt from the sacrifice; a clammy ooze
Reeked from the thighs, and 'mid the ashes dripped,
Smoking and sputtering; the gall disparted,
And on the air was spent; and the thigh-bones   1010
Of the enfolding fat fell stripped and bare.
This from this boy I heard, whose eyes beheld
The failing signs of sacrifice obscure:
Others by me are guided, I by him.
And by thy will we are afflicted thus.
For now our hearths and altars every one
Have ravening dogs and birds fouled with the flesh
Of this poor fallen son of Oedipus;
And so no flame of victims burnt may move
Gods any more to hearken to our prayers,   1020
And birds obscene flap forth a bodeful cry,
With fat of human carrion newly gorged.
Slight not, my son, such warning. For all men,
Both great and small, are liable to err:
But he who errs no more unfortunate
Or all unwise shall be, if having tripped
He rights the wrong nor stubbornly persists.
He who persists in folly is the fool.

Give death his due : stab not the fallen foe :
What valour is in this, to slay the slain ?   1030
Wisely I speak and well; and sweet it is
To hear good counsel, when it counsels gain.

   Cre. Old man, ye all, as bowmen at a mark,
Shoot at this man, and with your prophecies
Ye practise on me too, and mine own kin
Mere merchandise and salework make of me.
Go to, get gain, and barter, if ye will,
Amber ye buy from Sardis, and fine gold
Of Ind : but him, I say, ye shall not bury :
No, not if eagles, ministers of Zeus,   1040
Should bear him piecemeal to their Master's throne,
Will I, for fear of such pollution, grant
Leave for his burial ; knowing well that men
Soil not the stainless majesty of heaven.
But, aged seer, the wisest of mankind
Dishonourably may fall, who fairly speak
Dishonourable words, and all for gain.

   Teir. Alas !
Who knows, or who considers, in this world—

     Cre. What wilt thou say ? What commonplace is this ?

     Teir. How prudence is the best of all our wealth? 1050

     Cre. As folly, I suppose, our deadliest hurt.

     Teir. Yet with this malady art thou possest.

     Cre. Reproaches I'll not bandy with the prophet.

     Teir. Saying that I falsely prophesy, thou dost.

Cre. So are all prophets; 'tis a covetous race.
Teir. Greed of base gain marks still the tyrant-sort.
Cre. Knowest thou that of thy rulers this is said?
Teir. I know; for thou through me didst save the state.
Cre. Wise in thy craft art thou, but false at heart.   1059
Teir. Secrets, fast-locked, thou'lt move me to disclose.
Cre. Unlock them, only speaking not for gain.
Teir. So, for thy part indeed, methinks I shall.
Cre. Think not that in my purpose thou shalt trade.
Teir. But surely know that thou not many more
Revolving courses of the sun shalt pass,
Ere of thine own blood one, to make amends,
Dead for the dead, thou shalt have rendered up,
For that a living soul thou hast sent below,
And with dishonour in the grave hast lodged,
And that one dead thou holdest here cut off   1070
From presence of the gods who reign below,
All rites of death, all obsequies denied—
With whom thou shouldst not meddle, nor the gods
In heaven, but of their due thou robb'st the dead.
Therefore of Hades and the gods for thee
The Avengers wait, with ruin slow yet sure,
To take thee in the pit which thou hast dug.
Do I speak this for gold? Thyself shalt judge:
For, yet a little while, and wailings loud
Of men and women in thy house shall show.

Think, of each city too what gathering rage, 1080
That sees its mangled dead entombed in maws
Of dogs and all fierce beasts, or borne by kites
With stench unhallowed to its hearth-crowned heights.
So like a bowman have I launched at thee
In wrath, for thou provok'st me, shafts indeed
To pierce thy heart, and fail not, from whose smart
Thou'lt not escape.   But now, boy, lead me home,
That he may vent his spleen on younger men,
And learn to keep a tongue more temperate,
And in his breast a better mind than now. 1090

   Chor. The man has prophesied dread things, O king,
And gone: and never have I known—not since
These temples changed their raven locks to snow—
That aught of false this city heard from him.

   Cre. Yea, this I know, and much am I perplexed:
For hard it is to yield, but standing firm
I fear to pluck swift ruin on my pride.

   Chor. Son of Menoeceus, be advised in time.

   Cre. Say then, what must I do? and I'll obey.

   Chor. Go, from her prison in the rock release 1100
The maiden, and the unburied corpse inter.

   Cre. Dost thou think this, and wouldst thou have me yield?

   Chor. Yea, king, and quickly; for the gods cut short
With sudden scathe the foolishness of men.

Cre. Hardly indeed, but yet with forced consent
I'll do it, stooping to necessity.

Chor. Do it, and go; leave not this task to others.

Cre. Even as I am, I'll go; and, servants, haste,
That hear and hear me not: axes in hand,
All to yon spot, far-seen, make good your speed.   1110
But I, since this way now my mind is bent,
Whom I myself have bound, myself will loose.
For now my heart misgives me, he lives best,
Whose feet depart not from the ancient ways.

Chor. Worshipped by many names—   [*Strophe* 1.
Glory of Theban Semele,
Child of loud-thundering Zeus—
Haunting the famed Italian fields,
Whom as a prince the hospitable vale   1120
Of the Eleusinian Dame reveres—
Bacchus, that hast thy home
In Thebes, the home of Bacchanals,
Beside Ismenus' fertile stream,
Where the fell dragon's teeth of old were sown:
O'er the two-crested peak,   [*Antistrophe* 1.
With nymphs Corycian in thy train,
By springs of Castaly,
The streaming levin lights thy path: 1130
And from steep Nysa's hills, with ivy clad,
And that green slope, with clustering grapes
Empurpled to the sea,

When thou wouldst visit Theban streets,
A jocund company divine
With acclamation loud conducts thee forth.
Thebes of all cities most thou honourest, [*Strophe* 2.
Thou with thy mother, whom the lightning slew:
And now, when Thebes is sick, 1140
And all her people the sore plague hath stricken,
Hear us and come with healing feet
O'er the Parnassian hill,
Or the resounding strait:
Come, whom fire-breathing stars in dance obey, [*Ant.* 2.
The master of the voices of the night,
Of Zeus the puissant son—
Come at our call, girt with thy Thyiad troop, 1150
That follow, with thy frenzy filled,
Dancing the livelong night,
Iacchus, thee their lord.

 Mess. Neighbours of Cadmus, and the royal house
Of old Amphion, no man's life would I,
How high or low soever, praise or blame,
Since, who to-day has fortune, good or ill,
To-morrow's fortune lifts or lays him low;
No seer a constant lot foresees for men. 1160
For Creon before was happy, as I deemed,
Who saved this land of Cadmus from its foes,
And the sole sovereignty of Thebes receiving
Prospered therein, with noble children blest.

Now all is lost. For, when the joys of life
Men have relinquished, no more life indeed
I count their living, but a living death.
For in thy house heap riches, if thou wilt;
Keep kingly state; yet, if no joy withal   1169
Thou hast, for all things else, compared with pleasure,
I would not change the shadow of a smoke.

   Chor. Of what grief now of princes wilt thou tell?

   Mess. That one lies dead, whom those who live have slain.

   Chor. Say, who is slain? And what man is the slayer?

   Mess. Haemon is dead: his death no stranger's act.

   Chor. Slain by himself, or by his father's hand?

   Mess. Wroth with his pitiless sire, he slew himself.

   Chor. O prophet, how thy prophecy comes true!

   Mess. These things being so, consider of the rest.

   Chor. Lo, hard at hand the miserable queen,   1180
Eurydice: who from the house comes forth
Either by chance, or hearing of her son.

   Eur. Good townsmen all, your conference I heard,
As to the doors I came, intending now
Of Pallas to entreat her heavenly aid.
Even as I loosèd the fastenings of the gate,
That opened wide, there smote my ears a word
Of sorrow all my own: backward I swooned,
Surprised by terror, in my maidens' arms:

But tell me now your tidings once again—   1190
For, not unlearned in sorrow, I shall hear.
   Mess. Dear mistress, I will tell thee what I saw,
And not leave out one word of all the truth.
Why should I flatter thee with glozing words,
Too soon found false? Plain truth is ever best.
Thy husband hence I followed at the heels
To that high plain, where torn by dogs the body
Of Polyneices lay, unpitied still.
A prayer we said to Hecate in the way
And Pluto, their displeasure to refrain,   1200
Then, sprinkling with pure water, in new-stript boughs
Wrapped round and burned the fragments that re-
      mained.
A lofty funeral-mound of native earth
We heaped for him; then sought the maiden's bed,
Her bridal bed with Hades in the rock.
And from afar a voice of shrill lament
About the unhallowed chamber some one heard,
And came to Creon, and told it to his lord.
And in his ears, approaching, the wild cry
Rang doubtfully, till now there brake from him   1210
A word of sharp despair, 'O wretched man,
What fear is at my heart? and am I going
The wofullest road that ever I have gone?
It is my son's voice greets me. Good servants, go,
Go nearer quickly; and standing by the tomb,

Even to the throat of the vault peer through and look,
Where the wrenched stonework gapes, if Haemon's voice
I recognise indeed, or by the gods
Am cheated!' Crazed with his fear, he spake; and we
Looked, as he bade; and in the last of the tomb   1220
We saw the maiden—hanged: about her neck
Some shred of linen had served her for a noose:
And fallen upon her, clasping her, he lay,
Wailing his wasted passion in the grave,
His fatal father, and his luckless bride.
His father saw, and crying a bitter cry
Went in, and with a lamentable voice
Called him, 'O rash, what is it that thou hast done?
What wouldst thou? On what madness hast thou rushed?
My son, come forth: I pray thee—I implore.'   1230
But with fierce eyes the boy glared at his sire
And looks of loathing, and for answer plucked
Forth a two-hilted sword, and would have struck,
But missed him, as he fled: and in that minute,
Wroth with himself, in his own side amain
Thrust deep the steel, unhappy; and conscious still
Folded the maiden in his fainting arms;
Then, gasping out his life in one sharp breath,
Pelted her pale cheek with the crimson shower.
Dead with the dead he lies, such nuptial rites   1240
In halls of Hades, luckless, having won;
Teaching the world, that of all human ills

With human folly is none that may compare.

    Chor. How should one deem of this? The queen, without
A word, of good or evil, has gone hence.

    Mess. Indeed, 'tis strange: but yet I feed on hope
That to lament in public for her son
She will not deign; but, as for private sorrow,
Will charge her women in the house to weep.
She is well tried in prudence, not to fail.   1250

    Chor. I know not; but to me the too-much silence,
No less than clamorous grief, seems perilous.

    Mess. I will go hence to the house, and know, if aught
Of secret purpose in her raging heart
She hath kept locked from us. Thou sayest well:
The too-much silence may bode mischief too.

    Chor. Lo, the king comes hither himself, in his hands
The record, not doubtful its purport, bearing;
No grief (I dare to say) wrought by another,
But the weight of his own misdoing.   1260

    Cre. Alas, my purblind wisdom's fatal fault, [*Strophe.*
Stubborn, and fraught with death!
Ye see us, sire and son,
The slayer and the slain.
O counsels all unblest!
Alas for thee, my son,
So young a life and so untimely quenched—
Gone from me, past recall—

Not by thy folly, but my own! 1269
   Chor. Ah, how too late thou dost discern the truth!
   Cre. Yea, to my cost I know: but then, methinks,
Oh then, some god with crushing weight
Leapt on me, drave me into frantic ways,
Trampling, alas for me,
In the base dust my ruined joy.
O toil and trouble of mortals—trouble and toil!
   Sec. Mess. Trouble, O king, thine own and none but
      thine,
Thou comest, methinks, part bearing in thy hands;
Part—in the house thou hast, and soon shalt see. 1280
   Cre. What more, what worse than evil, yet remains?
   Sec. Mess. Thy wife is dead, with desperate hand ev'n
      now
Self-slain, for this dead son for whom she lived.
   Cre. O harbour of Hades, never to be appeased, [*Ant.*
Why art thou merciless?
What heavy news is this?
Harsh news to me of grief,
That slays me, slain before!
A woful word indeed, 1290
Telling of slaughter upon slaughter heaped,
To me, the twice-bereaved,
At one fell swoop, of son and wife!
   Chor. Behold and see: for now the doors stand wide.
   Cre. This second grief, ah me, my eyes behold.

What fate, ah what, remains behind?
My son I hold already in my arms:
And now, ah woe is me,
This other in my sight lies dead:
Mother and child—most piteous both to see! 1300

 Sec. Mess. Heartstricken at the altar as she fell,
Her swooning eyes she opened, and made moan
For Megareus, her son, who nobly died
Before, and for this other, and with her last
Breath cursed, the slayer of her children, thee.

 Cre. Ah me, will no one aim
Against my heart, made wild with fear,
With two-edged sword a deadly thrust?
O wretched that I am, 1310
Fulfilled with sorrow, and made one with grief!

 Sec. Mess. She did reproach thee, truly, ere she died,
And laid on thee the blame of both their deaths.

 Cre. What was the manner of her violent end?

 Sec. Mess. Pierced to the heart, by her own hand, she died,
Hearing her son's most lamentable fate.

 Cre. All, all on me this guilt must ever rest,
And on no head but mine.
O my poor son, I slew thee, even I:
Let no one doubt, but that the deed was mine. 1320
O servants, lead me quickly, lead me hence;
And let me be as one who is no more.

Chor. 'Tis counselled well, if well with ill can be :
For bad is best, when soonest out of sight.
    Cre. I care not, let it come :
Let come the best of all my fate,   1330
The best, the last, that ends my days :
What care I ? come what will—
That I no more may see another day.
    Chor. Let be the future : mind the present need,
And leave the rest to whom the rest concerns.
    Cre. No other wish have I ; that prayer is all.
    Chor. Pray not at all : all is as fate appoints :
'Tis not in mortals to avert their doom.
    Cre. Oh lead me hence, unprofitable ; who thee
Unwittingly have slain,   1340
Child, and my wife, unhappy ; and know not now
Which way to look to either : for all things
Are crooked that I handle, and a fate
Intolerable upon my life hath leapt.
    Chor. First of all happiness far is wisdom,
And to the gods that one fail not of piety.
But great words of the overweening
Lay great stripes to the backs of the boasters :   1350
Taught by adversity,
Old age learns, too late, to be wise.

ELECTRA

PERSONS.

ORESTES.
PYLADES. (*Mute.*)
AEGISTHUS.
PEDAGOGUE *or* ATTENDANT.
CLYTAEMNESTRA.
ELECTRA.
CHRYSOTHEMIS.
CHORUS OF ARGIVE MAIDENS.

Electra.

Ped. SON of that Agamemnon, who round Troy
       Gathered the hosts of Greece, now with thine eyes
May'st thou behold all that thy heart desired.
This is the ancient Argos of thy longing—
The precinct this of Ino, frenzied maid:
Named of the god, the Slayer of the wolf,
The Place Lyceian see, Orestes, here—
Hera's famed temple yonder on the left:
But, whither our feet are come, deem that thou seest
None other than Mycenae, the rich city—
Mycenae, rich in gold; and, rich in slaughter, 10
Stand there the halls of the Pelopidae—
Whence from the slaying of thy sire, that day,
By thine own sister trusted to my hands,
I bore thee forth, and saved thee, and have reared,
Till lo thou art grown a man—thy sire's avenger.
Now, then, Orestes, and thou, best of friends,
Pylades, counsel quickly of the way.
For see, the sun is risen, and his beam
Wakes clear the matin voices of the birds,

And the murk night of stars is overworn.
Then linger not till folk come from the house,   20
But straight confer; since, where we stand, is now
No time for tarrying, but high time for deeds.

Or. O good old servitor, how well appears
By certain proof thy loyalty to us;
For, as a noble steed, though he be old,
In extreme peril pricks erect his ear,
Forgetting not his valiant strain, so thou
Both hastenest us and followest first thyself.
Hear then how I advise, and to my words
Give thou good heed; then let thy better wit   30
Correct me, if in aught I miss the mark.
When to the Pythian oracle I came
Inquiring of the god how best I might
Join issue with the murderers of my sire,
Phoebus to me made answer—mark me, how.
By guile, alone, aidless of shields or host,
He bade me snatch the retributive stroke.
So spake the voice prophetic. Therefore go—
Soon as occasion bids thee, enter straight—
Know all that is a-doing in the house;   40
Then, of thy knowledge, bring us certain word.
So old and lapsed in years, fear not that folk
Will know thee, or suspect, besprent with grey.
Be this thy word, thou art a stranger come
From Phocis, sent by Phanoteus their friend—

Friend and ally more potent have they none.
Then tell them, and confirm it with an oath,
Orestes by hard stroke of doom is dead—
At Delphi, in the race of whirling wheels,
From chariot flung: so let the story stand.   50
Meanwhile my father's tomb—our task prescribed—
We with libation first will duly crown
And wealth of tresses shorn, then back return,
An urn of brass uplifted in our hands—
Whereof thou knowest, in safe covert hid—
So to announce our welcome tidings false,
Tidings that this my body is no more,
But calcined now and charred to nothingness.
Since what offends me here, when death in name
Proves life indeed to me and wins renown?   60
Words fraught with gain, I trow, cannot be ill.
Have I not heard of wise men, not a few,
Dying in an idle rumour? Back they come—
Great out of knowledge straightway are they grown.
So living, doubt not, from this falsehood's cloud
I on my dazzled foes, starlike, shall break.
But, O my fatherland, and native gods,
Receive me prospering in my home-return;
And ye, halls of my fathers; for I come
With justice charged by heaven to make you clean;   70
And send me not dishonoured from the land—
Let me begin its wealth, and right my house.

My say is said; thee let it now concern,
Old man, to go, and of thy task have heed—
And forth will we; for so occasion bids,
The sovereign ruler of all deeds of men.
    El. Ah me, alas!
    Ped. Hark—from the doors sounded a woman's voice
Weeping, meseemed—some servant of the house.
    Or. Is it the sad Electra? shall we bide   80
Here for awhile, and hearken her lament?
    Ped. Not so: nought else let us attempt before
The bidding of the god we have performed,
Our work's inauguration—to pour out
Libations to thy sire; for this imports
The victory ours, and prospers all we do.   [*They go out.*
    El. O holy light of heaven,
And Earth's coequal, Air,
How many a mourning song of me,
And buffeting of how many a blow
Upon my bleeding bosom have ye heard,   90
When night, your dusky robe, ye leave behind!
And well ere now this house of horror knows,
And my detested couch,
What night-vigils I keep—
For my unhappy sire what dirge I make,
Whom, from a barbarous land returned,
From entertainment 'scaped of Ares fierce,

My mother and her paramour,
Aegisthus, ev'n as woodfellers an oak,
With murderous axe hewed to the nape ;
And no compassion for these things,
Father, for thy so hideous piteous end,
From other lips than mine escapes :
But nowise will I fail
Of weeping and lamenting sore,
Till from my sight the shimmering sheen of stars,
And this fair daylight, fail ;
But, as a nightingale
For Itys unconsoled,
From these ancestral doors will I
Still utter forth in all men's ears
A lamentable voice.
O home of Hades and Persephone,
O ghostly Hermes and thou sovereign Curse,
And dread divine Erinyes,
Whose eyes behold the foully slain,
And those adulterously spoiled—
Hearken and come and help,
Our father's murder foul avenge,
And speed my brother home to me—
To me, whose single strength
No more can countervail
This downward-dragging weight of woe.
    Chor. Child of the guilty one,

Electra, how dost thou still
Waste in inveterate grief thy strength away
For Agamemnon, trapped, how long ago,
By cursed treachery of thy mother false,
And to the cowardly blow betrayed—may he
Who planned it perish—so God pardon me the word ! 129

El. O noble hearts, your coming soothes my pain.
I know and understand full well—
Nothing escapes me that ye say—
Yet would I not give o'er,
Not cease from weeping for my hapless sire.
But ye whose love responsive beats
To every mood of mine,
Allow my raving thus—
Ah me—for pity !

Chor. But not with sobs or prayers
Thy father shalt thou bring
Back from the dark inevitable flood.
Yet thou with ceaseless tears dost lose thyself 140
In sorrow beyond reason uncontrolled—
Wherein is no remission of thy pain.
Why wilt thou woo thy misery ?

El. Fool, who forgets a parent's piteous loss !
She fits my fancy rather,
That passionate and melancholy bird,
The messenger of Zeus, that makes her plaint

For Itys, Itys, evermore.
O queen of sorrow, Niobe,
I hail thee goddess—thee
Who, rock-ensepulchred,
Art weeping, weeping still.

Chor. To thee, thee single in the world,
Daughter, no grief has come,
Touching thee more than those within—
Blood of thy blood, thy sisters both,
Chrysothemis and Iphianassa, who yet live—
And he too lives, his young life screened from sorrow,
Blest, whom our famed Mycenian land
Shall one day welcome home, her noblest son,
In God's good time returning,
Returning home—Orestes.

El. For whom I waiting, ah the weary while,
Poor wretch, no mother and no wife,
Fail still for waiting, wasted with my tears—
And see my lot, sad without end of sorrow:
But he forgets
What he endured, and what has heard:
For what to me
Of tidings comes, not soon belied?
For always he desires,
But yet desiring heeds not to appear.

Chor. Courage, O daughter, courage: still
High Zeus in heaven is king,

Who sees and governs all;
To whom thine all too bitter wrath committing,
Neither forget thy foes nor hate them overmuch.
Time as a god makes rough ways smooth:
For neither Agamemnon's son,
Who by the sea with Crisa's herdsmen bides,
Hath all forgotten thee,
No, nor the god by Acheron who reigns.

El. But now almost in dull despair
My days are fled, my strength is spent;
My wasted frame no parents tend,
No loving champion shields from wrong;
Lodged as an alien, scarce allowed
Beneath my father's roof a home,
Clad in this mean attire,
And standing by a table scantly spread.

Chor. O piteous voice, proclaimed his home-return—
Piteous, whenas he lay at feast,
When through the temples of thy sire
The steely jaws remorseless flashed and struck.
'Twas guile that planned, and lust that smote,
Whereof the dire embrace
A direful act engenderèd—
By whomsoever this was done,
A mortal or a god.

El. O bitter, bitter day,
Beyond all days to me:

O night—O utter agony
Of that unutterable feast:
And O the hideous sight my sire beheld,
Those hands uplifted of the murderous twain,
Whose treason sapped my life, and murdered me:
For whom, supreme Olympian king,
Prepare such retributive fate,   210
Shall turn to dust the glittering prize,
Their deed achieved.

   Chor. Be advised to speak no more:
Hast thou not wit to mark,
Wherefrom into this low estate,
Into what woes self-gotten,
Thou art fallen so miserably?
No light excess of pain thou to thyself procurest,
Still in thy brooding soul
Conceiving war; but war 'tis none,
To struggle with the strong.   220

   El. I must, upon a dread compulsion must:
Nay, I know, my own heart full well I know;
But, whilst the dread is on my soul,
Not for the sake of life shall act of mine
Set to these miseries an end:
For what, kind hearts, but most unseemly words,
To all, to all that see aright,
Should then of me be spoken?
Ah, comfort, comfort, let me be:

For cureless shall my case be called, 230
Nor ever shall I cease from pain,
From pouring sigh on sigh.

Chor. Nay, but in love I counsel thee,
Ev'n as a careful mother might,
Add not to sorrows sorrow self-conceived.

El. But of my wretchedness what bound?
Shall we forget the dead? Were this then well?
Is there in men ingratitude so deep?
Never may I of such an one have praise;
Never may I, if still to any good 240
I cleave, in selfish ease abide therewith,
Checking, neglectful of my sire,
The pinion strong of passionate lament.
Because if he, being slain, woe worth the day,
Sleeps 'neath the earth, and is no more,
And those his enemies
Pay not their blood for his,
Then both regard of man and fear of God
From earth shall cease. 250

Chor. Daughter, I came, zealous alike for thee
As for myself; but if I speak not well
Have thou thy way, for I will follow thee.

El. I am ashamed, O ladies, if ye deem
Impatient overmuch my oft complaining:
But, since necessity compels my grief,
Chide not. How were it noble not to grieve,

Seeing my father's house oppressed with woe—
Yes, and I see the trouble day and night
Not ceasing, but prevailing more and more: 260
Who from the mother who bore me have found, first,
Hatred for love; then, under my own roof
I with my father's murderers abide;
They rule me, and from them comes all I have—
My having and my wanting, both are theirs.
Bethink you next, what sort of days I pass,
Seeing Aegisthus seated on the throne
That was my father's—seeing him clad in robes
That once my father wore, and pouring out
Libations at the hearth whereat he slew him, 270
And seeing this their crowning insolence,
The murderer couching in our father's bed
Beside our wretched mother—if we must
Call her our mother, wedded to this man;
Shameless she is, and with the guilty one
Dwells, fearing no Avenger of these things;
But, even as though she gloried in her deed,
Hath found her out that fatal day, whereon
Our father by her treachery she slew,
And honours it with dances, and each month 280
To the Saviour Gods makes sacrifice of sheep.
And I, beholding, wretched, in the house
Wear out my strength with weeping, and lament
For the unholy feast, named of my sire,

Myself in secret: for I may not have
Even of weeping all my heart desires.
For then this woman—nobly can she speak—
With words of fierce reviling taunts me thus:
'How, impious and abominable girl?
Hast thou alone to bear a father's loss?
Are there no mourners in the world but thou? 290
My curse upon thee! May the gods below
Give thee no riddance of thy present griefs!'
So she insults me: save when one brings word
Orestes will come home; that makes her mad—
Standing, she thunders forth: 'Thou art the cause,
For is not this thy work, who from my hands
Didst steal Orestes, and convey him hence?
But know that thou shalt have thy fit reward.'
Such words she shrieks; and with her, at her side,
Her glorious partner prompts her, word for word, 300
This utter coward, this villain unredeemed,
Who fights his battles with a woman's help.
And all my life ebbs from me, waiting still
Until Orestes come to bid them cease.
So has he wrecked, still meaning, never doing,
Hopes that I had and had not, all alike.
So faring, O my friends, of modesty
Or reverence I wot not; help is none—
I must in evil plight learn evil ways.

    Chor. Say, is Aegisthus near us in the house, 310

While thus we talk together, or gone abroad?
   El. Doubt not of that. Think not that, were he near,
I to the doors had come. He is afield.
   Chor. So with a better courage might I hold
Converse with thee, if this indeed is thus.
   El. As in his absence, ask: what wouldst thou know?
   Chor. I ask thee then: how sayest thou of thy brother—
That he will come, or lingers? Let me know.
   El. He says; but, saying, does not what he says.   319
   Chor. One well may pause, who has great work to do
   El. And yet I paused not when I rescued him.
   Chor. Courage: he's noble—will not fail his friends.
   El. I trust, or else I had not lived so long.
   Chor. Speak now no more: for at the doors I see
Chrysothemis, thy sister, of one sire
With thee, one mother, and to the tomb she bears
Gifts, such as to the dead men use to give.
   Chrys. Sister, what voice again art thou come here
To utter in the doorway of the house?
Not even in all this time wilt thou be taught   . 330
Not idly to indulge a barren wrath?
Yet this I know, that I myself am grieved
To see the things I see: soon would I show
What love I bear them, could I find the strength.

But now ride out the storm with shortened sail
I must, nor dream of harm I cannot do.
And such a prudent course I would were thine.
Justice, I know, is not as I advise,
But as thou choosest: but, to keep my life
Free, I must yield in all things to the strong.   340

   El. Oh strange, that thou, the daughter of such a sire,
Forgettest him, and carest for thy mother!
For all these admonitions that I hear
Are taught of her, and nothing of thyself.
And yet—choose which thou wilt, to be unwise,
Or, being prudent, to forget thy friends:
Who sayest now that, couldst thou find the strength,
What hate thou bearest these, should soon be seen:
But I avenge my father all I can,
Unhelped by thee—I do, and thou dissuadest.   350
Is not this bad, and cowardly besides?
For teach me, or by me be taught, what gain,
Ceasing from lamentation, should I have?
I live: though ill, yet well enough for me,
And they are vexed, and honoured is the dead,
If there is any comfort in the grave.
Prate not to me of hating—vain pretence,
While with thy father's murderers thou abidest:
Never would I consent—not for the chance
Of all those gifts of thine that make thee proud—   360
To stoop myself to these: I grudge thee not

The wealthy table, the abounding life.
Not to offend myself, be this alone
My meat and drink : I covet not thine honours :
Nor thou, if thou wert wise. Men might have called thee
Child of the noblest father in the world:
But now be named thy mother's. So indeed
To many men thy baseness shall appear,
False to thy father's memory and thy friends.

  Chor. Oh speak not aught in anger : for the words
Of both are profitable, couldst thou consent   370
To learn from her, and she again from thee.

  Chrys. Used, ladies, to my sister's speech am I :
Nor on this theme should I have entered now,
Had I not heard of mischief threatening her,
Great mischief, that shall end her loud complainings.

  El. Tell me your worst; withhold not. Of aught worse
Than this if thou canst tell me, I give in.

  Chrys. I will say out the whole of what I know.
They purpose, if thou wilt not cease from weeping,
Thither to send thee, where thou shalt not see   380
The sunlight, but a prisoner all thy days
Sing in the dark thy sorrows, banished hence.
Therefore bethink thee, and blame not me hereafter,
When falls the blow. Time to be wise is now.

  El. Are they so purposed ? Will they use me thus ?

  Chrys. Ay truly, when Aegisthus is returned.

  El. If that be all, so may he come with speed !

Chrys. O hapless one, what speech, what prayer is this?
El. That he may come, if this he means to do.
Chrys. That thou may'st suffer—what? Where are thy wits? 390
El. That far from sight of you I may escape.
Chrys. And hast thou of thy present life no thought?
El. A fair and admirable life is mine!
Chrys. It might be, didst thou know how to be wise.
El. Teach me not thou, how to be false to friends.
Chrys. I teach thee not, but to the strong to yield.
El. Be it thine to flatter thus—'tis not my way.
Chrys. But not to fall through folly were no shame.
El. If I must fall, I will—my sire's avenger.
Chrys. I know my father will forgive me this. 400
El. Such words are fit for traitors to applaud.
Chrys. Wilt thou not hearken, and be ruled by me?
El. Long may it be before my wits so wander.
Chrys. Then I will do my errand and begone.
El. Whither art thou going? these offerings are for whom?
Chrys. My mother bids me pour them on the tomb.
El. How? on the tomb of him—her enemy?
Chrys. Slain by her very hand—so thou wouldst say.
El. Which of her friends advised? whose wish was this?
Chrys. Warned as I think by a terror of the night. 410
El. Gods of our house—now aid me—now at last!
Chrys. Does this that has scared her give heart to thee?

El. Tell me the vision, and I'll answer that.
Chrys. I know not, nor I cannot tell thee much.
El. Tell what thou knowest. Often a little word
Hath marred men's fortunes—and oft made them too.
Chrys. I hear them say that she beheld again,
Revisiting the light, our father's form,
His very presence, and that he took and on the hearth
Planted that sceptre which he wielded once, 420
But now Aegisthus: and from this there shot
Upward a fruitful bough, whose shade waxed great
Above Mycenae, and covered all the land.
Such tale I heard from one recounting it,
Who heard her tell the dream to Helios:
But more than this I know not, save that she
Has sent me hither by reason of this fear.
Now by the gods who keep our house, I pray thee,
Hearken to me, and fall not through thy folly;
For, spurn me now, thou'lt seek me sorrowing. 430
El. Good sister, of all thou bearest in thy hands
Touch not the tomb with aught: for funeral gifts
Of this fell woman men nor gods allow
Thou to thy sire shouldst offer, or pour out
Libations: to the winds or to the dust
Deep-delved commit them, where they shall not come
Near to my father's bed: against her death,
Let them be treasured under ground for her.
Most shameless woman of all women is she,

Or else she had never thought, on him she slew 440
To pour libations, not of love but hate.
How think you? Seems it he will take these gifts,
Her buried lord, take and be pleased to take,
Even at her hand who slew him cruelly
As foe not friend, and mangled having slain,
And for ablution on his temples wiped
The blood-stains. Think you this which here you
 bear
Shall serve her for the quittance of her guilt?
It cannot be. Fling then these gifts away:
Cut rather from thy head its topmost tress
And give to him, and give (small gifts indeed, 450
But yet my best), give him from hapless me
This one poor lock, unfit for suppliant use,
And this my girdle, with no bravery decked;
And pray to him and bid him from the earth
Come graciously to help us from our foes,
And that Orestes with victorious strength
May live to trample down his enemies;
That so henceforth with wealthier hands than now
More costly gifts we to his tomb may bring.
Nay, for methinks, methinks his care it was
That visited her with such ill-favoured dreams. 460
Yet, sister, do this thing; so shalt thou help
Thyself and me, and help thy sire and mine—
Yea, even in the grave, our dearest still.

Chor. 'Tis piously advised: and, daughter, thou
Wilt do this service, if thy heart be right.

Chrys. Be it so: for of the right unmeet it were
We twain should wrangle, hastening not the deed.
Only, adventuring to do this thing,
I charge ye, friends, that ye betray me not;
For, if my mother hears it, well I know 470
That I shall rue my venture ere 'tis done.

Chor. Either a seer of dreams am I   [*Strophe.*
Of wit and wisdom void,
Or Justice straight shall come,
The sovereign Seer, by whom I see,
Crowned with the might of a righteous deed—
Shall come, my child, and make no tarrying;
So is my heart grown strong,
Since this fair dream made music in mine ears.   480
For now I know, thy sire remembereth,
Lord of the hosts of Greece;
Nor hath forgetfulness made dull
The ancient axe two-edged with biting steel,
That struck him down with outrage and with shame.
With the tramp of an army's tread,   [*Antistrophe.*
With multitudinous menace of lifted hands,
She shall come, the Erinys, whose feet are brass— 490
From her dreadful ambush shall start and come.
On the impious ones there fell
Lust, and adulterous haste

To a bed forbidden, a bridal cursed.
Therefore I know, for this
We not, ah not in vain shall look;
Not unaghast the murderous pair shall see
Nearer and nearer the horror creep:
Or else there is no art of men
To interpret dreams of fear, 500
And words oracular,
Unless this dream shall turn to good.
O woful charioting [*Epode.*
Of Pelops long ago!
O curse abiding, on this land that fell!
For, since beneath the wave
Sank Myrtilus on sleep,
From the chariot all of gold 510
With rash outrageous hand
Flung headlong forth,
Not from that day to this
Out of this house hath ceased
The tale of outrage, woe on woe.

 Clyt. At large once more thou rangest, as it seems,
Aegisthus absent—he who kept thee still
From gadding thus abroad to shame thy friends.
But, now that he is hence, thou hast no heed
Of me: although to many, many a time 520
Thou hast complained that I, unjust and harsh,

Provoke thy spirit, insulting thee and thine.
What insult, when I do but give thee back
Taunts for the ceaseless taunts I hear from thee?
Thy father—father still, thy one pretence—
By me was slain. By me? I know it well:
'Tis true, past all denying, so he was.
For Justice slew him, not my hand alone:
And, wert thou not past feeling, thou'dst have helped,
When this thy father, for whom still flow thy tears,   530
Dared slay thy sister for a sacrifice—
Of all men he—who only was her father,
And had not borne for her a mother's pangs.
Instruct me now, for whom paid he such price—
My daughter's blood? Thou'lt tell me, for the Greeks?
To slay my daughter was no right of theirs.
For Menelaus then, his brother, he slew
My child—and should not answer me for this?
Had not that brother two children of his own,
Who should have rather died, children of him,   540
Yea and of her, for whom our ships were launched?
Or was Death's appetite so nice, to feast
Upon my children's flesh and not on hers?
Or did this most unnatural father love
His brother's offspring, careless for his own?
Why, what a father—senseless and dull—was this!
However we may differ, so think I:
And so would say the slain one, might she speak.

So now for this deed's sake that I have done
My heart fails not: and, if thou'rt unconvinced,   550
Be just thyself before thou judgest me.

   El. This time thou scarce wilt say that I began
The bitterness, and then by thee was chidden:
Give me but leave, I'll plead and plead aright
Both for my father and my sister too.

   Clyt. Permission's thine: and, hadst thou always been
So humble, I had not loathed to hear thy voice.

   El. Thus then. My father thou hast slain. What word
More damning is there of thy guilt than this—
Justly or not, no matter. But I shall prove,   560
Just deed 'twas none—but thou wast won to it
With wooing of a traitor, now thy lord.
Ask huntress Artemis, what angered her
At Aulis so to check those thronging winds.
Or, since from her thou canst not, hear from me.
I hear it said, my father roamed one day
Her glades light-hearted, and with his footfall scared
An antlered stag with dappled skin, and spoke
A boastful word, and shot, and pierced its throat.
Therefore Latona's daughter being wroth   570
Held back the Greeks until thy sire should give
For the slain beast his daughter, life for life.
And so he slew her: for no otherwise
Homeward or Troyward had our fleet release.

Therefore on hard compulsion, loth to yield,
He slew her, nowise for his brother's sake.
Yet, were it as thou hast said, had he done this
All for his brother's cause, yet even so
Shouldst thou have slain him? By what law were this?
Take heed, appointing such a law for men, 580
That thou appoint not sorrow for thyself.
For, if blood must be shed for blood, thou first
Shouldst die, if justice should be done on thee.
But see to it, if thy pretext be not false.
For tell me, an thou wilt, for what cause now
We see thee do most shameful deeds of all,
Who dost beside that murderer couch, with whom
Thou didst conspire before to slay my sire,
And bear'st him children, and hast cast out for him
The stainless children of thy stainless lord. 590
How shall I praise this thing? Thou'lt tell me, this,
This also is the price of daughter's blood?
'Tis foully done, say as thou wilt. To wed
Foes, for a daughter's sake, is no fair thing.
Nay but one may not speak nor counsel thee,
Who sparest no words to tell, how I thy daughter
Am still thy slanderer: yea, and I deem thee less
A mother than a mistress unto me,
Who live a grievous life, and sore beset
With all hard usage of thy lord and thee. 600
But out of reach the other, scarce escaped,

The sad Orestes, wastes a hapless life:
Of whom I hear thee rate me that he lives
Reared up by me, for vengeance. Could I this,
Be sure indeed I would. If this be all,
Cry, cry aloud, and call me as thou wilt
Unnatural, loquacious, unabashed.
For if indeed I know such deeds as these,
Methinks of such a child thou shouldst be proud. 609

   Chor. I see, she breathes out fury: but, if her words
Chime still with justice, this she heeds no longer.

   Clyt. And why should I have any heed of her,
Who me her mother has with such words reviled—
She a mere child besides? Seems she not one
To go all lengths and never blench or blush?

   El. Nay, that I blush for this, I'd have thee know,
Although thou thinkest not; too well I see,
Unseemly and ill-timed my words have been.
But thy unkindness, and thine acts to me,
These in my own despite have made me mad. 620
For shameful deeds by shameful deeds are taught.

   Clyt. Thou shameless thing, my words and acts and I,
Methinks, have made thee over-garrulous.

   El. My speech is thine, not mine: thou doest the deeds,
And 'tis the deeds that find themselves the words.

   Clyt. So help me Artemis, but thou shalt rue
This boldness, when Aegisthus comes again.

El. So you fly out in anger—though you gave me
Leave to speak all my mind; but you'll not hear.

Clyt. May I not sacrifice without thy clamour, 630
Now, having left thee free to say thy say?

El. Hinder, not I: I pray you, sacrifice!
Chide not my speaking, for I'll speak no more.

Clyt. Who does my bidding, let her lift on high
The gift of every fruit, that I may pray
To Phoebus here to rid me of my fears.
Protector, Phoebus, hear and understand,
Although my speech be darkened. For I speak
In no friend's ears, nor with this maiden near
Must I unfold my meaning to the light, 640
Lest she with spite and rumour, thousand-tongued,
Through all the city scatter false report.
But hear me thus: thus I will dare to speak.
The vision which in doubtful dreams this night
I saw, O lord Lyceius, let it be
Accomplished, if 'tis sent me for my good;
If harm, upon my enemies let it fall:
And suffer not whoever deem by guile
To cast me down out of this high estate:
So let me live a life exempt from ill, 650
Possessing still the sceptre and the house,
And dwelling with the friends with whom I dwell
Lead peaceful days—and of my children those
Who neither bear me spite nor cause me sorrow.

Phoebus, Lyceius, hear me graciously,
And be it to all of us as I desire.
The rest, although my lips pronounce not, yet
I deem that thou, being a god, dost know.
All things are open to the sons of Zeus.

Ped. Ladies, I pray you tell me, is this house   660
The palace of Aegisthus, of the king?

Chor. No other, friend; thyself hast guessed aright.

Ped. And do I rightly deem this lady here
His wife? who looks none other than a queen.

Chor. As thou hast said; thine eyes behold the queen.

Ped. Lady, all hail. Bearing glad news I come
To thee and to Aegisthus, from a friend.

Clyt. I hail the word: and who with these glad news
Has sent thee hither?—this I first would know.

Ped. From Phocian Phanoteus I bear great tidings.   670

Clyt. What tidings, friend? speak, for from one so kind
Kind words that thou wilt utter, well I know.

Ped. Orestes—briefly to tell my tale—is dead.

El. O woful day, a fatal tale to me!

Clyt. How, sirrah—how say you? Hearken not to her.

Ped. I said and say, Orestes, lady, is dead.

El. O fatal tidings, how am I undone!

Clyt. See to thyself: but, sirrah, thou to me
Speak all the truth, and tell me how he died.

Ped. Thou shalt hear all, for therefore was I sent.   680
To the pride of Greece, the festival renowned,

For Delphic contests' sake Orestes came;
And when he heard the proclamation loud
That heralded the foot-race, first of trials,
He entered bright the lists, worshipped by all,
And ran, till starting-point and goal were one,
And crowned with honour and victory came thereout.
Few among many I know not how to tell
Of the victorious feats of such a man:
But this I say—that of no trial the judges 690
Proclaimed decision, single or double race—
Pentathlon also, all the fivefold custom—
But he of one and all bore prize away,
By men hailed happy—he an Argive styled,
By name Orestes, Agamemnon's son,
Who of all Greece gathered the famous host.
These things indeed were so: but, when a god
Stops the strong runner, hardly shall he flee.
For he, another day, when charioteers
At sunrise matched their speed in the swift race,
With many another entered for the prize. 700
One was Achaean, one from Sparta, two—
Masters of yokèd cars—were Libyan-born;
And he with these driving Thessalian mares
Came fifth; next him with chestnut colts the sixth,
Aetolian; a Magnesian was the seventh;
Aenian by race the eighth, and white his steeds;
A ninth came thither from Athens, built by gods;

One more Boeotian, making the chariots ten.
So, standing where their place the appointed umpires
Assigned them by the lot, and ranged their cars, 710
All at the trumpet's sound they started: all,
Chiding their horses on, shook loose the reins
Together, and the plain at once was filled
With din of rattling cars, and dust that rose
Skyward; and all together in a throng
Spared not the goad, when one from out the press
Shot past their axles and the snorting steeds.
For all about their backs and rolling wheels
The breathings of the horses foamed and smote.
And ever, against the pillar where they turned, 720
Orestes grazed his axle, and his traces
Loosed on the right and tightened on the left;
And all the chariots held erect their course,
Till those unbridled colts by the Aenian driven
From all restraint broke loose, and made the round
A sixth time, but the seventh, swerving, full
Against the team Barcaean dashed their foreheads:
And so from one disaster each against each
Crashed and heeled over, and with the chariot-wrecks
All the Crisaean plain was overstrewn. 730
This he from Athens, wise in his charioting,
Marked, and pulled sideways, and so rode out the storm—
Letting its surge seethe past him in mid-course.
Last drave Orestes, holding back his colts,

And trusted still his prowess at the close:
But, when he saw that other left alone,
His steeds in the ears with one sharp cry he smote,
And so, full speed, came after; until abreast
The chariots raced, and of the charioteers
Now this, now that, with head thrust forth, showed first. 740
And safe till now Orestes every round
Steered still, ill-starred, steadfast his steadfast car;
But the last time, loosing the left-hand rein,
Even while the horse turned, struck and knew it not
The edge of the pillar, and the rim o' the nave
O' the axle splintered; and himself behind
Slipped 'twixt the rails, and tangled all amid
The dainty reins: and down he fell on the plain,
So that his colts were scattered in mid-course.
And when the people saw him from the car
Fallen, a cry of pity outbrake to see 750
What deeds the youth had done, and how he fared,
Now dashed to the earth, and now feet uppermost
Tossed to the sky; until the charioteers,
Scarce having checked the fury of his steeds,
Loosed him all bleeding, all his poor limbs torn
And battered past all knowing of his friends.
Him on the pyre we burned, and hither now
Come chosen men from Phocis, in one small urn
Bearing the sad dust of that mighty form,
That in his native earth he may have rest. 760

There is no more to say. A piteous tale
To tell, but in the seeing, to us who saw,
Greatest of all evils that ever I have seen.

Chor. Ah me, for now, I think, the race and name
Of my old masters is from earth evanish'd!

Clyt. Zeus, what shall I say—this is glad news to me,
Or dire news and yet good news? oh 'tis bitter,
That by my own calamities I live!

Ped. Lady, why does thy heart fail for this hearing?

Clyt. 'Tis dire to be a mother—howe'er unkind,
The child of one's womb one cannot learn to hate.

Ped. Then all in vain it seems that we have come.

Clyt. Nay, not in vain. How shouldst thou say in vain?
If hither you bring to me proof of his death—
His death—whose life from my life sprang, but he
Would none of my milk, and from my nursing fled
And lived an alien, and since he went from hence
Saw me no more; but called me murderess
Of his father, and with dire reckoning menaced me,
So that the kind sleep neither by night nor day
Covered my eyes, but still the tyrannous time
Seemed ever to drag me onward to my doom.
But now, for on this day I am rid of fear
From him and from this maiden, who, worse plague,
Dwelt with me, sucking from me day by day
My sheer heart's blood—now, now methinks in peace,

Untroubled by his threats, my days shall pass.

El. Ah woe is me : for now, Orestes, now
I may lament for thee, when, being thus,
By thy mother thou art mocked. Is it not well? 790

Clyt. Not well with thee: but well, being thus, does he.

El. Nemesis of the dead—scarce dead—oh hear!

Clyt. Who should be heard, she heard; and well ordained it.

El. Mocker, mock on : this is thy triumph's hour.

Clyt. Thou and Orestes shall not spoil me this.

El. Nay, we are spoiled, no talk of spoiling thee.

Clyt. Much thanks indeed, friend, should thine errand win,
If she is silenced of her noisy grief.

Ped. So let me take my leave, if this is well.

Clyt. Not so; for so not worthily of me, 800
Or of the friend who sent thee, shouldst thou fare.
Come thou within; and let this maiden here
Proclaim aloud her sorrows and her friends'.

El. Seems she not, like one grieved and sick at heart,
This miserable mother, for her son
So slain to make dire weeping and lament?
Nay, laughing she is gone. O me, alas,
Orestes, dearest, thy death is death to me!
With thee are gone, plucked from my heart away,
All hopes that tarried still to comfort me, 810
That thou wouldst come, living, to avenge thy sire

P

And me, unhappy.   Now whither shall I go?
For now I am alone—now thou art lost,
Thou and my sire.   And henceforth in the house
Of these my father's murderers, whom I hate,
The life of a slave is mine.   O goodly lot!
Ah no, but never any more will I
Live 'neath their roof, but at their gate will lay
My withered, friendless life until I die.
Now therefore let them kill me, those in the house,   820
If they are weary of me: death is sweet,
But life is grievous—I have no heart to live.

 Chor. Where, Zeus, are thy lightnings—O Sun-god,
  where is thy beam—
If ye, these things beholding, hide them, all heedless?
 El. Woe and alas!
 Chor. O daughter, why art thou weeping?
 El. Alas and alas!
 Chor. No rash word utter.
 El. Thou'lt be my death.
 Chor. How?   830
 El. If for the dead, dead past all doubt,
Hope ye still shall suggest,
On me, consumed with my sorrow,
The more ye shall trample.
 Chor. Nay, for I know that King Amphiaraus,
By reason of golden snares of women,
Was buried alive; and now

Under the earth—
    El. Alas the day! 840
    Chor. In fulness of force he reigns.
    El. Alas!
    Chor. Alas indeed! for the murderess—
    El. Was slain?
    Chor. Yes.
    El. I know it, I know it,
For the mourner a champion arose:
But to me no champion is left,
For the one who remained is lost,
Snatched hence and gone.
    Chor. Unhappy thou art, hapless thy plight.
    El. I also know this, too well I know it, 850
Who lead a life, month after month,
All blindly surging
With troubles dire and dark.
    Chor. We saw indeed whence flowed thy tears.
    El. No more then, oh no more,
Entreat me where——
    Chor. What wouldst thou say?
    El. Where now no more shall visit me
Comfort of any hope of him,
My brother—son of my noble sire. 860
    Chor. To all men death must come.
    El. Even as it came to him, the hapless,
Amidst the tramplings of racers' hoofs—

To encounter with dragging of dainty reins?

Chor. O outrage, baffling thought!

El. So is it, if in the land of strangers
His ashes rest, not by my hands entombed,
Neither burial nor tears having won from me. 870

Chrys. Joy wings my feet, O sister, hitherward,
So that I come in haste, and heed not how:
For joyful news I bring, that makes an end
Of all thy days of sorrow and of tears.

El. How shouldst thou find help for my sorrows, thou,
Whereof no cure is possible to see?

Chrys. Know, for I tell thee, Orestes is returned—
His very self, plain as thine eyes see me.

El. What, are you mad, you who are miserable,
And would you mock our sorrow, yours and mine! 880

Chrys. No, by our father's hearth, no bitter jest
Is this—but fact; he has come back to us.

El. Alas, poor fool, and from whose lips I prithee
Heard you this tale that you so rashly trust?

Chrys. My own eyes told me, they alone: plain proof
They saw, and what they told me I believe.

El. Poor soul, what proof saw you? what sight was this,
That kindled in thy heart this fatal fire?

Chrys. 'Fore heaven, hear what I saw: that, having heard,
Then you may deem me wise, or else a fool. 890

El. Nay then, speak on, if speaking comforts thee.

Chrys. Forthwith I'll tell thee all that I have seen.
When to our father's ancient tomb I came,
At top of the mound libations freshly poured
Of milk I saw, and all the sepulchre
Wreathed round about with every flower that grows;
And seeing it I marvelled, and I looked,
Lest some one should be near me, at my side;
But when I saw that I was all alone,
Nearer the tomb I crept, and on the edge   900
Of the mound beheld a lock of hair, new-shorn;
And at the sight was borne upon my soul—
As it were a well-known form—it seemed a sign
From him whom most of men I love, Orestes:
And in my hand I took it, and my tongue
Refrained, but tears of joy o'erflowed my eyes:
And now full well I know, as then I knew,
That this fair tress of hair was none but his.
Who else should set it there, except us twain?
And 'twas not I who did it, that I know,   910
Nor thou—how shouldst thou? when thou canst not even
Go forth, unchidden, to the gods to pray.
Our mother then? When was she minded ever
To do such things? how could she, we not knowing?
But from Orestes' hand these offerings came.
Sister, take heart. No constant law of heaven
Deals to the selfsame life the selfsame doom.
Our lot before was bitter: but full-fraught

Perchance with lasting good this day shall prove.

El. Alas thy folly : I hear thee, pitying. 920

Chrys. How: are they not glad tidings that I bring?

El. Thou knowest not whither, unto what dreams thou'rt borne.

Chrys. Do I not know that which mine eyes have seen?

El. Fool, he is dead : of safety as from him
There is an end : to him look thou no more.

Chrys. O hapless—from what tongue heardst thou such news?

El. From one who when he died stood by and saw.

Chrys. Where is this witness? wonder overcomes me.

El. Welcomed within—not grievous to my mother. 929

Chrys. Out and alas! by whom then had been sent
Those lavish offerings to our father's tomb?

El. Most likely, to my thinking, they were brought
In memory of Orestes who is dead.

Chrys. O luckless: and I hasted with such joy
Such news to bring : not knowing as it seems
Our plight, how woful : but, having come, I find
Trouble on trouble—ills both old and new.

El. So stands thy case ; but hearken now to me—
This weight of present woe thou soon wilt lighten.

Chrys. What? shall I bid the dead arise and live? 940

El. Nay, there was no such folly in my thoughts.

Chrys. What wouldst thou have, that I have strength to do?

El. I'd have thee do my bidding and be bold.
Chrys. If in the doing is gain, I'll not refuse.
El. Look to it: without the striving nought succeeds.
Chrys. I see it: command my help, whate'er I can.
El. Then hearken, what to do I am resolved.
Thou knowest, I think, that countenance of friends
Now we have none: of all we had, we are
By death bereft—bereft, and left alone. 950
Now therefore I, who, while to me came news
My brother lived and prospered still, had hope
That he would come, avenger of my sire—
I turn, since he is gone, to whom but thee—
The murderer of our father bidding thee
With me thy sister tarry not to slay,
Aegisthus: for 'tis time I should speak out.
How long wilt thou be patient—in what hope—
When all our hopes are wrecked? thou who shouldst
    grieve,
Being disinherited of thy father's wealth, 960
And shouldst lament, that, all thy life till now,
Thy youth is spent unwedded and unloved.
Nay, and to marriage hope not any more
Thou shalt attain: for not so void of wit
Is this Aegisthus, as to let children spring
From thee or me, a certain harm to him.
But, if to my advice thou dost consent,
I tell thee first, pious thou shalt be called

Both by thy father and thy brother dead:
And free, as thou wast born, thou shalt be called 970
Henceforth, and worthy marriage shalt obtain,
For to the noble all men are wont to look.
Bethink thee, too, what honourable report
For thee and me, consenting, thou shalt win.
Who, countryman or stranger, seeing us,
Shall not with suchlike praises honour us—
'Behold ye these two sisters, O my friends,
Who wrought deliverance for their father's house,
Who against foes firm-planted in their pride
Drew sword the foremost, sparing not their lives: 980
These ye should love, these twain should all revere:
Yea, in all feasts and high solemnities
These women, brave as men, let all men praise.'
Such things of us shall everywhere be spoken;
Living or dead, our glory shall not fail.
O sister, then, be counselled, for thy father
Strive, for thy brother endure, and rescue me,
Rescue thyself from sorrow, minding this,
Ignoble life is shame for noble men.

   Chor. For one who speaks alike and one who hears, 990
Forethought is helpful in such case as this.

   Chrys. Were she not bent on folly, O my friends,
Ere she had spoken thus, she would have first
Remembered caution, which she remembers not.
For, on what hopes intent, dost thou so arm

Thyself with rashness, and call me to follow?
What, art thou blind? Woman, not man, art thou,
And for thine enemies in strength no match.
And them their fortune prospers day by day;
Ours ebbs and dwindles ever, and comes to nought. 1000
Who then shall think to vanquish such a man,
And yet come off unscathed, nor rue his folly?
Look well, lest, if they hear what thou hast spoken,
Our evil plight be soon exchanged for worse.
It steads us not nor profits us at all,
To win fair fame and yet ignobly die.
For not to die is worst, but when to die
One craves, and even this he may not have.
Nay, I entreat, or ever past retrieval
We perish, and leave desolate our house, 1010
Refrain thine anger. All that thou hast spoken
Will I unsay with silence, and defeat.
But oh, thyself learn prudence, though so late,
Not to contend, so weak, with them so strong.

 Chor. Hear her. For men there is no gain to get
Better than prudence and a sober mind.

 El. Thou hast spoken nought unlooked for. Well I
  knew,
Thou wouldst reject the proffer that I made,
But single-handed and alone this deed
I needs must do: it shall not go undone. 1020

 Chrys. Alas!

Would thou hadst been so minded in that day
Our father died: what might'st thou not have done?
   El. My heart was right, but feebler were my thoughts.
   Chrys. Study to keep such thoughts thy whole life long.
   El. This counsel purports then no help from thee.
   Chrys. Of rash attempts disaster needs must come.
   El. I praise thy wisdom, hate thy cowardice.
   Chrys. Even thy praise with patience I will hear.
   El. Never of me shalt thou have that to bear.   1029
   Chrys. To prove that 'never' craves the coming time.
   El. Begone, I say: thou art unprofitable.
   Chrys. Not so: 'tis thou that art incorrigible.
   El. Go, to thy mother all the tale repeat.
   Chrys. Nor do I hate thee with so dire a hate.
   El. But know at least how thou dishonourest me.
   Chrys. Dishonour thee—not I, but care for thee.
   El. And must I follow then thy rule of right?
   Chrys. For, when thou'rt wiser, *then* be guide to both.
   El. Strange that, who speaks so well, should speak amiss.
   Chrys. Thy words have hit the fault whereto thou
       cleavest.   1040
   El. How? what I speak, seems it to thee not right?
   Chrys. But sometimes what is right is mischievous.
   El. By such a law I do not choose to live.
   Chrys. Persist in this, and thou shalt praise me yet.
   El. Persist I shall, no whit dismayed by thee.
   Chrys. Must it be so? Wilt thou not think again?

El. Most hateful 'tis to think, and think amiss.
Chrys. It seems thou wilt not heed what I advise.
El. Not now, but long ago I have resolved.   1049
Chrys. I leave thee then: for neither thou my words
Nor I thy temper can endure to praise.
El. Why then, go in: I shall not follow thee,
Howe'er thou may'st desire it: since withal
Much folly it is to follow a fruitless quest.
Chrys. Why then, if in thine own eyes thou art
  wise,
I to thy wisdom leave thee: by and by,
Standing in evil plight, my words thou'lt praise.
Chor. Why, though the true-hearted birds of the air
  they see   [*Strophe* 1.
Careful to cherish those
Who give them life and all good things—
Oh, why do men likewise   1060
A like devotion fail to pay?
Nay, but not long delayed
(By the lightning flashed from the hand of Zeus,
By heavenly Themis, no!)
The day of reckoning comes.
O voice that soundest
To the dead beneath the earth,
In the ears of the sons of Atreus
Proclaim it there, a piteous cry
A joyless tale of shame: 1069

That the strength of their house is waxen faint, [*Ant.* 1.
And of their children now
With daily interchange of love
Discordant strife no more agrees.
Electra forsaken breasts the storm alone,
Unhappy, like the all-plaintive nightingale,
Lamenting always for her sire,
And recking not of death,
Ready to yield her life,
Might she but triumph o'er the twofold curse : 1080
What child her nobleness shall match ?
For no one who is noble deigns [*Strophe* 2.
Basely to live, and cloud
With obloquy fair fame—
O daughter, daughter, ev'n as thou
Hast chosen all thy days
To weep with them that wept,
That so one day, when the unlovely deed
Was armed and ready, thou mightest win
A twofold praise in one,
Wise and most noble of daughters to be called. 1089
Oh may I see thee living yet [*Antistrophe* 2.
As far in might and wealth
Above thy foes, as now
Beneath their hand thy life is crushed:
Since I have found thy feet
Set in no goodly lot ;

But, touching nature's highest laws,
I see thee bear away
The meed of the noblest, for that thou fearest Zeus.

Or. Ladies, have we heard true, and do we bend
Our steps aright, whither we fain would come?

Chrys. What seek you, and with what intent come hither? 1100

Or. To the house of Aegisthus I have asked my way.

Chrys. Your goal is reached; your guide shall forfeit nothing.

Or. Which of all you would tell to those within
The longed-for coming of our company?

Chrys. This maiden, if the nearest should announce it.

Or. Go, lady, and tell them in the house, that men
Are come from Phocis, who would see Aegisthus.

El. Out and alas! of rumour that we heard
It cannot be ye bring us proofs to see?

Or. Thy tale I know not: aged Strophius 1110
Hath charged me, of Orestes to bring tidings.

El. What tidings, friend? How I grow chill with fear!

Or. He is dead: a little dust is all of him,
Which here, thou seest, in this small urn we bear.

El. Woe's me, now all too clear, this grief, it seems,
My hands may handle, and my eyes behold.

Or. If for the fate of Orestes flow thy tears,

Know that within this urn his ashes rest.

El. Friend, in my hands, I pray thee, if it holds
Him, let me take this urn, that I may weep   1120
And wail my fill, not for this dust alone,
But for myself withal and all my house.

Or. Bring hither and give to her, whoe'er she be:
For not as one who loved him not she asks,
But either a friend, or born his kinswoman.

El. O poor last relic of Orestes' life,
Dearest of men to me, with hopes how other,
Than forth I sent, do I receive thee back!
Now in these hands I take thee, and thou art nought;
But beautiful and bright I sent thee forth,   1130
Child, from thy home. Oh would that I had died,
Or ever to a strange land I sent thee hence,
And stole thee in my arms, and saved from death,
That on that day thou mightest have lain dead,
And of thy father's tomb have earned a share.
Now, far from home, in a strange land exiled,
A woful end was thine, no sister near:
And, woe is me, I neither laved thy limbs
And decked with loving hands, nor, as was meet,
Snatched this sad burthen from the scorching fire: 1140
By hands of strangers tended thou art come,
A little handful in this little urn.
Alas me for my nursing long ago,
Unprofitable care, that with sweet pain

I ofttimes spent for thee; for thou wast never
Thy mother's darling, rather mine; nor they
O' the house—but I it was, whom all were wont
Sister at once to call and nurse of thee.
Now thou art dead, and all in a day these things
Have ceased to be—all with thy passing swept   1150
As by a whirlwind hence. Thy father is gone,
And I am dead, thy sister; and thine own life
Has past from earth. Our foes laugh us to scorn,
Our mother, nay no mother, is mad with joy:
Of whom so often thou didst send secret word,
Thou'dst come to be avenged on her; but now
Hard fortune, thine and mine, robs me of this,
Sending me hither, in thy dear body's stead,
Mere dust and shadow of thee, and good for nought.
Ah me, alas!   1160
O piteous ashes! alas and woe is me!
O sadly, strangely—
Alas, my brother!—
Thus journeying hither, how me thou hast undone!
Undone—undone indeed, O brother mine!
Therefore to thy dark chamber take me in;
Me, dust to dust, receive; that I may dwell
Henceforth i' the dark with thee. For, living, I shared
With thee, and shared alike; and now in death
Not to be sundered from thy tomb I crave,
For in the grave I see that grief is not.   1170

Chor. Mortal, Electra, bethink thee, was thy sire,
Orestes mortal : moderate thy grief :
This is a debt we all of us must pay.

Or. Alas, what shall I say? what words attempt,
Where all words fail? No more can I refrain.

El. What is your trouble? Why have you spoken this?

Or. Is this Electra's form, far-famed of men?

El. It is no other, in most distressful plight.

Or. Alas then for thy lamentable case!

El. Surely, good friend, thy tears are not for me? 1180

Or. O form defaced with foul and impious wrong!

El. On none but me, friend, thy reproaches light.

Or. Alas me, for thy loveless hapless life!

El. Why dost thou bend thy weeping eyes on me?

Or. How less than nothing of my wrongs I knew!

El. Wherein, of what was said, discerned you this?

Or. Reading in thy face the blazon of thy grief.

El. And yet of all my wrongs you see but few.

Or. How could there be more hateful sights than these?

El. That 'neath one roof with the murderers I
    dwell—— 1190

Or. Of whom? from whence hast thou this hint of
    crime?

El. My father; and me, perforce, they make their slave.

Or. Who are they that constrain thee to their will?

El. One called my mother, no mother by her deeds.

Or. With blows, or cruelty in thy life? Say, how?

El. With blows and cruelty, and every wrong.
Or. And hast thou none to help, and hinder this?
El. Not I, for, whom I had—his dust is here.
Or. O hapless, how thy sight hath stirred my pity!
El. Thou art the first that ever pitied me.   1200
Or. I am the first that ever shared thy grief.
El. Art thou some kinsman, that I have not known?
Or. This I could answer, if these are friends who hear me.
El. Yes, friends they are, whom speaking you may trust.
Or. Set down this urn then, and I'll tell thee all.
El. Friend, bid me not do this—so help thee heaven!
Or. Do as I say, thou shalt not do amiss.
El. I do entreat thee—take not my dearest from me.
Or. I say thou shalt not.
El.   Ah woe is me for thee,
Orestes, if thy burial is denied me.   1210
Or. Cease; for it is not right that thou shouldst weep.
El. How wrong, to weep my brother who is dead?
Or. 'Tis not for *thee* to use such words of him.
El. And am I so dishonoured by the dead?
Or. No man dishonours thee: this is not thine.
El. How, if I hold the body of Orestes?
Or. 'Tis none of his, save as our words have feigned it.
El. Where is the tomb of my most luckless brother?
Or. No tomb has he; we bury not the living.
El. How say you, boy?   1220

Q

Or. All that I say is true.

El. Orestes *lives?*

Or. If there is life in me.

El. What, art thou he?

Or. Look here upon this seal
That was my sire's, judge then if I speak true.

El. O blissful day!

Or. Blissful, my heart attests!

El. Voice, art thou come?

Or. Come back, the voice replies.

El. Home to my arms come back?

Or. My home henceforth.

El. O all ye women, my neighbours and good friends,
Look on this man Orestes, who was feigned
Dead, and by feigning is alive again. 1229

Chor. We see him, daughter; and for this happy chance
My eyes run over with excess of joy.

El. Dearest to me of all men ever born,
This hour come back to find—
Come back to see—me whom thy heart desired!

Or. Yes, I am come; but for awhile keep silence.

El. What fearest thou?

Or. Silence is best, lest those within should hear.

El. Nay but, by maiden Artemis,
I shall not stoop to fear the women there, 1240
The stay-at-homes, vain cumberers of the house.

Or. But yet take note, that even in breasts of women

May Ares lodge; as thou too well hast proved.

El. Alas and woe is me!
Thy words find out my sorrow,
Not to be hidden, not to be done away,
That never its own burthen can forget. 1250

Or. Sister, I know; but, when occasion bids,
These things must then be thought on; now, forbear.

El. All time, all time for me
Is present time and fit
To speak—and speak the truth:
For scarcely now my tongue at last is free.

Or. And so think I; therefore remember this.

El. What must I do?

Or. Wait; and while time is short, let words be few.

El. But how, when I have found 1260
Thee, is it fit, that speech
For silence I should change—
Now, having seen thee, whom to see
Seemed once past thought or hope?

Or. Then didst thou see me, when heav'n bade me come.

El. Yea, for this boon beside, and best of all,
That heaven hath brought thee home,
Thank heaven, say I, for this. 1270

Or. Loth am I to restrain thy joy; but yet
This overmuch rejoicing moves my fear.

El. Absent so long, but now, when time was ripe,

Returned, O glad return, to bless my sight—
Oh see what I have borne,
And do not, do not now——

 Or. What must I not?

 El. Not take from me, nor bid me yet forego,
The comfort of thy face.

 Or. Unmoved, I could not see another do it.

 El. Dost thou consent?   1280

 Or. How could I not?

 El. O friends, the voice is in my ears,
I had not hoped to hear.
[Thou wouldst not come, they said :]
And I refrained my speech,
And heard and answered not,
Unhappy. But I have thee now:
Now thy dear face hath shined on me—
Thy face, which not in darkest days
Could I again forget.

 Or. All superfluity of words let go,
And neither tell me of my mother's sins,
Nor how Aegisthus drains my father's house,   1290
And spills and spends at random all its wealth.
Such tale might well forbid all count of time.
But tell me now, what suits the present hour,
Where if we hide, or by appearing where,
Our enemies' mirth our coming shall confound:
And have a care thy mother note thee not

With thy glad face, when we are come within:
But, as for that false tale of dire mischance,
Let thy tears flow.   Not until all is well,
Shall our rejoicing or our smiles be free. 1300

   El. Nay, brother, but, even as it pleases thee,
So also will I do: for all my joy
I gat not for myself, but gat from thee.
Nor would I choose to grieve thee ne'er so little,
Myself to win great gain; for so but ill
Fortune, that now befriends us, should I serve.
But, what comes next, thou knowest.   Hast thou not heard
Aegisthus is not now within the house,
Only thy mother? and fear not thou that she
Will see my face lighted with joyful smiles. 1310
For my inveterate hate sticks deep in me;
Nor shall I since thy coming have had time
To dry my gladsome tears.   Must I not weep,
I who have seen thee in this one day come home,
Dead and alive?   O most bewildering change!
Stood now my sire before me as he lived,
I should not deem it strange, but should believe.
Now therefore, wondrously as thou art come,
Command me as thou wilt: since I alone
Of two things had not failed; for either nobly 1320
I should have saved myself, or nobly died.

   Chor. Keep silence; for I hear steps at the door
Of some one coming out.

El. So, friends, go in;
Bearing withal a gift that may not be
Rejected—no, nor yet a welcome gift.

Ped. O ye most foolish and of sense bereft—
What, do ye tender now your lives so cheap,
Or are of native prudence so devoid—
When now ye stand, not on the brink of danger,
But in the peril's midst, and do not know it? 1330
Nay, had not I kept watch here all the time
Close by the doors, your business would have been
About the house ere you yourselves were there:
But I bestowed the caution that ye lacked.
And now of many words make brief despatch,
And of this noisy and insatiate joy,
And enter quick: for in such work as this
To linger is to lose; this craves despatch.

Or. And having entered—can I then proceed? 1339
Ped. You can: secure, that you are known to none.
Or. I think that you have told them of my death.
Ped. You in the house are numbered with the dead.
Or. Is this glad news to them? how took they it?
Ped. I'll tell thee that to end with; as it is,
All that they do is well, although not well.
El. I pray you, brother, tell me, who is this?
Or. You know him not?
El. I know not, nor can guess.
Or. Do you not know to whom you gave me once?

El. What say you? who?

Or.   He who, as you devised,
Conveyed me hence to Phocis in his arms.   1350

El. Can this be he, whom when my sire was slain
Alone of all men I found faithful still?

Or. 'Tis even he: be brief and ask no more.

El. O kindly light, and one deliverer
Of Agamemnon's house, how came you here?
And are you he who saved us at the worst?
O dearest hands, O thou whose feet were sweet
And serviceable, how hast thou talked with me
Unknown and undiscovered, and thy words
Did slay me, but thy deeds were sweet to me?   1360
Hail, father; for in my eyes thou seem'st no less:
All hail—and know that in this selfsame day
Thee most of men I hated and I loved.

Ped. Let this suffice: the story of the past—
Many revolving nights and days shall serve
To talk this over, and make all things plain.
But now why stand ye here? this is the time
For deeds; now Clytaemnestra is alone,
No man is now within; but, if ye loiter,
Bethink you that with these ye'll have to fight,   1370
And better men than these, no equal fight.

Or. Now, Pylades, not many words of us
This work should crave, but in the house forthwith
To enter, meet obeisance having paid

To the shrines of the gods, who keep my father's
    doors.

El. To these, Apollo, lend a gracious ear
To these and me, who oftentimes have thee
With suppliant hand entreated of my best;
And now, bright god, Apollo, of all I have
I pray thee, I entreat thee, I implore,   1380
Oh prosper thou our handiwork to-day,
That men may know, when impious deeds are done,
From righteous heaven what retribution falls.

Chor. See there how step by step   [*Strophe.*
Goes Ares to his work,
And from his nostrils breathes
Resistless slaughter forth.
Beneath the roof of the house ev'n now
The swift inevitable hounds are gone,
Following fast on the scent of sin:
Nor long the dream of my heart shall tarry,
Hovering doubtfully.   1390
For now the avenger of the slain   [*Antistrophe.*
With stealthy pace into the house
Follows as he is led—
The ancient stately halls of his father enters—
With keen-edged murder in his hands:
And Hermes, son of Maia, leads him in,
Who with concealment wraps him round,
And to his goal conducts him straight,

And tarries not.

El. O dearest women, while I speak, ev'n now
They are about it : but in silence wait.

Chor. Say, how ? what do they now ?   1400

El.   She decks the urn
For burial, and they stand over her.

Chor. Why came you forth ?

El.   I must keep watch, for fear
Without our knowing Aegisthus should come in.

Clyt. (*within.*) Alas !—O house
Void of all friends and full of murderers !

El. Some one in the house cries out. Friends, do ye
    hear ?

Chor. I heard and shuddered, and shut my ears for
    horror.

Clyt. Ah woe is me ! Aegisthus, where art thou ?

El. Again one cries, and loudly.   1410

Clyt.   O son, my son,
Have pity on thy mother.

El.   But not from thee
Did this thy son find pity, nor his sire.

Chor. O city, O hapless house,
The fate that dogged thee day by day,
Is dying, is dying now !

Clyt. Ah, I am stricken.

El.   Strike, if thou canst, again.

Clyt. Ah me again !

El. Would that it were 'Ah for Aegisthus' too!

Chor. The curse fulfils itself: the dead live still.
They who were slain long since
Drain from the slayer the blood   1420
Ordained for blood to flow.
Lo here come they, with hands
Blood-red, that reek of sacrifice
To Ares, so as no words can tell.

El. Orestes, how have ye sped?

Or.   Here in the house
Well, if Apollo's oracle spake well.

El. Dead is the guilty one?

Or.   Fear not henceforth
Thy mother's pride shall flout thee any more.

Chor. Cease, for I see Aegisthus full in view.   1429

El. Rash boys, will ye not back?

Or.   Where see ye him?

El. From the suburbs of the city, lo in our power—
He comes, exulting.

Chor.   For the vestibule
Make with what speed ye may; that, having now
Bestowed the first work well, so may ye this.

Or. Fear not: we shall not fail.

El.   Haste, where thou'rt going.

Or. See, I am gone.

El.   What's here, belongs to me.

Chor. In this man's ear a few

Soft words were not amiss :
That he may blindly close 1440
And grapple with his doom.

   Aeg. Which of all you knows of the Phocian strangers,
Who, as I hear, came hither to announce
Orestes slain amidst the chariots wrecked ?
You there, 'tis you shall tell me : you who were
So bold before : methinks it should concern
You most ; you best should know, and tell me this.

   El. I know ; else were I careless of the woes
Of her who is of all my friends to me
Most near. 1450

   Aeg.   Then tell me where they are.

   El.   In the house :
To the heart of their hostess they have found their way.

   Aeg. Do they in very truth report his death ?

   El. No mere report they bring, but show him dead.

   Aeg. May then my eyes inform me of the truth ?

   El. They may indeed, and 'tis a sorry sight.

   Aeg. Such joyful greeting you are not wont to give.

   El. Of this your joyful news I give you joy.

   Aeg. But now be silent, and throw wide the gates,
And let all Argos and Mycenae see,
That, whoso buoyed themselves with empty hopes 1460
Of this man's life, now seeing he is dead,
May take my bit in their mouths, and not perforce
Get wisdom, getting chastisement from me.

El. Forthwith my part is done; for now at last
I have learnt to do the bidding of my betters.

Aeg. Zeus, 'twas thy wrath whereby this sight befell:
But be the word unsaid, if it offends.
Take off the face-cloth from the face; this life
Was near to mine, and claims some grief from me.

Or. Lift it thyself: thine office this, not mine,   1470
To look, and speak kind speech to what lies here.

Aeg. Well said, and as you say I'll do: meanwhile
Go call me Clytaemnestra through the house.

Or. She is beside thee: look not far off for her.

Aeg. What sight is this?

Or.   So scared? Is the face strange?

Aeg. Who are the men, into whose net I have
Thus helpless fallen?

Or.   Hast thou not yet discerned,
Thou dost accost the living as the dead?

Aeg. Ah—so I read thy riddle. Orestes surely—
He and no other it is, who speaks to me.   1480

Or. So wise a prophet, and yet fooled so long?

Aeg. Oh lost, undone! Yet suffer me to speak
A word, no more.

El.   In heaven's name, my brother,
Let him say no word more, nor waste the time,
Talking. When men must grapple with their fate,
What gain of time to one condemned to die?
But straightway slay him, and fling his body forth

To find such burial as 'tis meet it should—
Out of our sight.   For this and nothing else
For all my wrongs of old can make amends. 1490

   Or. With speed get thee within : the issue now
For thee is not of words, but of thy life.

   Aeg. What need of darkness, if this deed is fair?
Why lead me in, not strike at once and here?

   Or. Dictate not, but come with me where thou slewest
Our father, that ev'n there thy blood may flow.

   Aeg. Is it ordained these walls must see all woes
O' the house of Pelops, now and in time to come?

   Or. Thine must they : perfect prophet am I of that.

   Aeg. The art you boast derives not from your father.

   Or. You bandy words; our going is delayed : 1501
Set forth.

   Aeg.   Lead, you.

   Or.   'Tis you must go the first.

   Aeg. Lest I should fly from *thee?*

   Or.   Rather lest thou
Shouldst choose the fashion of thy death.   I needs
Must keep death's bitterness, perfect for thee.
Would that, for all, this justice tarried not ;
Whoever dares to deal in lawless deeds,
For that man, death.   So should not crimes abound.

   Chor. O house of Atreus, how from all thy griefs
Now into freedom's light thou hast leapt at last,
Crowned by this day's emprise ! 1510

TRACHINIAE

PERSONS.

HERACLES.
HYLLUS.
MESSENGER.
LICHAS.
OLD MAN.
DEIANEIRA.
IOLE. (*Mute.*)
NURSE.
ATTENDANT.
CHORUS OF TRACHINIAN MAIDENS.

Trachiniae.

Dei. THERE is a saying, time-honoured among men,
That of a man's life, till the day he dies,
Whether it be good or evil, none may know:
But what mine is, how troublesome and sad,
I know, or ever to death's doors I come;
Who, dwelling still in Pleuron with my father,
Oeneus, of marriage had such grievous fear
As never any Aetolian maiden had—
For a god of a river wooed me, Achelous,
And ever came to ask me of my sire, 10
Visibly, in three shapes—a bull, and now
A shining coiling snake, and now man-trunked,
Ox-headed, and ever from a shaggy beard
Streams of his fountain's water flowed abroad—
Such suitor entertaining, I, ill-starred,
Prayed still that I might die, or ever a bride
To such a couch I should be brought anear.
But then, O glad deliverance long delayed,
Came that great son Alcmena bare to Zeus:
Issue of battle with the monster joined 20

He, my preserver. How they toiling fought,
I cannot say—I know not: whoso there
Sat fearless of that sight, may tell the tale.
For me—I sat with terror all amazed,
Lest my fair face should win me only grief.
But Zeus, who ruled the fight, ordained it well—
If well: for since to Heracles I clave,
His chosen bride, fear after fear I nurse,
Careful for him. For one night brings a trouble,
And next night with a new one thrusts it forth.   30
And we have children, whom erewhile he saw
As sees the husbandman some field far off,
At seed-time, and in harvest, and no more:
Such life was his, that to and from his home
Upon a master's errands sent him still:
But now that he has vanquished all those toils,
Now most of all I have great cause to fear.
For, since he slew the might of Iphitus,
I here in Trachis live a banished life,
Lodged with a stranger; and of him no man   40
Knows, where he is. But, that he comes not, this
Lays to my heart full many a bitter pang.
Nay, I am sure some harm hath taken him:
For no brief time hath he been gone, but ten
Whole months and other five, and sent no word.
Some dreadful harm, I know: of such a purport
The writing that he left, which oftentimes

I pray the gods, boding no grief, I took.

 Serv. My mistress, Deianeira, I have heard thee
Often before with groaning and with tears
Lamenting for this absence of my lord:
Now, if one may with wisdom of a slave
Admonish ears free-born, let *me* say this:
How, being so rich in many sons, of these
Sendest thou none to seek thy husband forth;
And chiefly Hyllus, whom 'twere fit, if he
Cared of his father's prospering to think?
And to the house himself with timely step
Comes bounding: now, if I seem to thee to speak
A word in season, use my speech, and him.

 Dei. O child, my son, from humble lips I see
Advice may fitly fall. See now this woman:
A slave is she, but no slave's word has spoken.

 Hyll. What? Tell me, mother, if I may be told.

 Dei. That, of thy father tarrying so long
Not learning where he tarries, thou art shamed.

 Hyll. Nay but I know, if what is told is truth.

 Dei. Where, Hyllus, hast thou heard that he abides?

 Hyll. Last year, they say, the twelve long toilsome
  months,
He was the bondsman of a Lydian woman.

 Dei. Nought may we not hear, if he suffered this.

 Hyll. But now from this, I hear, he is released.

 Dei. Where now is news of him, living or dead?

Hyll. War in Euboea he makes or still intends,
Men say, against the city of Eurytus.

Dei. Knowest thou then, my son, of this same land
What certain oracles he left with me?

Hyll. What are they, mother? I know not what
    thou sayest.

Dei. That either he shall end his life, or else,
Achieving this last labour, shall henceforth
For all his time to come lead blissful days.
Then, whilst his fate so trembles in the scales,
Wilt thou not go to aid him, now that we
Are saved if he be safe, or lost with him?

Hyll. Nay, mother, I will go; and, had I known
What was foretold, I had been there long since.
Only his constant fortune suffered me not
To fear for him, nor overmuch to doubt.
Now that I know, trust me, I shall not spare
Pains in the quest, until I find the truth.

Dei. Go then, my son. Good news, though it
    come late,
So it might come at last, is fraught with gain.

Chor.   Thee, whom the starry night, [*Strophe* 1.
        Beneath the spoiler's hand
        Breathing her last, brings forth,
        Whom then she lays to sleep,
    Thee, Sun-god, thee, bright-burning, I implore—
        Oh tell me of Alcmena's son,

O thou, whose rays are as the lightnings bright,
       Where, where he dwelleth—
  Defiles of the Aegean threading,
Or from mid-strait beholding either continent—   100
     Oh tell me, god of keenest sight!
  For with an ever-hungry heart, they say,   [*Ant.* 1.
Fair Deianeira, she for whom the suitors strove,
     Like some unhappy bird,
    Lulls never into tearless sleep
      That hunger of her eyes:
      But unforgetful fear
      For him, her absent lord,
      She entertaining pines
    Upon her widowed couch of care,   110
  Ill-starred, foreboding all distressful chance.
For as, before the untiring blast of South or North, [*Str.* 2.
     Across the boundless sea
     We watch the march of waves
     That come, and ever come,
Even so upon this son of Cadmus' house attends,
     His hard life's toilsomeness
     Increasing more and more,
     Of troubles a Cretan sea.
     But from the halls of death
     Some god restrains his feet,
     Suffering them not to stray.   120
  Therefore I chide thee, and this word [*Ant.* 2.

Of contradiction, not ungrateful, I will speak.
    I say thou dost not well
    To kill the better hope.
   For think, a lot exempt from pain
   The son of Cronos, king who governs all,
    Ordainèd not for men.
  To all men sorrow and joy alternate come,
    Revolving, as in heaven
   The twisting courses of the Bear. 130
    For neither starry night [*Epode.*
  Abides with men, nor death, nor wealth—
    But quickly it is gone,
    And now another learns
   The changeful tale of joy and loss.
   Therefore I counsel thee, the queen,
   To keep this ever in thy hopes :
  For when was Zeus so careless for his sons? 140
Dei. Ye come, I must conjecture, having heard
My trouble ; but, how the trouble eats my heart,
Ye know not—may ye not by suffering learn.
In such a well-fenced place, in native soil,
The tender plant grows, where no sun may scorch,
Nor rain nor any wind is rough with it ;
Upward a painless pleasant life it lifts—
Until such time the maiden is called a wife,
And in a night her share of trouble comes,
By husband or by children made afraid. 150

Then, by your own experience taught, the grief
That at my heart is heavy ye may know.
For many sorrows have I often wept:
One now, whose like was never, I shall tell.
When on his latest journey Heracles
My lord went forth from home, then in the house
He left an ancient tablet, all inscribed
With such a writing as he deigned not else,
In all his rash outgoings, to reveal,
But went as if to victory, not death.   16
Now, like a man as good as dead, my portion
He bade me choose, and meted to his sons
Land for their heritage, his share to each,
Fixing a time, that, when he had been gone
Three months beyond the circle of a year,
Then either it was destined he should die,
Or having passed this crisis of his fate
Thence to the end should live a life unvexed.
Such issue of the toils of Heracles
He showed to me, issue by heaven ordained—   170
So by the voice of its twin doves, he said,
Dodona's ancient oak had spoken it.
And now waits confirmation of its truth
The voice prophetic, and the hour is come.
So that sometimes, O friends, from pleasant sleep
I start in fear—afraid, if I must live
My days out, widowed of the best of men.

Chor. Cease thine ill-omened words; for hither comes
One garlanded, as bearing joyful news.

Mess. Queen Deianeira, I first of messengers 180
Free thee from fear. Know that Alcmena's son
Both lives and triumphs, and from battle brings
Firstfruits of victory to his country's gods.

Dei. Old man, what tidings hast thou told to me?

Mess. That hither to thy doors will come full soon,
Illustrious, crowned with victory, thy lord.

Dei. Who, citizen or stranger, told thee this?

Mess. Lichas the herald proclaims it in the fields,
Our summer pastures, in the ears of many.
I heard and hasted, that, announcing first 190
Such news, I might have guerdon—thanks to boot.

Dei. Why comes he not himself, who brings glad
    news?

Mess. 'Tis not so easy, lady, all at once.
For round him all our Melian people press
Questioning, and he cannot move a step.
Their eagerness, each hungering to hear all,
Will not release him till they're satisfied.
So for their pleasure, not his own, with them
He tarries: soon thou'lt see him, face to face.

Dei. Zeus, of the unmown lawns of Oeta lord, 200
Joy long-delayed at last thou givest me.
Within the house, ye women, and beyond
The court, proclaim it—with what light new-risen

I bless myself, light of glad news unhoped.
  Chor. Shout clamorously to all the house
With joyful cries about the hearth,
O maidens—and let sound therewith
    Consenting voice of men—
    Apollo our protector,
    With his fair quiver, praise:
Withal a paean, girls, a paean lift— 210
To Artemis, his sister, cry aloud,
    Ortygian, huntress of the stag,
    Who holds in either hand a torch,
    And to the neighbour Nymphs—
    The passion lifts me—now,
    Now not the maddening flute
    Will I refuse to hear,
    O tyrant of my heart!
        Euoe!
  See how the ivy stirs my blood— 220
How it constrains me suddenly
    With Bacchanals to vie.
    Joy, joy, O Paean!
    See, see, dear lady, now
    The joyful news takes shape,
    And greets thee face to face.
  Dei. Yea, friends, I see, nor had my eyes so ill
Kept watch, not to descry this company.—
Welcome, O herald, whose coming, long-delayed,

Is joyful, if indeed thou bearest news.

Lich. Well are we come, O lady, and are greeted
Well, as our deeds have earned ;—since, who indeed 230
Prospers, he cannot fail to win good words.

Dei. O best of friends, first what I first would know—
Shall I receive my Heracles alive?

Lich. I left him strong enough, I warrant him—
Living and hale, plagued with no sickness, he.

Dei. Upon Greek soil, or foreign? tell me this.

Lich. There's an Euboean headland, where he traces
Altars to Zeus Cenaean, and fruitful dues.

Dei. Paying some vow, or warned by oracles?

Lich. A vow in battle, when he stormed and sacked 240
The city of these maidens, whom thou seest.

Dei. And these—I prithee, whose are they, and who?
Piteous—unless their plight deceives my heart.

Lich. Of the plunder of the city of Eurytus,
These for himself and for the gods he chose.

Dei. Was it before this city that he spent
All the incredible time, past count of days?

Lich. Not so: most part of it he was detained
In Lydia—by his own account, not free,
But sold and bought. Nor let the word offend, 250
When Zeus appears the author of the thing.

So a full year, as he himself avers,
He served the barbarous woman Omphale,
And the reproach so stung him to the heart
He laid an oath upon his soul and swore
The man who brought this trouble on his head
One day with wife and child he would enslave:
Nor idly spake—but, when his hands were clean,
Gathered a foreign host against the town
Of Eurytus. For Eurytus, he said,   260
Had had sole share in working him this woe:
Who with his voice, and with a spiteful heart,
Railed oft against him, when he came a guest—
Guest as of old into the friendly house—
That he, with those inevitable shafts,
Was yet in bow-craft for his sons no match—
And called him slave of a free master, cowed
And broken: last, at a banquet, hot with wine,
Had cast him from his doors. Therefore in rage,
When to the hill of Tiryns Iphitus   270
Came, following after horses that had strayed,
Him from the smooth top of the towering cliff,
Whilst one way went his eyes, his thoughts another,
My master flung. But for this deed the king,
Olympian Zeus, the Sire of all, being wroth,
Drave him a bondsman forth, nor suffered him,
Because this man alone of men he slew
By guile. For, open vengeance had he wreaked,

Zeus had allowed the violent deed as just:
Since gods no more than men love insolence. 280
But now they all, rank tongues and riotous,
Themselves are lodged in Hades, and their town
Enslaved; so that these maidens whom thou seest,
From prosperous fallen upon evil days,
Come here to thee.   Such charge thy lord enjoined,
And I, obedient to his word, fulfil.
Himself, when to his Sire for victory
The sacrifice is paid that clears his vow,
Expect to come.   For this, of all the long
Glad story, is the sweetest word to hear. 290

Chor. Now, lady, is thy joy made manifest,
Part present, and thou hearest of the rest.

Dei. Hearing this news of all my lord's success,
How should I not rejoice, who am true wife?
Needs must they go together, this and that.
Yet shall the prudent still find cause to fear,
Lest he who prospers now may sometime fall.
Friends, through my heart a pang of pity went,
Beholding these unhappy, fatherless
And homeless, outcasts in an alien land, 300
Who erst belike were children of free men,
But now a slave's life is the life they have.
Zeus, may I never—Averter of the ill—
See thee so visit any child of mine:
Be it, if it must be, not till I am gone.

Such fears arise in me, beholding these.
Thou hapless girl—speak, tell me who thou art?
Say, art thou maid or mother? By thy looks
All inexperienced of such things thou art,
And noble. Lichas, whose daughter is the maiden? 310
Who was her mother? what her father's name?
Speak out: for her I pity most of all,
Beholding her, of all most quick to feel.

   Lich. Nay, what know I? Why ask you me? Belike
Not of the meanest of the land her birth.

   Dei. Was she the king's? Had Eurytus a daughter?

   Lich. I know not, for I asked few questions, I.

   Dei. Hast not from her companions heard her name?

   Lich. Not I: I did my task, nor wasted words.

   Dei. Speak, hapless maiden, freely speak to me: 320
'Tis pity not to know *thee*, who thou art.

   Lich. Nought like her former mood, I wot, 'twill be,
If now she should prove liberal of her tongue;
Who spake no word before, or much or little,
But ever travailing with her weight of grief
Weeps, and still weeps, unhappy, since she left
Her windy home. Yet fortune, howso hard
On her it be, not therefore is to blame.

   Dei. Suffer her then, and let her go within
As suits her best, nor may she at my hands 330
To crown her present ills find grief on grief:

Enough is that she has. And let us all
Go in, that you may haste whereso you list,
And I may make all ready in the house.

Mess. Ay, but first tarry awhile, that you may learn,
Now these are gone, whom to your hearth you lead,
And things unheard may hear, that should be known.
For of these matters I am well apprised.

Dei. What is it? Why stand you thus to bid me stay? 339

Mess. Stand still and hear me. Not my former speech
For nought you heard, nor this, I think, shall hear.

Dei. Shall we then call those others back again,
Or is thy mind to speak to these and me?

Mess. To these and thee nought hinders: *they* may go.

Dei. Well, they are gone: now let thy say be said.

Mess. This man told now his tale, as using not
Straightforward truth; but either now is knave,
Or else before was no true messenger.

Dei. How say'st thou? Tell me plainly all thy drift:
What thou hast spoken is a dark speech to me. 350

Mess. I heard this man declare, loud in the ears
Of many men, that for this maiden's sake
Eurytus and Oechalia's lofty tower
Did Heracles o'erthrow, nor other god
Than Eros charmed him to these martial feats—
Of slavish toil for Lydian Omphale,

Or headlong death of Iphitus, no word—
So changed the story now, with Love left out.
And, when her father would not give consent,
Nor yield the maiden for a concubine, 360
Some trivial accusation he contrived,
And brought an army against her land, and there,
Said Lichas, sits on the throne of Eurytus,
Having the king her father slain, and sacked
Her city. And now he sends her, as thou seest,
Before him hither—not without a purpose,
Lady, nor as a slave—expect it not—
It is not likely, if he glows with love.
So it seemed good to me to show thee all,
O queen, that I myself have heard from him. 370
And this did many in the mid-marketplace
Of Trachis hear along with me, and can
Convict him. I am sorry if my words
Grieve thee : but I have told thee all the truth.

   Dei. Ah me, ill-starred ! In what plight stand I
     now ?
What veiled insidious plague beneath my roof
Have I received ? O hapless—is she then
So nameless, as he swore who brought her here ?

   Mess. Splendid her beauty and her birth alike—
Daughter of Eurytus, Iole by name, 380
She used to be, whose lineage he forsooth,
Because he never asked it, could not tell.

Chor. Perish—I say not all ill-doers, but who
Practise with guile ill deeds that should not be!
  Dei. Ah, friends, what must I do? this latest news
Hath sounded in my ears bewilderingly.
  Chor. Go in and question him; since, with constraint
If thou shouldst ask, belike he'll tell thee all.
  Dei. There's purpose in thy counsel. I will go.   389
  Chor. And we—shall we remain? or what do next?
  Dei. Remain: for here, self-summoned from the house,
He comes, called by no messengers of mine.
  Lich. What word, O lady, shall I bear my lord?
Tell me, since I am going, as you see.
  Dei. Much haste you make to go, who slowly came—
Nor give me time to talk your tidings o'er.
  Lich. If aught you would ask further, here I stand.
  Dei. Hold you the honesty of speaking truth?
  Lich. Be Zeus my witness, whatso truth I know.
  Dei. Who is this maiden, then, you have brought hither?   400
  Lich. Euboean born: her name I cannot tell.
  Mess. Sirrah, look here at me. Whom speak you to?
  Lich. You—might I know, why *you* have asked me this?
  Mess. Answer my question, if your prudence dares.
  Lich. To the most royal Deianeira, daughter

Of Oeneus, wife of Heracles, unless
My eyes have played me false, and to my mistress.
    Mess. Precisely this I wished to know. Your mistress
You call this lady?
    Lich. Yes, as in justice bound.
    Mess. How then? What, think you, are your *just* deserts,   410
If you have dealt *unjustly*—you, with her?
    Lich. Unjustly — how? What cunning speech is this?
    Mess. 'Tis none. The cunning speeches come from you.
    Lich. I must be gone. Fool, to have tarried thus!
    Mess. One question you shall answer, ere you go.
    Lich. You have a tongue: what is it that you want?
    Mess. The captive whom you brought into the house—
I think you know her?
    Lich. Yes: why do you ask?
    Mess. Did you not call her daughter of Eurytus,
Iole? whom now you see, and know her not.   420
    Lich. Yea, to what audience? Who and where's the man,
Attests you, he was there and heard me say it?
    Mess. Many of our townsmen heard it—all the crowd
In the mid-marketplace of Trachis gathered.
    Lich. Yes—this I said that I had heard. To quote

Opinion is not to affirm the fact.

Mess. Opinion! Said you not upon your oath
You brought her to be wife to Heracles?

Lich. I said I brought her for his wife? Dear lady,
I pray you, tell me, who this person is. 430

Mess. One, sirrah, who heard you say, that for her beauty
A city fell—which not the Lydian woman,
But love of *her*, outbreaking, overthrew.

Lich. Let him go hence, good lady: for indeed
Sane men prate not with madmen, such as he.

Dei. By Zeus I charge thee, whose clear lightnings shine
Down the high glens of Oeta, keep back nought.
To one not evil-natured wilt thou speak,
One who knows well, 'tis human to rejoice
Not in the same delight continually. 440
I know, they are not wise, who set themselves
To fight with Love, challenging him to blows.
For even gods he governs as he will;
And me—why not another, weak like me?
Oh, if I blame my husband that he suffers
This madness, mad indeed am I myself;
Or blame this maiden, cause with him of that
Which causes me no shame, does me no wrong.
I cannot blame. But now, if taught of him
You lie, no noble lesson have you learned; 450

Or, if you school yourself, take heed lest then
You be found cruel, when you would be kind.
Nay, tell me all the truth.   To be called false
Is for free men no honourable lot.
That you should 'scape discovery, cannot be:
Many are they who heard you, and will speak.
And, if you are afraid, you fear amiss:
For, not to know—this would afflict me; but
Fear not my knowing: hath not Heracles
Loved many another—most of all men he? 460
And never any of them bore from me
Harsh word or gibe; nor shall, howe'er she be
Consumed with love, this maiden; nay, for her
Most of them all I pity, having seen
That 'twas her beauty that made waste her life—
Poor soul, who sacked, unwitting, and enslaved
The city of her home.   But now I charge thee—
Heed not what winds blow whither—but be false
To others if thou wilt, to me speak truth. 469

 Chor. Obey good counsel.   Cause thou shalt not find
To blame this lady, and shalt have thanks of me.

 Lich. Nay then, dear mistress, since I see, being human,
Thou hast a human heart, that knows to feel,
I will keep nothing back, but tell thee all.
For so indeed it is, as this man says.
Huge passion for this maid smote through and through
My lord, and for her sake the ruined town,

Her home Oechalia, fell beneath his spear.
And this—so much for him I needs must say—
He nor himself denied nor bade conceal; 480
But I, O lady, who feared to grieve thy heart
With telling of these tidings, I alone
Have sinned, if sin thou holdest it, in this.
But, now that all the story thou hast heard,
Both for his sake and for thine own no less,
Suffer the maiden, and let concerning her
The words that thou hast spoken bind thee still.
For, as no triumph he hath not won save this,
So for her love no bondage he'd not bear.

Dei. My thoughts, to do thy bidding, are as thine; 490
I shall not wage weak strife with gods, and win
My neighbours' plagues for mine. Go we indoors :
That thou may'st bear a message to my lord,
And gifts for gifts, a fit and fair exchange,
May'st carry. Empty shalt thou not go hence,
Who camest hither with such a goodly train.

Chor. Great strength from victory   [*Strophe.*
  Doth Cypris ever bear away.
  I stay not now to speak of gods,
 And how the son of Cronos she beguiled
   I spare to tell, 500
  How Hades, lord of night and death,
   And how Poseidon, strong
   To shake the rooted earth.

But hear, to win this lady for a bride,
    What champions ready of limb
    Addressed themselves to fight—
  The fight and then the marriage-feast;
Ordeal of battle, blow and dusty fall,
    What rivals dared.
    A River's might the one,   [*Antistrophe.*
    In semblance of a bull,
    Four-footed, lofty-horned,
Great Acheloüs hight, who came from Oeneadae.   509
    From Thebè, loved of Bacchus, the other came,
With curven bow and spear and brandished club,
    Of Zeus the son.
  Who then together in the midst,
  Desiring that fair marriage, met:
    And in the midst was sitting
The single umpire, with an umpire's wand,
    Cypris who gives fair brides to men.
    Much noise of heavy hands was then,   [*Epode.*
    And much of bowstrings twanging,
And the horns of the other fiercely struck and clashed:
    And there were grapplings close-entwined—   520
    And murderous blows on foreheads ringing—
    And deep hard breath of both.
    And all the while she sat
  Upon a height where all might see,
  With her fair face and delicate mien,

   And waited for her lord.
  Methinks I note it as a mother might :
   How there the maiden's sweet sad eyes,
   They fight for, bide the issue still :
    Then from her mother's side,
  As when men tear a heifer from its dam,
   All on a sudden she is gone.   530
 Dei. A moment, whilst the stranger takes his leave,
Friends, of the captive maidens in the house,
To speak with you here to the doors I stole,
Part, what my hands have planned that ye may know,
And part, that ye may pity my distress.
I have received this maiden in my house—
Maiden I think no longer, but a wife—
As when the shipman takes an overfreight,
A bale that will make shipwreck of my heart.
And now we twain share one embrace, beneath
One mantle's folds abide.   Such the reward   540
That Heracles, whom men call good and true,
For my long careful housekeeping hath sent.
Yet to be angry I find not in my heart,
With him oft smitten with this amorous plague :
But dwell beneath one roof with her, and share
With her my rights of wife, what woman could ?
Her bloom of youth I see is ripening still,
But fading mine : and eyes of men, I know,
The flower of such young beauty love to pluck,

But ever from the other turn away.
This then I fear, that he my wedded lord, 550
But husband of the younger, will be called.
Enough : I said that anger ill beseems
A woman who is wise : how I shall grieve
This maiden for my riddance, ye shall hear.
A gift, from the ancient Centaur long ago
Received, hid in an urn of brass, I keep.
From shaggy-breasted Nessus, from his blood,
As he lay dying, I drew it yet a girl—
Nessus who in his arms for hire across
The deep Euenus flood bore men, nor rowed them
Upon their way with oars, nor hoisted sail. 561
By whom I also—when in those first days
After my marriage I with Heracles
Upon my father's sending followed forth—
Borne on his shoulders, when I reached mid-stream,
With wanton hands was touched, and cried aloud,
And quick the son of Zeus turned, and let fly
A feathered arrow, that went singing straight
To the lungs of the Centaur. Who, fainting in death,
Spake to me thus : 'Daughter of Oeneus old,
So much, because thou wast my latest charge, 570
An if thou hearkenest to my words, shalt thou
Be gainer by my ferrying of thee.
If with thy hands thou takest of the blood
That curdles round about my wound, ev'n there

Where the Lernaean monster-hydra dipped
Its rankling arrows, this shall be to thee
A charm to sway the soul of Heracles,
Nor on another woman shall he look
To love her more than thee.' This then, O friends,
Remembering, (for after he was dead
Locked up with care I kept it in the house,)
I dipped this tunic, minding all he said 580
While yet he lived—all's done, and nought left out.
No deed of guilty daring may I know
Or learn—who hate all women who are bold:
Only with charms put forth on Heracles
And spells, before this child to be preferred,
This have I schemed: but, if I seem to do
A wanton thing—why, then I will forbear.

Chor. Nay, if you may put trust in what you do,
Our judgment is that you have counselled well.

Dei. Such trust I have as likelihood inspires, 590
But nowise yet am conversant with proof.

Chor. In the effect's the proof; you cannot know,
Howe'er it seems, until you make assay.

Dei. Soon I shall know; for now I see the man
Come from the doors; and straight he will be gone.
Only be secret: even if shameful things
Be darkly done, one shall not suffer shame.

Lich. Command me, child of Oeneus, what to do:
Already I have tarried all too long.

Dei. Nay, to this end not idle have I been, 600
Whilst to the strangers there thou saidst farewell,
That thou shouldst bear me this well-woven robe,
My handiwork, a present to my lord;
And charge him, giving it, to let it be
Worn by no other but himself the first,
And let no sunlight, nor the sacred court
O' the altar, nor the flame upon the hearth,
Behold it, till what time in sight of all,
Upon a day when bulls are slain, he stands
Forth, and displays it for the gods to see.
For fitly in this tunic had I vowed, 610
If I should see or hear him safe returned,
To dress him, and present him to the gods,
New-dight in a new robe, their worshipper.
And on the seal's enclosure, plain to see,
This sign deliver him—which he will know.
But go now, and this rule, that messengers
Seek not to meddle, chiefly bear in mind;
Next, see thou find a twofold meed of thanks,
Not single, but united, his and mine.

Lich. Call me of Hermes no true follower 620
Or servant, if you find me fail in this,
To bring this casket to him as it is,
And add for proof the reasons you allege.

Dei. And now begone. I think you know right well
How at this time things are within the house.

Lich. I know and will report all safe and sound.

Dei. My welcome of the stranger—how I gave
Her kindly welcome—this you have seen and know?

Lich. So that for joy my heart was all amazed. 629

Dei. What need to tell aught else? I fear you may
Too soon tell of the yearning of my love,
Before you know if I am yearned for there.

Chor. Where from ship-harbouring rocks   [*Strophe* 1.
  Our warm springs flow,
 And whosoever dwells
 At foot of Oeta's crags,
Where inland furthest runs this Melian bay,
And where the golden-arrowed goddess owns
  The seaward shore,
 Where meet the Parliaments of Greece,
 Named of the Gates, renowned—   639
 Expect right soon the sweet-voiced flute, [*Ant.* 1.
 Not with loud dissonance of despair,
 But with a music most divine
 To the responsive lyre attuned,
  All heaven will fill.
 For hither hastes Alcmena's son,
  The son of Zeus;
 With trophies of all high exploit
  Hastes hither to his home.
 A full twelve months we thought of him   [*Str.* 2.
 A wanderer, citiless among men,

> Beyond the sea—
> We thought and waited, and no tidings came;
> And drowned in tears his loving wife 650
> Her aching heart consumed with patient pain.
> But, fallen now on sleep,
> Hath Ares of her day
> Of mourning made an end.
> So quickly, quickly may he come: [*Ant.* 2.
> So may the oars
> Of his ship-chariot tarry not,
> Till to these walls they bear him home,
> Deserting soon those island altar-fires,
> Where now he offers sacrifice,
> If fame be true:
> Thence may he come 660
> A long day's journey without pause—
> Come, having drunk through every vein
> The magic of the specious robe,
> Persuasion's sovereign chrism.

Dei. Friends, how I fear that overbusily
All that I lately did may have been done.

Chor. What mean you, Deianeira, child of Oeneus?

Dei. I know not, but I fear I shall be found
Fair hopes to have nursed, huge mischief to have wrought.

Chor. You speak not of your gift to Heracles?

Dei. Of that. No one henceforth should I advise
To dare a deed in blindfold confidence. 670

Chor. Tell, if it may be told, whence grows your fear.
Dei. That which has come to pass if I shall tell,
Friends, ye will marvel, hearing things undreamed.
Wherewith but now I smeared the investiture
O' the robe, a weft of wool, fleecy and white—
'Tis gone from sight, consumed, but by no hand
Of those within—no, self-devoured, it wastes,
Down on the slab-face crumbling. But hear all—
All, how 'twas done, I will unfold at length.
What warnings the brute Centaur, in his side   680
The bitter shaft then rankling, bade observe,
Of these I nothing lost, but minded all—
Gravure from brass page ineffaceable.
So 'twas prescribed and even so 'twas done.
He bade me keep from touch of fire or reach
Of the glowing sunbeam in the dark the drug,
Until, fresh-smeared, I put it to its use.
And so I did. But now, the time being come,
I smeared within-doors secretly at home   689
With wool—from fleece of the home-flock torn, a wisp—
And laid and folded from the sunlight close
The gift within its casket, as ye saw.
Returning I beheld—but how to tell
Sight unforeseen, bewildering to hear?
For so it chanced I flung my tuft of wool,
I smeared the robe with, out in the full blaze
Of the noon sunshine. Whence conceiving warmth,

All melts from sight now, crumbled on the ground,
Most like to view, as ye may see the dust
Shed from a saw's teeth when ye saw the wood. 700
Mere dust, it lies. But where that dust was strewn,
Boils upward from the earth thick-curded froth,
As when from vines of Bacchus on the ground
Ye spill rich juice of a grey vintage-tide.
Ah miserable, I know not what to think :
A fearful deed I see that I have done.
For whence or wherefore had the monster borne
Good will to me—dying—for whom he died?
He could not; no, but, minded to undo
His slayer, beguiled me : guile which all too late 710
I, when it helps not, win the wit to see.
For I, I only, (or else my thought flies wide
Of the mark,) I hapless, shall destroy my lord.
The shaft that flew, I know, ev'n to a god,
Cheiron, proved fatal, and, howso it touch,
To every beast is death; from wound whereof
This its black venom mingled with the blood
How now shall he escape? Nowise, I think.
But I am purposed, if harm comes to him—
Such rage I feel—myself with him to die. 720
For who, *called* guilty, would endure to live—
What wife that prizes innocence indeed?

 Chor. Mischief we needs must fear : but fortune still
Rules the event ; esteem not forecast more.

Dei. Forecast, of courage ministrant, is none—
Of hope no help, when men have counselled ill.

Chor. When men have stumbled all unwittingly,
Anger has pity—as 'twere fit you found.

Dei. So talks no partner of the evil deed,
But one upon whose heart no burthen weighs. 730

Chor. Silence from further speech of this were best:
Or will you speak to your own son? for here
He comes, who went erewhile to seek his sire.

Hyll. Mother, for thee I had chosen of three things one—
That thou wert dead this day, or if not dead
Then mother not of me, or else to get
Somewhence a better mind than this thou hast.

Dei. What is it, my son, in me mislikes thee so?

Hyll. Thy husband—shall I tell thee?—yea, and I call
Him father—know that thou hast slain this day. 740

Dei. Ah me, my son, what word hast thou announced?

Hyll. A word that fails not of fulfilment: for
The fact that's palpable who may undo?

Dei. My son, how say you? By what warranty
A deed so hateful say you I have wrought?

Hyll. Of eyes that saw my father's grievous case—
My own; no hearsay this, from lip to ear.

Dei. Where found you then, where stood beside, my lord?

Hyll. If you must hear, from first to last you shall.
From sack of Eurytus' fair town returned, 750
A victor with his trophies and his spoils—
Where the Euboean headland breasts the waves,
The cape Cenaean, there to his father Zeus
Altars he traced and leafage of a grove :
There first I saw him, glad, whom I desired.
To Zeus a hecatomb preparing then,
Came to him Lichas, his own herald, hence,
Who bore thy gift, the robe that proved his death.
For this he donned, fulfilling thy behest—
So to the sacrifice : twelve faultless bulls, 760
Prime of the spoil, were there; but, count them all,
He led a hundred victims, small and great.
And first of all—unhappy—in gracious mood,
Pleased with the pomp and goodliness, he prayed :
But when of high solemnities the flame
Blazed from the blood and fed with resinous pine,
Sweat bathed his skin, and round his body clung
Close, as if welded by some craftsman's skill,
Clasping each limb, the tunic : racked each joint
Convulsive pains.   But, when he felt the accurst 770
Fell serpent's venom battening on his flesh,
He cried aloud for Lichas, the ill-starred,
The guiltless of thy guilt, and bade him tell
The whole vile plot—wherefore he brought this robe.
But, what knew he, the miserable ? thy gift,

He said, thine only, as 'twas sent, he gave.
My father heard, and as he heard a wrench
Of that sharp torture caught away his breath :
Lichas he snatched by the foot, where the ankle plays,
And flung full at the sea-confronting cliff. 780
Out from his hair white oozed the brain : mid-crown
His skull was split, and weltered with his blood.
A cry of deprecation and of grief
Brake from the crowd—one murdered, and one mad.
And no man dared to stand before thy lord;
So, dragged by the pain, he grovelled and he leaped,
So rock to rock resounded shout and yell,
Headlands of Locris and Euboean cliffs.
But when, poor soul, he wearied, oft on the earth
Flinging himself, oft in that grievous voice 790
His ill-consorted marriage execrating
With thee, the guilty, and Oeneus' virgin-prize
How winning he had won what wrecked his life,
Then from the shrouding smoke distorted eyes
He lifted, and he saw me, 'midst the crowd,
Weeping, and gazed upon me, calling me—
'O son, draw near, shun not my misery,
Not though to touch involve thee in my death :
But bear me forth, and set me, if you may,
Somewhere far hence, quite out of all men's sight: 800
Hence, as you pity me, from this land at least
Ferry me quickly ; here I must not die.'

Nor slighted we his bidding, but mid-ship
Set him, and brought—but hardly brought—ashore,
Tortured, with groanings loud. And him full soon
Living ye shall behold, or lately dead.
Counsel and hand herein, mother, are known
Thine : whom may Justice visit for these things,
Erinys plague !   Gods, pardon me the prayer ! 809
And they do pardon : since pardon thou didst scorn—
The noblest man of all men on this earth
Murdering, whose like again thou shalt not see.

 Chor. Why pass you hence, not speaking ? Know
   you not,
Eloquent with the accuser silence pleads ?

 Hyll. So let her pass. A fair wind go with her—
Out of my sight so waft her, passing well.
Mere empty sound of the name what boots to swell
Of mother, since nowise mother-like her deeds ?
Pass she, and fare she well : such gladness as 819
She gives my father, may herself partake ! [*Strophe* 1.

 Chor. Lo how, O maidens, cometh to pass o'ersoon
The word prophetic in our sight
Of the immemorial Prescience,
By the Voice proclaimed ; that, when to its last month's
   end should run
The twelfth year out, should be of bearing toils an end
To the son indeed of Zeus :
Promise which now the God
   T

To its fulfilment wafts aright.
Since how can he, who no more sees
The light, in death have toilsome service any more? 830
For since Necessity, that wrought with guile   [*Ant.* 1.
O' the Centaur, steeps in clouds of doom
His limbs, to which the venom clings,
Gendered by death, and by the gliding snake conceived—
What hope that he upon to-morrow's sun shall gaze,
By the grim hydra-shape
Inextricably clutched:
And of the swart-haired beast therewith
Torment him sharp avenging pains—
Poison of treacherous speech, in every vein that boils. 840
Which she, his miserable wife—   [*Strophe* 2.
Seeing with swift and sore misfortune to her home
His novel passion sudden-fraught—
Part not considered; part by policy not her own
Ruining whose love she sought to save,
Breaks now, I ween, her heart with sobs—
Sheds now, I ween, from eyes surcharged
A tender dew of dripping tears.
Woe treacherous and huge 850
The coming fate foreshadows clear.
Broken is the fountain of my tears.   [*Antistrophe* 2.
Poured on his head, ye gods, this sickness! never yet,
Not from his foes, assailed my lord
Suffering so signal and so pitiable as this.

O blood-stained steel of vanward spear,
That barest hither from the fray,
When proud Oechalia's heights were won,
The maiden fleet, that fatal day!
Nay, Cypris, handmaid mute,   860
The veil is off—the guilt is thine!

   Chor. 1. Was the sound born of my fancy, or did I
     hear,
This minute, peal through the house some cry of grief?
Hark! . . . Am I right?

   Chor. 2. A wail of despair sounds nowise doubtfully,
Within: something in the house has gone amiss.

   Chor. 1. And hither see
With aspect strange who comes and troubled brow,
Poor aged soul, bursting with news to tell.   870

   Nurse. O girls, the gift to Heracles—the gift
We sent—where ends the trouble it began?

   Chor. What mischief more, mother, will you report?

   Nurse. Gone hence is Deianeira—gone, the last
Of all her goings—ay, nor budged a step.

   Chor. How—gone?   Dead, say you?
   Nurse.   There's no more to say.
   Chor. Poor lady!—dead?
   Nurse.   Once and again 'tis told.
   Chor. O most untimely end! how died she, say?
   Nurse. Most rashly, for the manner.
   Chor.   In what guise

Encountered she with death? 880
    Nurse. Herself she slew.
    Chor.   Remorse—or what fierce fit
Of madness was it, the fatal thrust
So murderously dealt?   How compassed she
Death piled on death—
Wild work for one weak hand to do?
    Nurse. One plunge of cursèd steel—'twas done.
    Chor. What, babbler, were you there?
Saw you the wanton deed?
    Nurse. Near as I stand to you, I stood and saw.
    Chor. How was it?   The manner?   Tell me all. 890
    Nurse.   Herself, and of herself, she did this thing.
    Chor. What do you tell me?
    Nurse.   Plain, the truth.
    Chor. Stranger, not thy fair face alone
Thou bringest, but born, yea born of thee,
A dire Erinys to this house!
    Nurse. Too true: but more, had you been there to see
The things she did—much more your tears had flowed.
    Chor. And daunted not such work a woman's hand?
    Nurse. A marvèl, truly: hear, and testify.
She came alone in the house, and saw her son   900
In the great chamber spreading forth a couch,
Deep-pillowed, ere he went to meet his sire,
Back; but she crept away out of his sight,
And at the altars falling moaned that she

Was desolate, and each chattel of the house,
That once she used, fingered, poor soul, and wept:
Then, hither and thither roaming, room to room,
Each face she saw of servants that she loved,
Unhappy lady, looked and wept again,
Upon her own hard lot exclaiming still,   910
And how her children were her own no more.
And, when she ceased from this, I saw her pass
Suddenly to the chamber of my lord:
I, screened by the dark, seeing, myself unseen,
Watched; and I saw my mistress fling, lay smooth,
Couch-coverings on the couch of Heracles,
Till all were laid: then from the ground she sprang
And sat there in the midst upon the couch,
And loosed the flood of scorching tears, and spake:
'O marriage-bed and marriage-chamber mine,   920
Farewell, now and for ever; never more
This head upon this pillow shall be laid.'
No more she said, but with a violent hand
Did off her robe, clasped by the brooch that lay,
Gold-wrought, upon her bosom, and made bare
All her left arm, and whiteness of her side.
Then I made haste and ran, with all my strength,
And told her son what way her thoughts were bent.
But lo, whilst I was gone, just there and back,
The deed was done—the two-edged sword we saw,   930
Quite through her side, midriff and heart had pierced.

Oh but he groaned to see it! For he knew
This deed, alas! his rashness had entailed—
Taught all too late by those o' the house that her
The Centaur lured to do she knew not what.
And now the boy—piteous!—of groans and tears
He knew no end, lamenting over her:
He knelt and kissed her lips; his side by hers
He laid along, and lay, complaining sore
That he had slain her with his random blame;   940
And weeping, his would be a double loss,
Bereaved of both his parents at one stroke.
So fares it here. Henceforth I know, two days—
And some do more—if any man computes,
He is a fool. To-morrow there is none,
Until to-day be prosperously got through.

 Chor. Nay, for of these two strokes of fate
Which first, which after, to lament—
Alas me, for I know not which!
The face of one is here to see—
The other dread is fancy-drawn—   950
'I see,' 'I shall see,' mix in one.
Oh that some wandering breeze of heaven [*Strophe.*
From hearth to frontier fresh would spring,
And waft me hence, and bear me far,
Or ere, the puissant son of Zeus
Of mere beholding suddenly,
I die, exanimate with fear:

So comes he, say they, to the doors,
Tormented in inextricable pain, 960
A thing to wonder at, and find no words.
As nightingales of sorrow sing—   [*Antistrophe.*
I sang of grief not far but near.
I hear the tread of alien feet.
Where are they bearing him? It sounds
Like march of mourners for a friend,
The heavy muffled tramp they keep.
Ah me! a speechless form they bear.
Alas! how frame conjecture of his state,
If this be death—so still he lies—or sleep? 970

  Hyll. Ah woe is me for thee, my father!
Miserable am I for thee!
What shall I do? How shall I help? Alas!

  Old Man. My son, keep silence, nor awake
The fierce infuriating pain:
There's life in the prostrate man. Bite hard
Thy lips—no word speak.

  Hyll.   How? he lives?

  Old Man. Nay, but wake not the slumber-bound;
Nor start and kindle into life
His raving dreadful malady. 980

  Hyll. O load intolerable of stifled agony!
O miserable me!

  Her.   O Zeus,
What land is here? among what men

Lay ye me, racked incessantly
With pain?—There, there—out and alas!
Again those cursèd fangs, again!

Old Man. Then didst thou learn, what gain it was
To hold thy peace, and not to scare 990
From head and eyes his sleep away?

Hyll. Patient I cannot be, not I,
Seeing this horror that I see.

Her. O thou Cenaean altar-pile,
A fair return for victims fair
Didst thou procure me, to my cost!
Zeus, what a wreck thou madest me!
O cursèd spite, that e'er mine eyes
Beheld thee, so beholding now
This frenzy's fever, passing cure! 1000
Nay for what sorcery, or what skill
Of leech-craft—save of Zeus himself—
Shall wield a spell to heal my hurt?
Scarce shall such marvel bless my sight.
Let be and let me sleep—
Sleep, and forget my grief—sleep, not to wake.
Where will ye touch me? What posture would ye have?
Each movement, every touch is death.
All sleep—whatever shuts an eye—ye have o'erthrown.
That clutch, off! Close again, close creeps my foe!
   And now,
Ye thankless men of Greece, who stirs of you— 1010

For whom so often on the deep,
And ridding every forest of its pest,
I daily died—and now, when I am sick,
Fire or the sword will no one turn this way,
To slay and ease me of my pain?
Come, friendly arm, and strike—
Strike thou my head and hated life atwain!

 Old Man. Son of the hero here, this task grows over-
  great—
Passing my strength. Help thou! With youthful sight
Undimmed—thou, where I fail, canst aid.

 Hyll. My hands—yes, I can help with them; 1020
But wit or wisdom have I none, to bid
The whole sound life forget its grievous woe:
Such issues are of Zeus alone.

 Her. O son, whose voice I hear, approach:
Raise me, and lay me on my side, to see.
. . . O fate, alas, alas!
Again with dreadful onset and fierce pain
The unapproachable malady 1029
Leaps, leaps upon its prey—to rend and not to spare!
Pallas, this torture must I bear again? But thou,
My son, have pity on thy sire, and draw
A blameless sword, and deeply strike
'Twixt breast and throat; and cure this maddening pain,
Thine impious mother's act—whom might I see
Fall'n in the selfsame case, none otherwise

Than me she slew. O Hades sweet,   1040
Brother of Zeus—with sudden death
Smite me, the miserable, and give me sleep—
O Hades, give me sleep!

  Chor. I shudder, friends, hearing the woful plight
O' the prince—so great a soul, afflicted so.

  Her. Full many, and full fierce, and sore to tell,
The labours of these shoulders and these arms:
But never yet the queen, consort of Zeus,
Proposed, no nor Eurystheus whom I hate,
Task like to this—this net by Furies woven,   1050
And by the false-faced daughter of Oeneus flung—
Fast on my shoulders—this, by which I die.
So, welded one with me, ev'n from the bone
It gnaws my flesh; and passages of my breath
Sucks, and with me inhabits; and my fresh blood
Has drained, till heart is dry, and all my frame
Wasted—by unconjectured chains enthralled.
Spears hurtling on the plain, gigantic force
Of the Earthborn, violence of savage beasts—
I have defied; lands Greek and barbarous   1060
Each of its scourge have rid—myself unscathed:
A woman, woman-hearted as her sex,
O'erthrows me, single-handed, with no sword.
O son, be thou my own, my very son,
Nor worship more the name of motherhood;
But in thy hands, go, bring her from the house—

To my hands give—thy mother: that I may know
If more it grieves thy sight my form to see,
Than hers, disfeatured, punished as is fit.
Go, son, be pitiless, pitiful of me,   1070
Whom many men might pity—like a girl
Moaning and weeping; as no man shall dare
Say that he ever saw me weep before;
But uncomplaining followed I my fate.
Now I am found womanish, so valiant once.
Come now beside me close, my son, and stand,
And see what plight it is that from myself
So moves me. See—for I will lift what hides.
Look at my poor maimed body, all of you:
Know what I suffer; see the piteous fact.   1080
Ah me, alas!
Through every limb glowed, thrilled again a throe
Of agony; rest from wrestling with my pain
Denies, 'twould seem, the dread devouring pest.
O Hades, lord, receive me!
Oh smite me, fire of Zeus!
Hurl forth, great king, thy bolt; full on my head,
Father, thy thunder! Save me from these fangs
O' the pain, full-blown once more, aggressive. Hands—
Hands, and ye shoulders, breast, and arms—my
 own—   1090
I see ye still, the selfsame thews, that erst
The scourge of herdsmen from his Nemean lair,

That lion, fierce to face, and grim to greet,
Grappled and conquered; and the Lernaean worm,
And that twiform, uncivil, horseman-host,
Monsters, lawless and rude, of might unmatched;
And the Erymanthian boar; and underground
At Hades-gate the dire three-headed whelp,
Echidna's spawn, resistless; and far i' the west,
The dragon-guarder of the golden fruit—   1100
These and a thousand toils beside I proved,
And no one ever flaunted spoils of me.
Now shattered thus, and tattered as ye see—
Fate dealt one blindfold blow—my strength lies prone;
Mine—whom men say the noblest mother bore,
Ay, and of Zeus in heaven proclaim me son.
But I—this surely know—nought though I be,
No step may move, on her that maimed me thus,
Ev'n thus, avenged will be. May she but come,
That, as I teach her, so she may report,   1110
Living and dead, ill-doers I chastised.

   Chor. Alas for Greece! what mourning I foresee
In store for her, if she shall lose this man.

   Hyll. Father—because you give me leave to speak—
Refrain and hear me, howsoe'er with pain.
What I shall ask, you shall in justice grant.
Incline to hear, not as thine anger chafes,
Impatient: vainly then were told, wherein
Thou cravest joy, wherein art grieved, amiss.

Her. Say all thy say, and cease: for, racked with pain, 1120
I know not what thy wordiness intends.

Hyll. My mother—I must tell thee how she fares
Now, and how nowise wilfully she sinned.

Her. O thou most base, thy father's murderess,
Thy mother—wilt thou talk to me of her?

Hyll. Being as she is, I may not well refrain.

Her. Truth, no, for that ill deed which late she did.

Hyll. Nor what she hath done this day—thou shalt confess.

Her. Speak, but have heed lest speaking prove thee base.

Hyll. Thus then. She lies dead—slain within this hour. 1130

Her. By whom? Harsh prophet of strange news art thou.

Hyll. No stranger's but her own hand struck the blow.

Her. Alas—she cheats me then of my revenge.

Hyll. Even thy heart 'twould melt, the whole tale to hear.

Her. Thou preludest a riddle. Tell me, how.

Hyll. All in a word—she sinned, intending well.

Her. Well, traitor, has she *done*—who slew thy sire?

Hyll. She saw the wife within there, thought to bind
Thy heart with spells—thought, and miscarried thus.

Her. Can Trachis boast a sorcerer so bold? 1140

Hyll. Nessus long since, the Centaur, gave advice
With such a charm to madden thy desire.

Her. Ah me unhappy, how am I undone!
Lost and undone and banished from the light!
Too well I see, hedged by what ills I stand.
My son, go, for thy father is no more;
Call me thy brethren hither, all the brood;
And call the miserable Alcmena, loved
Vainly by Zeus, that with my latest breath
I may declare what oracles I know. 1150

Hyll. So it hath chanced, thy mother is not here,
But dwells apart, at Tiryns by the sea.
And of thy children some she rears for thee
There, and of others learn lodged hence at Thebes:
But we, my father, as many as remain,
What thou requirest, hearing, will perform.

Her. Then hear me thou. Now is thy time to show
What stuff thou art made of, who art called my son.
My sire of old forewarned me of my end,
That by no living wight should I be slain, 1160
But by one dead, a dweller in the dark.
So now by this brute Centaur, as the god
Foretold, I die—the living by the dead.
Hear also, chiming all to one result,
New oracles that with the old agree.
For in the grove, whose priests the Selli make
Their home the mountain and the earth their bed,

There from the many-voiced, my father's oak,
I heard and wrote my doom—that at this time,
This living present, of my heavy tasks
I should be freed—and happy, I supposed—
But now I see this meant that I should die;
For on the dead is laid no burthen more.
Thus all to one conclusion plainly points.
Now therefore, O my son, I crave thy help:
Nor wait until thy waiting whets my tongue;
Help me, thyself consenting, having found
No law like this—for children, to obey.

 Hyll. Such words have passed between us—what comes next,
I fear: yet, father, speak—I shall obey.
 Her. But first thy hand—lay thy right hand in mine.
 Hyll. Why wilt thou fix me with this needless pledge?
 Her. Give me thy hand: dispute not, but obey.
 Hyll. Freely I give it; do with me as thou wilt.
 Her. Now, by the head of Zeus my Father, swear.
 Hyll. What thing to do? tell me, and I will swear.
 Her. That, what I shall prescribe, thou wilt perform.
 Hyll. I swear that so I will, so help me Zeus.
 Her. Pray that his curse may find thee, if thou fail.
 Hyll. So may it: I fear it not—I shall not fail.
 Her. Knowest thou the summit of Oeta—seat of Zeus?
 Hyll. Often have I climbed—and at his altar stood.

Her. Now ye must lift my body with your hands,
Thou, and what friends with thee thou wilt, and
    there—
Hew me great faggots out of ancient oaks
Deep-rooted, and male oleasters cleave
Nor spare, and lay my body on the wood,
Then take a blazing torch of resinous pine,
And set fire under. Mourn not for me, nor weep:
But do thine office, as thou art my son,   1200
Tearless, without a groan; lest from the grave
My curse be heavy upon thee all thy days.

    Hyll. What do I hear? What hast thou done to me?

    Her. Thou hast thy task: this do, or else be called
No son of mine—get thee another sire.

    Hyll. Alas my father, and again alas—
What wouldst thou? Shall I be thy murderer?

    Her. Nay, not a murderer, but with healing hands
The one physician of my dire disease.

    Hyll. Strange medicine thou cravest—this of fire.   1210

    Her. If this thou fearest, do for me all but this.

    Hyll. I shall not grudge to bear thee to the place.

    Her. And wilt thou heap the pyre, as I have said?

    Hyll. So that I do not touch it with my hands,
All else I will; thou shalt not lack, for me.

    Her. This shall suffice. Yet grant one boon beside,
And to the greater favour add the less.

    Hyll. Greater it cannot be than I shall grant.

Her. The daughter of Eurytus—thou knowest her?
Hyll. Of Iole thy speech is, as I think.   1220
Her. Of her. Hear now my will concerning her.
When I am dead, if thou hast any care
Not impiously to break thine oath to me,
Take her to be thy wife, nor thwart me here:
And let no other man have her but thee,
Seeing that beside thy father she hath lain,
But cherish her and take her for thine own.
Promise; for in a trifle to rebel
Forfeits the thanks of loyalty in much.
Hyll. Ah me, with a sick man one should be gentle;   230
Yet who could bear to see him so distraught?
Her. Thy muttering bodes no doing of my will.
Hyll. Who in my place, with the one woman who caused
My mother's death, and this thy grievous plight—
Who but one plagued with madness for a curse,
Would choose this? Better, father, I should die,
Than with my enemies ill-matched to dwell.
Her. So now it seems this man will not regard
Me, dying. But the gods live, and for thee,
O disobedient to my voice, their curse shall wait.   1240
Hyll. Ah, soon, I fear, thou'lt say thy pangs return.
Her. The pain had slept; thou dost awake me, thou.
Hyll. Unhappy, on all sides how am I perplexed!
U

Her. Yea, me thy father deigning not to hear.

Hyll. Shall I be taught to do an impious deed?

Her. Not impious, if thereby my heart is cheered.

Hyll. Shall then thy bidding clear me of the guilt?

Her. I call the gods to witness, thou art clear.

Hyll. Enough: I promise it. The gods have seen
What part herein is thine, nor will condemn   1250
Me, father, that I hearkened to thy voice.

Her. 'Tis well concluded. Show me then, my son,
This kindness quickly : and set me on the pyre
Now, ere the pain comes back to rend and sting.
Ho ye, make haste and lift me. Rest from trouble
Is none for me, save death that endeth all.

Hyll. All without hindrance, father, as thou wilt,
Since thy command is urgent, shall be done.

Her. Come, while the pain sleeps undisturbed,
Come, O thou stubborn heart, and bring   1260
A bit of steel, set sharp with stones,
And let no groan escape my lips—
Rejoicing, heart, to dare and do
The inevitable deed.

Hyll. Good henchmen, lift him : and of me
Have ye great pity in your thoughts;
But, for this deed that must be done,
Know that the gods are pitiless,
Who, though this man is called their son,
Yet let him suffer as ye see.

Shut is the future from our view : 1270
But grief the present hath for us,
And for the gods reproach ;
Yea, and for him, who bears his doom—
Was ever pain like his?
Come, maidens, follow, who have seen
Unknown dread forms of death to-day,
And sorrows manifold and strange :
And nought comes not from Zeus. 1278

AJAX

PERSONS.

AJAX.
ODYSSEUS.
TEUCER.
AGAMEMNON.
MENELAUS.
MESSENGER.
ATHENE.
TECMESSA.
CHORUS OF SALAMINIAN SAILORS.

Ajax

Ath. EVER, son of Laertes, I behold thee
Keen-eyed to snatch occasion of thy foes:
And now I find thee by the seaward tents,
Of Ajax, where at the camp's end he lies,
Like hunter on the trail, pausing to scan
His footmarks newly-printed, and discern,
Is he within or not.   Right to thine aim
Keen-scented footing as of a Spartan hound
Leads thee.   Here hath he entered even now,
His brows and slaughtering hands all drenched with
    sweat. 10
Now then within these doors no more is need
That thou shouldst peer, but say what brings thee hither,
Thus eager: I who know will tell thee all.
    Od. Voice of Athene, goddess best-beloved,
Albeit unseen, how well I know thy sound,
This that I hear and all my heart drinks in,
As of Tyrsenian trumpet brazen-tongued.
And now my foe, as thou hast deemed, I hunt,
This buckler-bearing Ajax, to and fro:
Him have I tracked so long, and none but him. 20

For he this night a deed that baffles thought
Has wrought against us, if the work be his:
Since nothing sure we know, but are in doubt.
And I my service offered for this quest.
For lo our captive flocks, and with the flocks
Their guardians also, by some violent hand
Slain and despoiled all newly have we found;
And all the camp charges on him this guilt.
Yea and a certain watcher came with word
And showed me how with smoking sword alone   30
He saw him leaping o'er the plain: whereat
I hasted on the track, and now conclude—
Now am perplexed—whose may the footprints be.
But in good time thou comest: for thy hand
Guides all my goings, and evermore shall guide.

   Ath. I knew it, Odysseus, and with good will came,
To go along with thee and watch thy quest.
   Od. On a true scent, dear mistress, do I work?
   Ath. Be well assured thou dost: he did this deed.
   Od. What to such work nerved his insensate hand? 40
   Ath. Wrath for Achilles' arms oppressed his soul.
   Od. How then in such strange wise fell he on flocks?
   Ath. Deeming on you he dyed his hands in gore.
   Od. And was this purposed for the Argive host?
   Ath. Purposed indeed and done, had I not watched.
   Od. What daring and what hardihood was this?
   Ath. Alone, i' the night, by stealth he went against you.

Od. And came he near us? at his goal arrived?
Ath. At the tent-doors of the two generals.
Od. How stayed he then his hand that craved for
blood?   50
Ath. I checked him, and I cast upon his sight
Distracting fancies of a desperate joy:
Against the flocks I turned him, flocks and herds—
The general spoil not yet distributed,
Which herdsmen have in charge—on these he fell,
And hewed great slaughter of the hornèd beasts,
Smiting all round him: and sometimes he deemed
He slew the two Atreidae with his hand,
Anon, of leaders fell on this or that.
Seeing him rave with madness in his soul,
I urged him, drave him to the toils of fate.   60
And, having rested from such work as this,
The living oxen now he bound with cords,
And all the sheep, and home he brought them all,
Thinking 'twas men, not beasts, he had for prey.
And now within, bound fast, he tortures them.
Nay, thou shalt see his madness with thine eyes,
That thou mayest tell the Greeks what thou hast seen.
Bravely await, expecting no mischance,
His coming: for his eyes' gaze I will turn
Another way, nor let him see thy face.   70
Ho, thou who straightenest out the captives' arms
With cords within there, come, I bid thee, forth—

Come forth, come hither, Ajax, out of doors.

    Od. What dost thou, mistress? Nowise call him forth.

    Ath. Hold thou thy peace, and be not cowardly.

    Od. I pray thee, be content, and let him stay!

    Ath. Lest what befall? Was he no man before?

    Od. Ay, and to me a foeman was, and is.

    Ath. To laugh at foes—what laughter is more sweet?

    Od. Content am I, he should abide within.   80

    Ath. A madman—and you shrink to see the sight?

    Od. I had not shrunk to face him, were he sane.

    Ath. But now, ev'n stand beside him, he'll not see.

    Od. How, if he sees with the same eyesight still?

    Ath. His eyes, although they see, yet I will blind.

    Od. All's possible indeed, when gods contrive.

    Ath. Stand and be silent: as thou art, remain.

    Od. I will remain; but would that I were hence.

    Ath. What, Ajax, ho: a second time I call,
So lightly thine ally dost thou regard?   90

    Aj. All hail, Athene! daughter of Zeus, all hail!
I thank thee for thy help. For this day's prize
With goodly spoils all-golden will I crown thee.

    Ath. 'Tis fairly spoken. But answer me to this:
Hast thou dyed well thy sword i' the Argive host?

    Aj. I'll not deny it; such boasting is my right.

    Ath. Upon the Atreidae did thine arm'd hand fall?

    Aj. So that these men will not slight Ajax more.

Ath. I read thy saying, that the men are slain.

Aj. Slain—of my arms let them defraud me *now!* 100

Ath. Good now: but of Odysseus—what of him?
In what plight stands he now? is he escaped?

Aj. The cursèd dog-fox—askest thou of him?

Ath. Yea, of thy foe, Odysseus, I would learn.

Aj. Sweetest of all, O queen, he sits i' the tent
My captive: for he must not die just yet.

Ath. Till thou dost what, or what more shalt have
gained?

Aj. Till being bound to a pillar of the court——

Ath. How wilt thou punish then the miserable?

Aj. His back shall bleed with scourging, ere he dies. 110

Ath. Nay, do not so torment the hapless one.

Aj. Have all save this, Athene, as thou wilt:
But so must this man suffer, no way else.

Ath. Why then, if it delights thee to do this—
Hold not thy hand, spare nought of thine intent.

Aj. I go to do it: only I charge thee this—
As now, so ever, help me at my need.

Ath. Seest thou, Odysseus, what the might of gods?
What man more prudent, or more prompt to do
The thing in season, couldst thou have found than he? 120

Od. I know not any. Yet must I pity him,
Being so unhappy, unfriendly though he be,
Bound with a fate so cruel hand and foot:
For in his state I see my own no less;

I see that all we living are nought else
But phantoms, or a shadow that escapes.

   Ath. So having eyes to see, keep thou thy lips,
And of the gods speak never a boastful word;
And show no swelling port, because thy hand
Is heavier than another's, or than his
Deeper the soundings of thy hoarded gold.   130
For a day lays low, and a day restores,
All human things: and humbleness the gods
Love, but all evil-doers they abhor.

   Chor. O son of Telamon, that hast
Thine island home at Salamis,
Firm-planted 'mid the waves,
In thy prosperity I am glad,
But when on thee some heavy blow
From heaven, or of the Grecian host
A furious slanderous rumour falls,
I shrink and cower—no fluttering dove
More timorous-eyed than I.   140
As, in this night now spent, all tongues
Are loud against us clamouring shame,
That flocks of the Greeks and herds—
What spoil of the conquering spear remained—
Ranging the meadows where
Our steeds run wild, thou didst destroy,
With flash of murderous steel.
Such false and whispered tale

Odysseus pours in ears of all,
Persuading all: for now   150
All men believe all things of thee,
And every one who hears exults
And triumphs in thine anguish, more
Than he who told.   One shall not miss,
Who at a mighty spirit aims:
But, should he speak such things of me,
None would believe him; envy still
Assails the fortunate.   Yet are
Small men no stable tower of strength,
Without the great: small joined with great,   160
Great helped by small, shall prosper best.
But fools, by step and step, to learn
This lesson who can lead?
So foolish is their clamorous spite;
And we without thee, prince, are weak
Their idle slanders to repel.
Nay, for so soon as from thine eye
They have escaped, they chatter loud,
Like flocks of noisy birds:
But, O great vulture, show thyself—   170
Straight they shall cower
Before thee, stricken dumb with fear.
Did Artemis incense thee so?   [*Strophe* 1.
Zeus' daughter, Tauric Artemis,
(O rumour huge, parent of shame to me!)

Upon the herds to fall, the people's kine—
Minding belike some day of victory,
To crown it now with bitter fruit,
When glorious battle-spoils she missed,
Or missed the wonted honours of the chase?
Or brazen-harnessed Enyalius is it perchance,
Who, for he blamed alliance lightly prized, 180
Conspiring with the darkness of the night,
Hath thus redressed the wrong?

For never, son of Telamon, [*Antistrophe* 1.
Didst thou of thine own counsel stray
In foolish paths so far, to fall on flocks.
Men are with madness smitten of the gods.
But now may Zeus and Phoebus both avert
This foul tale that the Argives tell!
And, if they speak a cunning speech,
A changeling lie—these mighty kings, or he 189
Who of the miscreant house of Sisyphus is sprung—
No more, our prince, keeping thy presence hid,
Here on the beach among the tents, no more,
Win me an evil fame!

Arise and sit no more, [*Epode*.
Where rooted in a stubborn idleness
Too long thou sitt'st already, absent from the war,
Kindling a flame of ruin high as heaven:
So fearlessly it flares,
Fire in a wind-swept thicket of the hills—

The fury of thy foes;
Whose scornful wagging tongues to thee
Are grievous—and for me abideth woe. 200

   Tec. Shipmates of the bark of Ajax—
Of the Erechthid race, sons of the soil—
We have tears for our shedding, we who care
For the house of Telamon, for the house far off.
For now the dreadful, the mighty,
Ajax the fierce and strong,
By madness—all one turbid stream—
Lies stricken.

   Chor.   What heavy deed
Has startled the night from its stillness?
Child of the Phrygian Teleutas, speak: 210
For thee, his consort, won with the spear,
He loves; and wild is his soul, but to thee
Is constant: so shouldst thou,
Not ignorant, hint the truth.

   Tec. How shall I utter a tale unuttered?
Yea, for like death is the grief ye shall hear.
Ah me, our glorious Ajax—
So stricken with madness, so all in a night
Wrecked and undone is he.
Such bleeding butchered victims 220
Sacrificed there in the tent thou'lt see,
Ev'n by no hand but his.

   Chor. Ah, of my fiery-hearted lord   [*Strophe.*

What tidings are these that thou tellest,
Not to be borne, nor yet escaped—
Told all abroad by the mighty Greeks,
Which Rumour extols as she tells, loud-voiced?
Ah me, for I fear whereto this tends.
Surely, discovered, the man will die,
Having slain together with frenzied hand, 230
Slain with the reeking sword together,
Sheep, and the horsemen who kept the sheep.

 Tec. Alas! thence then it was,
Thence that we saw him come,
Driving his captive flocks; and of part
He cut the throats on the ground within;
Some, hewing their sides, he tore asunder;
And two white-footed rams he took,
And of one shore off the head, and the tip
Of the tongue, and flung them
From him; and one upright 240
By its forefeet lashed to a pillar,
And then with a mighty thong
Of his horse's harness smote,
Doubling it into a sounding scourge,
Reviling him too with bitter words,
Which a god and no man had taught.

 Chor. Now it is high time, now, that one [*Ant.*
Should cover his head with a mantle,
And with his feet make haste to flee,

Or on swift benches of rowers sit,
And over the sea let the ship be gone. 250
Such threats do the two lords, Atreus' sons,
Threat after threat like our own oars' tune,
Ply against us: nay, and I fear to share,
Stricken with him, a death by stoning—
Whom unapproachable fate involves.

   Tec. But now no longer so: for now
The lightnings cease, and the gale is still,
That rushed so keen before.
Now, come to himself, new pain he suffers:
For looking on self-inflicted grief, 260
Wherein no other bore a hand,
Lays to the soul sharp pangs.

   Chor. Nay, all may yet be well, if this has ceased:
Soon we make light of troubles that are past.

   Tec. Yet which, if these were offered, wouldst thou
      choose,
To vex thy friends and to be glad thyself,
Or, partner of their grief, be grieved no less?

   Chor. The double grief, O lady, is the worse.

   Tec. Then by his sane mind are we losers now. 269

   Chor. How mean you this? I know not what you say.

   Tec. This man, this Ajax, whilst he still was mad,
Himself rejoiced in his own misery;
Ours was the grief who saw it and were sane:
But, since his madness gives him breathing-space,

x

Now with sore sorrow all his soul is vexed,
And we are grieved no less than formerly.
Is it not a twofold plague, two griefs for one?
  Chor. I'll not gainsay thee: but I fear, some blow
From heaven has fallen. Nay, how else, if, sane,
No whit more than distracted, he is glad?   280
  Tec. Be well assured and know that so it is.
  Chor. What first beginning of this evil fell?
Tell us, who share thy grief, whate'er has chanced.
  Tec. Yea, it concerns thee, thou shalt hear it all.
At dead of night, when evening fires were out,
With a sharp two-edged sword he armed his hand,
Bent on some bootless errand to be forth.
I spake and chid him: 'Ajax, what wouldst thou?
Why goest thou forth unbidden on this quest,
Called by no messenger, nor hearing voice   290
Of trumpet, but the host lies now asleep?'
Shortly he answered me, the old old tale:
'Woman, to be silent is a woman's crown.'
So taught, I ceased, and he rushed forth alone;
What chanced whilst he was gone I cannot tell,
But back he came with spoil into the tent,
Bulls, bound, and shepherds' dogs, and goodly flocks.
Some he beheaded, of some slit throat, back-bent,
Some hewed in pieces, some his prisoners
As men tormented, falling on senseless sheep.   300
Last, through the doors he rushed, bandying wild words

There with some phantom, of the Atreidae now,
Odysseus then—and still his laugh rang false,
How he had gone, wreaked scorn upon his foes.
Then swiftly back within the tent he came :
And there with pain, at last, came to himself :
And through that house of slaughter sent his eyes,
And smote his head, and cried aloud : and sat
A wreck amid the wrecks of the slain beasts,
And tightly clutched his hair with his bent hands. 310
Most of the time he sat without a word ;
But then at me broke forth with direst threats,
Should I hide from him aught of what had chanced ;
And bade me tell him in what plight he stood.
And I, O friends, afraid, told all the tale,
Far as I knew it, all that he had done.
Then did he cry out with a grievous cry,
Such as I never heard from him before ;
Ever till now he taught that such complaints
Were fit for cowards and men dispirited ;— 320
No sound of shrill lamenting would he make,
But moaned, as a bull might, beneath his breath :—
But now, in such ill plight, so overthrown,
There, without food or drink, fall'n midst the beasts
Slain by his sword, he sits, and holds his peace.
And past all doubt some mischief he intends :
There's some such meaning in his words and moans.
But, O my friends, for therefore came I hither,

Come in and help us, if ye have the skill;
Such men are governed by a friend's advice. 330

Chor. O daughter of Teleutas, a sore tale
You tell us, of this man made mad with grief.

Aj. (within.) Ah me, alas!

Tec. Not yet the worst, I fancy: heard ye not
What bitter cry there sounded from his lips?

Aj. Ah, woe is me!

Chor. The man, it seems, is mad, or, face to face
With sight of his past madness, grieves for that.

Aj. My child there!

Tec. Alas me: for Eurysaces he calls. 340
What means he? child, where art thou? hapless I!

Aj. What, Teucer! where is Teucer? will he be gone
Plundering for ever, and leave me to my fate?

Chor. There speaks no madman. Open ye the doors.
Ev'n sight of me may put him to some shame.

Tec. 'Tis done, the doors stand open. Now may
    ye see
His deeds, and see himself, what plight is his.

Aj. My mariners, my friends,   [*Strophe* 1.
My only, only friends who still,
Still by the upright rule abide, 350
Behold what circling tide is round me now,
Borne in by the deadly tempest's stress.

Chor. Ah, how thy testimony proves too true!
Too plain the deed declares its senselessness.

Aj. Shipmates who dipt the oar, [*Antistrophe* 1.
Good crew, staunch in the seaman's craft,
You have I seen and none but you
A bulwark still against calamity: 360
Come therefore, and slay me—me with these.

Chor. Refrain thy tongue: by curing ill with ill,
Increase not thou the sharpness of thy doom.

Aj. Ye see me here, the brave, the stout of heart,
The undismayed in battle with the foe—
Dealing on fearless beasts most valiant blows.
Alas the mockery, how am I cast down!

Tec. Ah, my lord Ajax, say not so, I pray thee.

Aj. Hence, woman, and begone out of my sight!
Ah me, alas! 370

Tec. Nay, by the gods, learn wisdom and submit.

Aj. Luckless, who spared to strike the guilty, the
   accursed, [*Strophe* 2.
But, falling on these hornèd kine and goodly flocks,
Poured out their purple blood.

Chor. Why shouldst thou grieve, now when the deed
   is done?
There is no way but that these things are so.

Aj. O seeing all, tool of all mischief ever,
Most false, most loathsome knave in all the host, 380
Now in thy triumph well I know that thou,
Son of Laertes, laughest loud and long.

Chor. As heaven ordains it, so men laugh or weep.

Aj. Yet might I see him—suffering as I am!
Ah me, alas!

   Chor. Speak no proud word. Bethink thee of thy
     plight.   [*Antistrophe* 2.

   Aj. O Zeus, my sire's progenitor, might I but slay
The cunning hated knave, and those twin-sceptred kings,
And then myself be slain!   390

Tec. Chor. When thou wouldst pray thus, pray withal for me
To die: why should I live when thou art dead?

   Aj. O night, my light—   [*Strophe.*
O Erebus, most bright, for me—
Take, take me hence, with you to dwell:
Take me: no longer am I fit
To look to gods for succour,
No, nor for any help of mortal men:
But me the child of Zeus,   400
The mighty goddess, plagues
To my undoing: then whither can I flee?
Or where, oh where, gone hence, shall I remain?
If all the past fades from me, O my friends,
And vengeance is at hand,
And on an idle triumph my heart was set;
And all the host, lifting both hands to strike,
Would strike me dead.

   Tec. Oh me unhappy, that a brave man should speak
Such words, words that before he had not deigned!   410

   Aj. O seaward caves,   [*Antistrophe.*

And paths beside the sounding wave,
And pastures sloping to the beach,
A long, a long, a weary time,
Beneath Troy-walls ye held me;
But now no more, no more with breath of life—
Let none but fools doubt that!
And, O Scamander's streams,
Ye neighbour streams, that to the Greeks were kind,
Ye shall not any more behold this man— 420
A man of whom I shall not fear to boast,
Troy hath not seen his like,
In all the host come hither from Grecian land;
But now, from height of glory fall'n so low,
Prostrate I lie.

    Chor. I cannot forbid, but how to let thee speak
I know not—so with misery beset. 429

    Aj. Alas me! who had thought my name one day
Would have such meaning, chiming with my fate?
For twice and three times now have I good cause
To cry Alas, fallen in such evil plight:
Whose father once in this Idaean land
Won by his prowess first prize of all the host,
And home departed crowned with all renown;
But I his son unto the selfsame Troy
Came, strong as he; yea, and, albeit I wrought
Like helpful deeds in battle with my hand,
I perish thus, dishonoured by the Greeks. 440

Yet surely I think that this one thing I know,
Had but Achilles lived to make award,
Whose prowess had deserved his arms for prize,
No other man had snatched them then from me.
But now the Atreidae to this utter knave
Have sold them, and my deeds they have despised.
And had not sight and thought, distorted both,
Swerved from my purpose, never more had they
Against another man giv'n sentence thus.
But now the stern-eyed maiden, child of Zeus,   450
Even whilst I armed my hand to strike the blow,
So mocked me, with such madness dazed my mind,
That on these poor beasts I imbrued my hands,
Whilst *they* exult to have escaped my clutch—
No fault of mine: no, when a god arrests,
The worse man from his better may escape.
What shall I do now? whom 'tis manifest
The gods hate, and the Greek host loves me not,
And all Troy hates me and these plains of Troy.
Home o'er the Aegean wave, from shore and camp,   460
Leaving the Atreidae helpless, shall I go?
Before the face of Telamon, my sire,
How shall I stand? how will he look on me,
Come back ungraced, come back without the prize,
With praise whereof he crowned his own brows once?
'Twere past endurance. What then? Shall I storm
Troy's towers, and fall alone on none but foes,

And do some valiant deed, and so be slain?
But the Atreidae would be glad of this.
It may not be.   Another kind of feat   470
Must I devise, whereby my sire shall know,
At least no coward in grain am I, his son.
Base is the craving for the longer life,
When life is misery, and unrelieved.
What joy has day that alternates with day,
And this brings nigh and that draws off from—death?
Too dear I count him at the cheapest rate,
Who warms his heart with visionary hopes.
Nobly to live or nobly die, there is
No choice for brave men else.   My say is said.   480

   Chor. No one shall say thy words rang counterfeit:
We heard thy whole soul, Ajax, in that speech.
But now let be : now let thy friends prevail
To bend thy purpose—and dismiss these thoughts.

   Tec. O my lord Ajax, of all things most hard
Hardest is slavery for men to bear.
And I was daughter of a sire freeborn—
No Phrygian mightier, wealthier none than he:
But now am I a slave.   For so the gods,
And so thine arm, had willed it.   Therefore now—   490
For I am thine, thy wife, and wish thee well—
I charge thee now by Zeus who guards thy hearth,
And by that couch of thine which I have shared—
Condemn me not, given over to their hands,

To bear the cruel gibes thy foes shall fling.
Bethink thee, on that day when thou shalt die,
And by that death divorce me, violent hands
On me the Greeks will lay, and we shall live
Henceforth the life of slaves, thy child and I.
And then at me shall some one of my lords   500
Shoot out sharp words, ' Lo ye, the concubine
Of Ajax, who was strongest of the Greeks—
Fallen from what pride, unto what service bound ! '
So they will talk. And me such fate will plague ;
But shame such talk imports to thee and thine.
Nay but have pity, and leave not thou thy sire,
So old, so grieved ; pity thy mother too,
Portioned with many years ; who night and day
Prays to the gods to bring thee home alive :
And have compassion on thy boy, O prince—   510
Think, should he live, poor child, forlorn of thee,
By unkind guardians of kind care deprived,
What wrong thy death will do to him and me.
Nothing have I to look to any more,
When thou art gone. Thy spear laid waste my home ;
My mother too and father Fate withal
Brought low, in the dark house of death to dwell.
What home then shall I find instead of thee—
What wealth ? My life hangs utterly on thee.
Nay even of me be mindful. Should not men   520
Remember, having tasted of delight ?

Ever from kindness should new kindness spring.
Who of past joy lets fade the memory,
Call me not that man noble any more.

Chor. Such pity, Ajax, as in my heart I have,
I would thou hadst: then wouldst thou praise her speech.

Aj. Yea, praise in plenty shall she win from me,
If but my bidding she is content to do.

Tec. Nay, O dear master, I will not fail in ought. 529

Aj. Bring then my child to me, that I may see him.

Tec. Nay, but for fear I did release him hence.

Aj. Now while this night's ill work was toward—or how?

Tec. Lest, hapless, had he met thee, he had died.

Aj. Yea, well indeed it would have matched my fate.

Tec. But, to avert this, I took care of him.

Aj. I thank thee for this prudence thou hast shown.

Tec. How may I serve thee, since these things are so?

Aj. Now let me speak to him and see his face.

Tec. Yea, in slaves' keeping he abides hard by.

Aj. What hinders him to be brought hither then? 540

Tec. O child, thy father calls thee. Let some slave
Whoever in safe hands keeps him, bring him here.

Aj. Comes he at call, or hears he not thy voice?

Tec. Here comes indeed a servant, bearing him.

Aj. Lift him, lift hither. He will not fear, not he,
To look upon this sight of blood fresh-spilt;
Not if he is indeed his father's son.
Best lose no time, but in his sire's rough ways

Break him in now, whilst nature takes the mould.
Child, happier than thy father mayest thou be; 550
But like him else—thou shalt not be amiss.
Nay, even now one thing I envy thee,
That of this misery no sense hast thou:
Life's sweetest time is thine, ere feeling comes—
For 'tis a painless evil, not to feel—
Whilst joy and sorrow are a lore unlearnt.
But, when thou art grown to this, my foes must know
Thee, what a son thou art of what a sire.
Meanwhile, by heaven's light breezes fanned and fed,
Nurse for thy mother's joy thy tender life.
None of the Greeks, I know, shall trouble thee 560
With their base spite—no, not though I am gone:
Such ceaseless care of thee shall Teucer have,
Whom I will leave, staunch warder of thy life,
Though now we miss him, hunting down his foes.
But you, my sailors, comrades of the shield,
On you I charge this kindness for your share—
Deliver to him my bidding, hence to my home
To bear this child, and there to Telamon
Show him, and to my mother Eriboea,
That he may nurse their old age to the last, 570
Until they come to Pluto's dusky realm;
And let no umpires offer (no, nor he,
Who wronged me) to the Greeks *my* arms for prize.
But thou, my son, Eurysaces, take thou

And wear my shield's self, whence thou hast thy name,
Wielding it by its strap of many thongs—
The sevenfold impenetrable shield;
But all my other arms must share my grave.
Now quickly take this boy and shut the doors,
And make no weeping here before the tent.
Good sooth, a woman is a plaintive thing. 580
Make fast with speed. No wise leech seeks to charm
With lamentation woe that craves the knife.

   Chor. I am afraid, hearing this eager haste:
Too keen-edged for my liking is thy tongue.

   Tec. O my lord Ajax, what is it thou wilt do?

   Aj. Ask not nor question. To be discreet is best.

   Tec. Ah, how I fear! By heaven, and by thy child,
I pray thee, hearken, and forsake us not.

   Aj. Thou weariest me. Knowest thou not, that I
Am debtor now no more to serve the gods? 590

   Tec. Refrain thy tongue.

   Aj.   Speak thou to those who hear.

   Tec. Wilt *thou* not hearken?

   Aj.   Thou'rt importunate.

   Tec. O prince, I fear thee.

   Aj.   Shut fast the doors on her.

   Tec. By heaven, relent.

   Aj.   I count thee but a fool,
If now to school my temper thou art bent.

   Chor. O glorious Salamis, I think that thou, [*Str.* 1.

Loved by the gods alway,
And of all eyes observed,
Abidest still, lashed by the surging sea.
But I, the miserable, how long, how long,   600
For my reward I wait
From these Idaean meadows, where I keep,
Losing all count of months, my nightly couch;
Worn out with waiting and the toilsome time;
Nursing a bitter hope,
That one day yet I shall come home—to the dread doors,
The darksome doors of death.

And now consorts with me another grief—   [*Antistr.* 1.
New foe that bides its time—
Ajax, alas me, lodged,   610
Past hope of cure, with madness from the gods;
Whom long ago thou didst send forth from thee,
In furious fight unmatched;
But now not so—brooding on lonely thoughts,
Great sorrow to his friends is he become;
And all the matchless deeds his hands wrought once
Have fallen, fallen dead,
And with the sons of Atreus, loveless, miserable,   620
Wake no response of love.

Methinks his mother, with life's long-drawn day   [*Str.* 2.
Familiar, and with white-haired eld,
When she shall hear how with a mind diseased
Her noble son was sick,

Will cry, Alas! woe worth the day!
And in her sorrow pour
No dirge of plaintive nightingale,
But loudly weep and wail, 630
All in a shrill-voiced song;
While on her breast a heavy sound
Shall fall of hands that smite—
With rending of her reverend hair.
Better in Hades hid from sight were he, [*Antistr.* 2.
Whose mind is sick without an aim,
He who, come hither, by lineage of his sire,
Best of the toil-worn Greeks,
To promptings of his natural mind
Is constant now no more,
With wild new thoughts grown conversant. 640
O wretched sire, for thee
What tidings are in store—
Fall'n on thy son a heavy curse,
Whose like no life nursed yet
Of the Aeacidae save his.

Aj. The long march of the innumerable hours
Brings from the darkness all things to the birth,
And all things born envelops in the night.
What is there that it cannot? Strongest oaths
Of men, and the untempered will, it bends:
As I, who lately seemed so wondrous firm, 650
See by this woman now my keen edge made,

As steel by dipping, womanish and weak;
So that it pities me among my foes
To leave her widowed, fatherless my child.
Now to the seaside meadows and the baths
I go to purge away my stains, if so
Athene's grievous wrath I may escape.
And I must go and find some spot untrodden,
And hide away this hated sword of mine,
Burying it in the earth where none may see;
Let night and Hades keep it under ground. 660
For from the day I took it in my hand,
From Hector, from my enemy, a gift,
Of Greeks I gat no honour any more:
But soothly says the proverb that men use—
Foes' gifts are no gifts—no, nor profitable.
Well—I shall know henceforth to bow to heaven,
And the Atreidae study to revere:
Men must obey their rulers. Nay, how else?
Things most august and mightiest upon earth
Bow to authority: the winter's storms, 670
Dense with their driven snow, give place at last
To fruitful summer; and night's weary round
Passes, and dawn's white steeds light up the day;
And blasts of angry winds let sleep again
The groaning sea: and tyrannous sleep withal
Holds not his prey, but looses whom he binds.
Then shall not *we* learn wisdom, and submit?

And I—this lesson I have learnt to-day,
To hate my enemies so much and no more,
As who shall yet be friends, and of a friend 680
I'll bound my love and service with the thought,
He's not my friend for ever. For most men find
A treacherous haven this of fellowship.
But for these things it shall suffice: and thou,
Woman, go in, and pray the gods that all
My heart's desire may be fulfilled in full.
And you, my comrades, honour me with her
Thus praying, and bid Teucer when he comes
Have care of me and all good will to you.
For I go hence whither I needs must go. 690
Do ye my bidding; so shall ye hear perchance,
That after all my troubles I am safe.

Chor. I tremble, I thrill with longing! [*Strophe.*
With joy transported, I soar aloft!
O Pan, Pan, Pan, appear!
Come hither, tossed by the sea, O Pan,
From Cyllene's rock-ridge scourged with snow—
The master in heaven of those that dance!
And unpremeditated measures here,
Nysian or Gnosian, fling with me! 700
For now on dancing my heart is set.
And far across the Icarian waters,
Lord of Delos, Apollo, come;
Come, plain to see, and partake my mirth—
Y

Gracious and kind to the end as now!
Lo, Ares the cloud has lifted; [*Antistrophe*.
Despair and dread from our eyes are gone!
Now, now, O Zeus, again
May stainless light of a gracious day
To our swift sea-cleaving ships come nigh: 710
When Ajax his sorrow again forgets,
And serves the gods with perfect piety,
Pays them their rites and leaves out none.
For all things ever the strong Hours quench;
And nought, I'll say, is too hard for saying;
Now when Ajax, so past all hope,
Against the Atreidae unbends his pride—
Rage and defiance outbreathes no more.

Mess. O friends, these tidings first I am fain to tell—
Teucer ev'n now is from the Mysian crags 720
Returned; and at the generals' tents, mid-camp,
By all the Greeks together is reviled.
Afar they learnt his coming, and they drew
Together, and thronged about him; and no man spared
To pelt him with reproaches right and left,
But called him, taunting him, that madman's brother,
His who conspired against the host—no help
But he should die by stoning, crushed and torn.
So far they went, that sudden swords outleaped,
Plucked naked of the scabbard, hilt to point. 730
Scarce in extremity the strife was stayed

By mediation of the old men's speech.
But where is Ajax—that he may hear my tale?
Him it concerns—needs must he know the whole.

Chor. Not here—hence ev'n now, having learnt to wed
New thoughts with new behaviour, is he gone.

Mess. Ah me, alas!
Upon too tardy an errand was I sent
By him who sent me—or I came too slow.

Chor. Say, what's the urgent business scanted here? 740

Mess. Straitly did Teucer charge me, that the man
Should not pass hence, till he himself should come.

Chor. Nay, he is gone on profitable thoughts
Intent, with the angry gods to make his peace.

Mess. These words of thine are full of foolishness,
If Calchas knows whereof he prophesies.

Chor. How prophesies? What should he know of this?

Mess. So much I know, for I was there and heard.
Forth from the synod of the assembled chiefs,
Without the Atreidae, Calchas came alone, 750
And grasped the hand of Teucer as a friend,
And spake and charged him, with all skill he had,
Until this day's sun should be set, to keep
Ajax in tent, nor let him go at large,
If he would see him living any more.
For this one day—he said—and only this
Shall bright Athene's anger follow him.
For the overgrown unprofitable life

From heaven with dire disasters is o'erthrown—
So said the prophet—whoso of mortal race 760
Forgets his birth, more than a mortal proud.
And he at once, ere he set forth from home,
Made foolish answer to his sire's wise speech.
For 'O my son,' said Telamon, 'have care
Thy spear prevail—but with consent of heaven.'
Who with a fool's speech vaunting made reply,
'Father, with gods to help, a man of nought
May get him honour: but I trust that I
Shall pluck this glory ev'n without their aid."
So spake he, boasting: and another time, 770
At bright Athene, when exhorting him
She bade turn on his foes his reeking hand,
Dread words, unutterable, back he flung:
'O queen, go stand beside the other Greeks;
Never near me shall battle break our line.'
Athene's hot displeasure by such words,
And thoughts for man too high, did he provoke.
Only, if this day he lives, so it may chance
We yet shall save him—if the gods consent. 779
These things said Calchas. From the council straight
Teucer arose and bade me bear this charge,
For thee to keep. But if our care is mocked—
The seer saw false, or Ajax is no more.

Chor. O poor Tecmessa, born to misery,
Come forth and learn the tidings of this man:

For sorrow hard at hand this tale imports.

Tec. Why will ye startle me from rest again,
Who found so late peace from my ceaseless griefs?

Chor. Come, hear this man, what tidings he has brought
Of Ajax—grievous news for me to hear.

Tec. Alas, what news? Speak, man, are we undone?

Mess. I know not of thy plight; but, if this hour
Ajax is hence, I fear concerning him.

Tec. Thy words distract me: hence indeed he is.

Mess. Teucer enjoins us straitly, in the tent
Indoors to keep him—nor let him range alone.

Tec. But where is Teucer, and wherefore says he this?

Mess. He is returned ev'n now; and he forebodes
That this outgoing of Ajax ends in death.

Tec. Alas me, miserable! whence learnt he this?

Mess. From Thestor's son, the seer, this very day—
Wherein to know imports him death or life.

Tec. Ah me, my friends, help now my helpless state:
Hasten, some to bid Teucer come with speed:
Search, some the western, some the eastern bays—
His rash outgoing search until ye find.
For now I know myself by him beguiled,
And of his sometime favour dispossessed.
Ah, child, what shall I do? I must not sit.
I will go there, I too, with all my strength.
Let us make haste and go—no idling now—
To save this man who is in love with death.

Chor. Not words shall prove me ready for the quest;
Quick act and nimble foot shall answer speech.
(*The scene changes. Ajax is seen, alone, by the sea-shore.*)
　Aj. So stands my cut-throat fitliest for its work—
Give me but time to think this matter out—
First, as 'tis Hector's gift, of all my friends
Worst foeman, and most hateful to my sight;
Then, as 'tis planted in Troy's hostile soil,
New-whet on whetstone hungry for the steel:　　　　　820
And delicately, with care, I planted it,
With best good will to give me speedy death.
So all is ready, and so, my part being done,
Thou, Zeus, be first to help me, as is fit.
'Tis no great boon of thee that I shall ask:
Send now some messenger and let him bear
The ill-news to Teucer, that no hand ere his
May lift me fallen about this reeking sword:
And let no enemy behold me first
And fling me forth, to dogs and birds a prey.　　　　　830
Zeus, unto thee my prayer is said: but thou,
Hermes, good guide to deathward, give me good sleep—
With unconvulsive and with sudden bound,
Leaping upon this sword to pierce my heart.
Moreover, I call to aid the virgins ever,
Whose eyes fail never of seeing wrong done on earth,
Far-striding, dread Erinyes—to see
How by the Atreidae, hapless, I am undone:

And with a swift perdition sweep them off,
An evil portion for their evil deeds— 840
As by this fatal and unnatural hand
They see me die, grant them to perish so,
Unnaturally, by their own children slain.
Come, vengeful Furies, swift Erinyes,
Spare not, but glut your will on all the host.
And thou that chariotest the steeps of heaven,
When on my native land falls next thy gaze,
Awhile, O Sun-god, draw thy golden rein,
And tell the old man my father—let him know,
And my sad mother, my sufferings and my death.
Poor soul, I think that, when she hears the tale, 850
Loud weeping through the city she will send.
But now what use lamenting, all in vain?
Quick as I may, let me begin this deed.
O death, death, death, come now and look on me!
Nay rather—for I shall commune *there* with thee—
This present radiance of the shining day,
Now I invoke, and Helios, charioteer,
Thee with my latest breath, and never more.
O light, O sacred soil of Salamis
My home, and firm-set hearth of my father's house, 860
And glorious Athens, and the kindred race,
Founts and these rivers, and ye plains of Troy—
All ye have nursed my life—to all farewell!
His latest word to you thus Ajax speaks:

To ghosts in Hades shall the rest be said.

(*Falls on his sword, and dies.*)

Semi-Chor. 1. Trouble on trouble new trouble heaps!
Where, where,
Where have I not made search?
But, that I learnt its lore, no place attests.
Lo there, 870
Again a tramp of feet!

Chor. 2. 'Tis we—your friends—and comrades of the
    fleet.

Chor. 1. What have ye done?

Chor. 2. No ground's untrod to westward of the ships.

Chor. 1. And have ye found?

Chor. 2. Found toil in plenty, and nothing more to see.

Chor. 1. Nay, and no less upon this eastern road,
Too plain it is, he's nowhere to be seen! [*Strophe.*

Chor. Will no one tell me, either some toilsome fisher,
Busy about his sleepless quest, or nymph 880
Haunting Olympian heights,
Or streams toward Bosporus that flow—
Will no one see him,
The stubborn-hearted, somewhere roaming,
And tell me that he sees?
For hard, too hard, it is that I,
I who have wandered far in toilsome search,
Still baffled, to no prosperous course attain,
But look to find the man unmanned— 890

And evermore in vain.

Tec. Ah me, alas!

Chor. What cry broke there from covert of the glen?

Tec. Ah me, unhappy!

Chor. I see the luckless captive of his spear,
Tecmessa, yonder, in lamentation plunged.

Tec. Friends, I am lost and ruined and undone.

Chor. What ails thee?

Tec. Ajax, my lord, lies here, this moment slain,
With buried sword enveloped in his fall.

Chor. Alas my hopes of home! 900
Me, prince, thy shipmate, has thy death destroyed:
Unhappy that I am! and miserable
'Mong women, too, art thou.

Tec. Lament thy fill, for all these things are so.

Chor. Say, by whose hand did he the fatal deed?

Tec. Plainly, his own. His sword whereon he fell,
Planted in the earth, convicts him of the guilt.

Chor. Oh fatal deed for me—
How was thy blood poured out, no friend to help! 910
And I, the all-dull, the all-witless, took no heed.
Where lies he, where—alas—
The wayward soul, Ajax, the luckless name?

Tec. Look not on him: him out of all men's sight
Here in this mantle's folds will I enwrap:
Since none who loved him might endure to see,
From that red gash, and out at nostril, how

Spouts from the self-dealt wound the darkened blood.
Ah for some friend to lift thee: what can I? 920
Where is thy brother? to compose thy limbs
How timely now his coming—might he come!
Poor Ajax—from what height fallen how low!
How fit to win compassion of thy foes!

   Chor. Was this indeed for thee, unhappy Ajax, [*Ant.*
Stubborn of soul, at last to be the end
Of all thy cruel fate
Of measureless affliction—this?
To this have brought thee
The fierce complainings of thy hatred,
Which all night long I heard 930
Thee pour, and in the daylight too,
Against the Atreidae nursing deadly rage?
A great beginner of troubles was that day,
Which contest of stout hands proposed,
The hero's arms to win.

   Tec. Ah me, alas!
   Chor. The generous pang goes to thy heart, I know.
   Tec. Ah me, alas! 939
   Chor. Once and again full well thy grief may sound,
Lady, of such a friend this day bereft.
   Tec. Ye deem of things, that I too deeply feel.
   Chor. I'll not gainsay thee.
   Tec. Alas, my child, how hard a yoke our necks
Shall carry, toiling beneath such masters' eye.

Chor. Ah me, this last distress,
That thou deplor'st, imports a nameless deed
Of the Atreidae, of the ruthless pair;
Which yet may gods avert! 950
   Tec. These things had not stood thus, were gods displeased.
   Chor. They wrought an all too heavy weight of woe.
   Tec. But dreadful Pallas, child of Zeus, it is,
Who for Odysseus' sake breeds all this woe.
   Chor. Doubtless he triumphs now,
The patient hero, in his gloomy soul,
And laughs loud laughter at our frantic grief.
Alas, and, hearing this,
With him the kingly pair, the Atreidae, laugh. 960
   Tec. So let them laugh, exulting in his fall.
For haply, whom they loved not in his life,
Dead, in some battle-need, they may deplore.
For foolish men have treasure in their hands
And know it not, till from their hands 'tis dashed.
Bitter his death to me, or sweet to them,
Himself it pleases. What he longed to find,
He has it now, death that his soul desired.
Why then shall these exult against him now?
His death concerns the gods, not them, not them. 970
An empty triumph let Odysseus vaunt;
Ajax for them is not: but in his going
Sorrow and anguish he has left to me.

Teuc. Ah me, alas!

Chor. Hush—'tis the voice of Teucer, as I think,
Loud with a strain regardful of this woe.

Teuc. Dear to my sight, O Ajax, O my brother—
Hast thou indeed fared, as the fame is rife?

Chor. Dead, Teucer, is thy brother, doubt it not.

Teuc. Woe then to me—a heavy lot is mine.   980

Chor. Yea, for these things are so.

Teuc.   Ah me, alas!

Chor. Good cause for tears!

Teuc.   O over-passionate haste!

Chor. Too rash, too rash indeed.

Teuc.   Woe's me! but say,
Where in this Trojan land is now his child?

Chor. There, at the tents, alone.

Teuc.   Will ye not then
Make haste and bring him, ere his foes shall steal him,
As when men rob the lioness of her cubs?
Haste now and help and spare not! all men love
To mock the slain foe, prostrate at their feet.

Chor. Yea, Teucer, and the hero while he lived   990
Laid upon thee this charge, which thou dost seek.

Teuc. Oh of all sights my eyes have ever seen
To me most grievous, this which now I see—
And bitter to my heart, beyond all ways
That I have trod, this way that led me hither—
When, O my brother, I had learnt the truth,

And knew it was thy death I tracked and sought.
For a swift word of thee, as from some god,
Sounded throughout the host, that thou wast dead.
And hapless I who heard it, being far off, 1000
Made weeping low, but now the sight is death—
Ah, woe is me!
Come now, uncover, let me see the worst.
O thou most hideous, rash, and fatal sight—
What anguish has thy death bred now for me!
For whither can I go, among what men,
Who, when thou wast afflicted, lent no hand?
I think that Telamon, thy sire and mine,
Would welcome me with glad face graciously,
Come home without thee. Doubt it not—whose brow 1010
Lights with no smile—no, not in joyful days.
What will he hide? or what reproach not utter
Of me the bastard, son of the captive woman,
Whose baseness and whose cowardice betrayed
Thee, O my brother—or else of treachery,
That sceptre and house might pass from thee to me.
So will he chide me, choleric, peevish now
With age, at trifles heated into spleen.
Last, he will thrust me out and banish me,
Proved by his taunts no freeman but a slave. 1020
At home such welcome waits me, and here at Troy
Are many foes, and few things serviceable.
And all these things thy death hath done for me.

Alas what shall I do? how pluck thee hence
From this sharp shining sword-point—this whereby
Ebbed out thy life, thy murderer? didst thou see
How by dead Hector thou shouldst at last be slain?
Consider, I pray, the fortunes of these two.
Gripped by the girdle which this man gave to him,
The body of Hector at the chariot-rail   1030
Was mangled on and on until he died.
And Ajax, who received this gift from him,
By this lies dead, slain by the fatal fall.
Was it not some Erinys forged this sword—
Hades the girdle, grim artificer?
These things and all things ever, for my part,
I needs must think the gods contrive for men.
But, whoso in his heart deems otherwise,
By his belief shall hold, I hold by mine.

    Chor. Cut short thy speech: bethink thee how this man   1040
Shall now be buried, and how thou wilt reply.
For lo, an enemy, who comes, I trow,
To mock our misery with his miscreant mirth.

    Teuc. What man, of all the host, beholdest thou?

    Chor. Menelaus, for whom our ships sailed here to Troy.

    Teuc. I see him, on nearer view not hard to know.

    Men. Sirrah, I bid thee lend no hand to bear
This body hence: but leave him where he lies.

    Teuc. Yea, to what purpose was this good breath spent?

Men. Such is my will, and his who rules the host. 1050
Teuc. And might we hear what reason you pretend?
Men. This: that we deemed we brought him from his home
To the Achaean host ally and friend,
But found on trial no Phrygian more our foe:
This man, who purposed death to all the host,
And set on us, for midnight murder armed:
And, but some god had foiled his enterprise,
The fate that he has found had e'en been ours,
Slain and o'erthrown by most ignoble death,
And he were living now. But some god turned 1060
From us his fury, on sheep and flocks to fall.
And for this cause the man lives not, whose strength
Shall so prevail, to give him burial;
But on the yellow sand his corse shall lie,
Cast out unburied, for sea-birds to devour.
Now therefore lift not thou thy blustering rage.
Since, if we could not govern him, alive,
Yet surely, dead, do what thou wilt, we shall,
And with our hands shall guide him. For, while he lived,
No word that I could speak he'd deign to hear. 1070
Nay, 'tis no good man's part, who should be subject,
To shut his ears against authority.
How shall a city have good government,
Wherein established is no wholesome dread?
Nor can there be good order in the camp,

That lacks defence of fear and reverence.
Yea, though men's limbs wax mighty, let them think
A little harm may mar their mightiness.
For, with such fear and with such shame withal
Hedged round, alone is safety—of this be sure.   1080
But, where licence and pride go unrebuked,
Mark well that city; one day she shall sail,
Sail with fair winds to waft her—to the depths.
Be seasonable fear my strong defence:
Let us not think, doing what most delights,
We shall not pay whatever most may grieve.
For Fortune's wheel runs round.   This man before
Was hot and headstrong: mine is now the pride.
Therefore I bid thee not to bury him,
Lest, burying him, thou too shouldst find a grave.   1090

  Chor. Wise maxims, Menelaus, well premised,
Wilt thou entreat so wantonly the dead?

  Teuc. Never, friends, shall I marvel any more,
That men who spring from nothing should transgress;
When those whom all men deem our noblest-born
Such bold transgressors in their speech are found.
What, may it please you say the same again—
You say you brought him here to help the Greeks?
Sailed he not hither himself, lord of himself?
How owed he thee allegiance? where's thy right   1100
To rule the people whom he brought from home?
Thou camest Sparta's king, no lord of us.

No privilege of sovereignty was thine,
More to dictate to him, than he to thee.
Captain of others, not over all supreme,
Didst thou sail hither, that Ajax should obey thee.
Rule whom thou rulest, and with thy solemn words
Chastise them: me thy speech shall not affright;
Thou, and my lord the other, may forbid;
My duty's plain, and I shall bury him.   1110
Think not that for thy wife's sake, like the rest,
The men bowed down with toil, he joined the host:
No, but by reason of the oaths that bound him,
And not for thee: he scorned all nobodies.
Now therefore bring more heralds: come again—
Come with the general back; but yet thy noise,
For all thou'rt Menelaus, I shall not heed.

  Chor. Such speech in such sore plight I blame no less—
Harsh words offend, however just the cause.

    Men. The bowman thinks not meanly of himself. 1120
    Teuc. For 'tis no base employment that I boast.
    Men. Couldst thou but wear a shield, what boasting then!
    Teuc. Light-armed, I'd match me with thy shield and thee.
    Men. Fierce is the courage that inspires thy tongue.
    Teuc. Justice to friend, well may a man be proud.
    Men. How just, that this my murderer should have honour?

Teuc. Murderer! 'tis strange, if you, the murdered, live.

Men. The gods have saved my life, no thanks to him.

Teuc. If gods saved thee, dishonour not the gods.

Men. Could *I* arraign the ordinance of heaven?   1130

Teuc. When you deny the burial of the dead.

Men. Yea, of mine enemy: it must not be.

Teuc. Why, on what field encountered he with thee?

Men. He hated me, I him: you knew it well.

Teuc. You tricked the votes, and stole from him his own.

Men. The umpire's fault, not mine—his failure there.

Teuc. 'Tis like thy knavery—to steal and hide.

Men. To some one's sorrow shall this prating turn.

Teuc. Not more, I think, than sorrow I shall cause. 1139

Men. One word for all: this man must not be buried.

Teuc. And one word back—to tell thee that he shall.

Men. I saw a man once who was bold of speech,
Who chid his sailors on to face the storm,
And lo, when by the tempest he was caught,
The man lay speechless, covered with his cloak,
For all who would to trample under foot.
And so with thee, and thy intemperate speech—
Out of a little cloud perchance shall blow
A mighty storm, shall quench thy blustering.

Teuc. And I have seen a man so full of folly,   1150
That he would triumph if his neighbour fell:

And one like me, of temper just like mine,
Saw him and warned him, speaking words like these—
'Friend, have a care, and do the dead no wrong:
For know that, wronging them, thou'lt come to harm.'
So did he speak, and warned the luckless one.
And lo I see him, and methinks he is
None other than thyself. Canst read my riddle?

 Men. I'll stay no longer. All would cry shame who heard
That I used chiding where I might use force. 1160

 Teuc. Therefore begone. Me too it shames to hear
Words of a babbler, prating worthlessly.

 Chor. Hard-fought this strife shall prove:
But, Teucer, lose no time—
Find for this man with speed a grave, dug deep enough,
Wherein not unremembered he shall keep
His mouldering tomb for evermore.

 Teuc. And see where near at hand, and just in time,
The hero's child comes hither, and his wife,
To deck the poor dead limbs for burial. 1170
O child, come hither, and stand close beside,
And to thy father as a suppliant cling.
Then sit in suppliant guise, with hair of three,
Mine and thy mother's and thine own the third,
Such wealth to back entreaty. If any man
By force should drag thee from thy father's side,
Knave, for his knavery may they fling him forth

Unburied from the land, with all his race
Consumed for ever, and levelled, root and branch,
Even in like manner as this lock is shorn.
Take it, O child, and keep it, and let no man   1180
Remove thee hence: fall suppliant here, and cling.
And ye—no women prove, but men at need,
Ready and near to help, until I come,
Having prepared his grave—whoe'er forbids.

   Chor. What shall be the sum,   [*Strophe* 1.
And when shall be the ending,
Of the tale of restless years,
Bearing for me continually
Of battle-toil the ceaseless doom,
Here on Troy's spacious plains—   1190
O dire disgrace to Greece!
Would that the void air,   [*Antistrophe* 1.
Or all-receiving Hades,
Had enveloped first the man
Who taught the Greeks with hateful arms
To league themselves for war: that man—
O toil surpassing toil—
Laid waste the lives of men.
No joy of garlands or of goblets deep   [*Strophe* 2.
Gave he—O wretched man—to crown my life,   1200
No, nor sweet din of flutes,
Nor boon of night-long sleep,
And all my days from love, ah me,

From love divorced.
And none heeds how I lie;
And night by night with the thick-falling dews
Of heaven my hair is wet:
Nights for whose sake I shall
Remember bitter Troy. 1210
And once indeed from terrors of the night [*Antistr.* 2.
And driven darts fierce Ajax was my shield:
But he to a cruel fate
Has fallen now a prey.
What joy to me then any more,
What joy shall be?
Oh that I might be where
The wooded wave-washed foreland breasts the sea,
'Neath Sunium's level heights, 1220
That I the sacred towers
Of Athens thence might greet!

Teuc. I saw, and came with haste—saw posting hither
Whom but the general, whom but Agamemnon?
Some mischief, as I think, he comes to vent.

Ag. Were thine the blustering words whereof I hear,
The licensed jaws that gaped 'gainst us so wide?
What, sirrah, thou—son of the captive woman—
Surely, if thy mother had been some noble one,
Loud had thy talk been then, dainty thy steps— 1230
Thou nothing, that for this nothing wouldst stand up,

And didst protest that not for Greeks or thee
Leaders of ships or armies came we hither,
But Ajax sailed, thou saidst, himself supreme.
Is't not too much—such challenge from a slave?
What man was this of whom you boast so loud?
Where went he, or where stood, but I was there?
What, have the Greeks no men now he is gone?
Well may we rue the day when to the host
We set for prize the Achillean arms,   1240
If, come what will, Teucer shall prove us base,
And, howso beaten, ye will not be content
To acquiesce in what the more judged right;
But either will revile and never cease,
Or, for the slight's sake, stab us in the dark.
But, grant such licence, never any more
Could be of any law establishment,
If we the rightful winners thrust aside,
And those that lag the hindmost drag to front.
It must not be; for not the burly ones,   1250
The broad of shoulder, are your safest men;
On every field 'tis prudence that prevails.
How mighty-ribbed the ox, how small the goad
That drives him straight, the way that he should go!
And such good medicine shall be thine ere long,
Unless thou comest to a saner mind—
Who of a shadow, of one who is no more,
Dost vainly prate, bold words and unabashed.

Go to, be wise: learn who and what thou art;
And find some man free-born, and bring him here,　1260
And let him plead thy cause instead of thee:
Thou'lt waste thy words if thou spend'st more on me—
I do not understand thy barbarous tongue.

　Chor. I wish to both the wisdom to refrain:
There's nothing better for either to be wished.

　Teuc. Alas! how fast the gratitude of men
Fades, and is proved a traitor to the dead!
As, Ajax, now no memory has this man,
Not even in slight respects, of thee,—whose life
On many a hard-fought field was risked for him:　1270
But all is now as if it had not been.
O of all speakers most fluent and most vain,
Hast thou so soon forgot that day, whereon
This man, when you were shut within your lines,
Your battle broken and yourselves as nought,
Alone stood forth and saved you, when the flame
Had wrapt your fleet, and round the seamen's thwarts
Shot upward, and when Hector cleared the trench
At one high bound, and swooped upon the ships?
Who saved you then? Was not your champion he,　1280
Whose foot thou sayest went ne'er with thine to battle?
Did ye not thank him for staunch service then?
Or when alone in single fight he met
With Hector, unbidden, singled by the lot;
For in the midst no shirking lot he flung,

No clod of crumbling glebe; but one that should
Leap lightly first out of the well-plumed helm—
'Twas he who did these things, and I was with him,
The slave, the son of the barbarian mother.
Why, wretch, what face hast thou to say such things? 1290
Hast thou forgot who was thy father's father,
Pelops of old, the Phrygian, the barbarian—
And Atreus who begat thee—who, most impious,
Before his brother set his children's flesh?
And thou wast son of a Cretan mother, of her,
Whom with her paramour her father found,
And to dumb fish consigned her for a prey.
Born of such breed, tauntest thou me with mine—
Whose sire was no worse man than Telamon,
Who for his prowess, he of all the host, 1300
Won for his bride my mother, a king's daughter,
Child of Laomedon: her to my sire,
Best of the spoil, gave Heracles for prize.
Thus of two noble parents nobly born,
How should I do dishonour to my kin—
To him whom, fallen in this sore plight, thou wouldst
Thrust forth unburied, and hast no shame to say it?
But know that, if ye fling his body hence,
Hence must ye fling the bodies of us three.
Far better I should die in serving him, 1310
Die in the sight of all, than for thy wife
In battle—thine or thy brother's, what care I?

Now therefore for thyself, not me, be wise.
For, if thou harmest me, thou'lt wish anon
A coward thou hadst been—not bold with me.
 Chor. In season, lord Odysseus, thou art come—
So thou wilt help, not tie the knot, but loose it.
 Od. What ails ye, friends? far off I heard loud speech
Of the Atreidae o'er this valiant dead.
 Ag. Yea, for what shameful words from this man's lips,   1320
My lord Odysseus, have I heard ev'n now!
 Od. What words? since one who hears himself reviled
I shall not blame for waging wordy war.
 Ag. Taunts I flung back, for he flung taunts at me.
 Od. What word, so fraught with mischief, has he said?
 Ag. He says this body shall not be unburied,
But he will bury it in my despite.
 Od. What, may a friend speak now, and speak the truth,
Yet be thy fellow even as before?
 Ag. Say on: for else were I but foolish—since   1330
Of all the Greeks I hold thee staunchest friend.
 Od. Then I will speak. I charge thee by the gods,
Think not to fling thus pitilessly forth
This man, unburied: nor let passion sway
Thy soul to such extreme of hate, to set

Thy foot on justice.   Once to me no less,
In all the army, since to me were given
The Achillean arms, worst foe was he :
But not for all his hate of me could I
Do him so much dishonour as gainsay
That, save Achilles, of all Greeks who came   1340
Hither, none have I seen so brave as he.
It is not right thou shouldst dishonour him.
Not at this man, but at the laws of heaven
Such blow were aimed.   Brave men, if they be dead,
Howe'er we hate, it is not good to hurt.

Ag. Wilt thou stand up for him—Odysseus, thou?
Od. Yea, though I hated him, whilst this was well.
Ag. Shouldst thou not trample now upon him, dead?
Od. Such gain were loss : Atreides, love none such.
Ag. A monarch may not always fear the gods.   1350
Od. Yet may he heed good counsel of his friends.
Ag. What the king speaks, let all good men attend.
Od. Give o'er : to yield to friends is victory.
Ag. Bethink thee what he was, whom thou wouldst serve.
Od. My enemy, but noble, was he once.
Ag. What wilt thou do? honour a dead foe thus !
Od. Far does his worth to me outweigh our quarrel.
Ag. Unstable still the world calls men like thee.
Od. Yet many a friendship turns to bitterness.

Ag. Are these the friends whose friendship thou
    wouldst praise?   1360
Od. 'Tis not my way to praise a stubborn mind.
Ag. Cowards thou'lt make us seem this day to be.
Od. Men rather, in the eyes of Greece found just.
Ag. Thou bidd'st me then to let them bury him?
Od. Yes: for I too one day shall come to this.
Ag. 'Tis even so: each works but for himself.
Od. Whom should I work for, rather than myself?
Ag. Thy doing then, not mine, it must be called.
Od. 'Tis a good deed thou'lt do, howe'er 'tis done.
  Ag. Nay but of this be sure, that, though to thee 1370
This grace and more than this I'd gladly do,
Dead or alive, all's one—my enemy
I count this man. But be it as thou wilt.
  Chor. If any man, Odysseus, doubts that thou,
Who hast done this, art wise, unwise is he.
  Od. Yea, and henceforth to Teucer I profess
Friendship as true as was my former hate—
And I would fain help bury the dead man here,
Share in the toil, and nought leave out, of all
Toil that for bravest men 'tis fit to spend.   1380
  Teuc. O good Odysseus, be thou thanked for this
With the best thanks I have; so hast thou quite
Belied my fear. Thou wast his enemy,
Thou, most of all, but now thy hands alone
Have holpen him, nor him the fallen foe,

Living, didst thou dare with loud mirth to mock—
As came my lord the general, crazed with pride,
Came with his brother, and with him would fain
Have cast him out unburied and disgraced.
Therefore may Zeus, lord of the heaven above,
Justice who strikes, Erinys who remembers,   1390
Slay them for their deservings—these who would,
Outraged, dishonoured, have cast forth this man.
But yet, O son of old Laertes, thee—
I fear to let thee meddle with these rites,
Lest in so doing I should offend the dead:
Help us in all save this; and, whomso else
In all the camp thou'dst bring, we shall not grudge:
I'll grant thee all the rest: but thou herein—
Doubt not at all, thou hast been good friend to us.

   Od. This had I wished: but, if it likes thee not   1400
That so I should, I go; have thou thy way.

   Teuc. Enough: too long already is time
Prolonged.   Haste, some to dig his grave,
And some to place the high-set caldron
'Mid wreathing flames,
All for the pure ablution ready:
And let one band bring from his tent
All armour that his shield enwrapt:
And thou, child, with what strength thou hast,
Touch lovingly and lift with me   1410
Thy father's body; for warm with life

Each channel still its sanguine tide
Spouts upward.   Come, whoso is here,
That calls himself a friend—let him
Make haste and come—come serve this man,
All-brave, than whom
None better yet was served on earth—
Better than Ajax none, say I,
Whilst life was his.

 Chor. Full many things shall mortals learn
By seeing : but, before he sees,
No man is prophet of his fate,
To know how he shall fare. 1420

PHILOCTETES

PERSONS.

ODYSSEUS.
NEOPTOLEMUS.
PHILOCTETES.
HERACLES.
SAILOR (*disguised as Merchant*).
CHORUS OF SAILORS.

Philoctetes

Od.   T̲HIS is the beach of that sea-cinctured land,
        Lemnos, untrodden and no home of men,
Where, oh by noblest of Greek fathers reared,
Son of Achilles, Neoptolemus,
The Melian son of Poeas I set ashore,
And did the princes' bidding, and left him here,
Sick with the sore that ran, and gnawed his foot:
When at libation or at sacrifice
No quietness he gave us, none—but still
Filled with his fierce upbraidings all the camp,   10
Loud-voiced and dolorous.   But these things what need
Now to recount?   No time for many words
Now, lest he learn our coming, and I waste
Good wit, that else should snare him suddenly.
Deeds now, not words: thine, to perform the rest,
And seek, not far from hence, a cave that looks
This way and that, whereof at either mouth
A man may sit, to feel the winter's sun;
And breezes cool in summer, fraught with sleep,
Course through the tunnelled chamber of the rock.
And lower down a little, on the left,   20

A springing fountain mark, if still it flows.
Go softly now, and bring me word of this,
If near at hand it be, or further hence.
So shalt thou hear, and I disclose, the rest;
That to one end together we may work.

Ne. The errand, lord Odysseus, is not far:
Such cave as thou describ'st methinks I see.

Od. Above us, or below? I see it not.

Ne. 'Tis here, above thee: and no footfall sounds.

Od. See that he lie not in the cave asleep.

Ne. I see an empty chamber, no man there.

Od. See you within no comforts of a home?

Ne. A bed of leaves, pressed down, where one has slept.

Od. And is the dwelling empty, save of this?

Ne. There is a cup, some sorry craftsman's work,
Of mere rough wood: some fuel too lies near.

Od. These are the household treasures of the man.

Ne. Alack, and there, spread in the sun to dry,
Are rags withal, stained with some sore disease.

Od. This must be then the place wherein he dwells,
And he hard by: for how should he go far,
With foot so crippled by an ancient hurt?
But either he is gone in quest of food,
Or for some painless herb whereof he knows.
Set thy companion then to keep the watch,
That he surprise me not. To find me here—

Me, more than all the Greeks—the man would choose.

Ne. Enough; I send him: he will guard the path,
And now thy further purpose I attend.

Od. Son of Achilles, not thy body alone 50
Noble in this day's business must be proved:
Paid must the service be, for which thou camest,
Though strange its sound in unaccustomed ears.

Ne. What is thy bidding?

Od. Words, which thou shalt speak,
The soul of Philoctetes must beguile.
When he shall ask thee, who and whence thou art,
'Son of Achilles,' answer: hide not this:
But say thou sailest homeward, having left
The Grecian host, incensed with bitter hate,
Because with prayers they called thee from thy home, 60
Seeing that without thee Troy they could not take,
Yet, at thy coming, thought not good to give
Thy father's arms to thee, who claim'dst thine own,
But gave them to Odysseus: and therewith
Foulest of foul reproaches heap on me:
Thy words I shall not feel: but, this undone,
Grief thou wilt lay on me and all the Greeks.
For this man's bow and arrows we must have,
Or hope not thou to sack the Trojan town.
Why freely with no danger thou, not I, 70
Canst with the man hold converse, thou shalt hear.
Bound by an oath to no man thou hast sailed,

Nor of constraint, nor with the first that came:
But none of all these things can I deny.
Therefore, if, bow in hand, he lights on me,
I die, and shall involve thee in my death.
But those resistless shafts to steal from him,
This is thy task; this compass with thy wit.
I know thee, that thy nature is averse
From lying words, or practice of deceit; 80
Yet, for the prize, success, is sweet to win,
Consent: some other day shall prove our truth.
Now for one little shameless hour be mine,
Give me thyself to-day: and then be called,
Thy whole life long, most scrupulous of men.

   Ne. What in the telling grieves my ears to hear,
Son of Laertes, that I loathe to do.
My nature is not to deal treacherously—
No, neither mine, nor, as men say, my sire's.
But I am ready, not by guile but force, 90
To bring the man: for with his one sound foot
Against so many his strength shall scarce prevail.
And yet indeed, sent hither for thy help,
I fear to be called traitor: but, O king,
I'd rather nobly fail than basely win.

   Od. Son of brave sire, I also in my youth
Was slow of tongue, and ready with my hand;
But, since I came to trial, I have seen
Tongue still go foremost in this world, not deeds.

Ne. What dost thou bid me other than to lie? 100
Od. Let Philoctetes be entrapped, I say.
Ne. And why entrapped—why not persuaded rather?
Od. Thou'lt not persuade him, and thou canst not force.
Ne. Relies he then on strength so formidable?
Od. On shafts inevitable, and winged with death.
Ne. Not even to approach him may one dare?
Od. Not till we first have trapped him, as I say.
Ne. Seems it to thee no shameful thing to lie?
Od. If lying brings us safety, surely not.
Ne. Why, with what face shall I outbrazen this? 110
Od. From profitable deeds one must not shrink.
Ne. To me what profit, he should come to Troy?
Od. That by these arrows only Troy is taken.
Ne. Then I am not its conqueror, as ye said?
Od. Thou with their aid shalt conquer, they with thine.
Ne. They are a worthy prize, if this is so.
Od. Know, that this deed twofold reward shall win.
Ne. Yea, what reward? tell me, and I will do it.
Od. Both wise and brave together shouldst thou be called.
Ne. Come what come may, I'll do it, and cast off shame. 120
Od. Dost thou remember then how I advised?
Ne. Trust me for that, having consented once.
Od. Now then remain, and wait his coming here,
Whilst I go hence; not to be seen with thee,

And to the ship send back our sentinel.
And, if ye seem to tarry overlong,
Back comes again the same good messenger,
But dressed in sailor-fashion, and disguised
Out of your knowledge. From whose lips, my son,
Charged with a riddling speech, fail not to catch   130
The pregnant sentence ever and anon.
So to the ship will I, and leave thee here:
And may good Hermes guide, who brought us hither,
God of all craft, and she who is my friend,
Athene Polias, Victory herself.

   Chor. Strange in a strange land, O my lord, [*Strophe* 1.
What shall I, what shall I hide, or what
Say to the man, suspecting harm?
Instruct me.
Better than other men's skill
Or other judgment, is his, to whose wielding
Is committed the Zeus-given sceptre divine: 140
As to thee has descended, my son, from of old,
Such sovereign power: now therefore tell me,
How shall I serve in this?

   Ne. First, for I doubt not ye fain would see
Where on the island's skirts he dwells,
Look without fear:
But, when he comes, who from yonder cave
Terribly journeying forth is gone,
Keep on where my hand shall point you still,

And seek to help as the time may crave. 149

   Chor. Care I have cared for all the time,   [*Antistr.* 1.
Prince, thou hast charged me withal, to keep
Vigilant watch for the moment's need:
Now tell me,
Lodged in what lair he dwells:
His home, where is it? his haunts—reveal them:
No ill-timed knowledge were this to win,
Lest from ambush he fall on me unawares:
What place? what lair? and now where walks he,
Within-doors or without?

   Ne. The house there, with its portals twain,
Of his caverned bed, behold.   160

   Chor. Where now is the cave's sad inmate gone?

   Ne. I doubt not, somewhere hard at hand
In quest of food he trails his steps.
In such evil fashion, rumour saith,
He lives his life, and with pain and grief
Slays beast and bird with his wingèd shafts,
And no physician of his woe
Comes, and the years go by.

   Chor. Needs must I pity him, to think   [*Strophe* 2.
How, with no man to care for him,   170
And no companion's form to greet,
How helpless, ever alone,
And with fierce sickness plagued,
His mind is racked from hour to hour,

The instant craving to supply.
How hapless, how does he endure?
O dark designs of heaven!
O luckless tribes of men,
Doomed to extremes of fate! 179
He whom no scion of noblest house   [*Antistrophe* 2.
Belike might have disdained of yore,
Robbed now of all that life requires,
Dwells out of all men's sight,
With beasts for company,
Of dappled hide or shaggy fell—
Piteous, with hunger and with pain,
Oppressed by cares that find no cure:
And Echo's babbling voice,
Dolorous from afar,
Chimes to his shrill lament. 190

  Ne. Not wonderful is this to me.
From heaven, unless my thoughts are vain,
Those woes upon him at the first,
From the unpitying Chryse, fell:
And, far from help what now he bears,
It must be that some god designed,
Lest against Troy too soon he might
Shoot his resistless shafts divine,
Ere the time came, whereat, men say,
It shall by them be overthrown. 200

  Chor. My son, keep silence.   [*Strophe* 3.

   Ne.   Wherefore?
   Chor.   Comes a sound—
Such sound as might pertain to one afflicted so,
Somewhere approaching, here, or here.
A noise indeed strikes, strikes upon my ears,
Of one who walks with laboured tread;
And, nowise indistinct, escapes me not
A voice of lamentation borne from far,
A voice of wasting pain, a grievous voice.
But frame, my son. . . .   [*Antistrophe* 3.
   Ne.   Say, what?
   Chor.   Some purpose new: 210
For now the man, not far from hence, but near at hand,
No music of the pastoral pipe,
As when a shepherd drives his flocks to fold,
Brings with him, but a bitter cry
Far-sounding, as he stumbles painfully,
Or on the haven looks, no friend to ships:
A dreadful cry precedes him, ere he comes.
   Phil. O friends,
Who are ye, that with sea-dipt oar have touched   220
These desert and inhospitable shores?
Your country and your race how should I name,
And name aright? The fashion of your garb
Is Greek indeed—most welcome sight to me:
Yet would I hear your voices: and shrink not
With fear and dread away from me, grown wild,

But, pitying one so wretched and forsaken,
Lone as ye see and friendless, at my call
Speak to me, if indeed as friends ye come.
Nay, answer me: for so much courtesy   230
I should not miss from you, nor ye from me.

  Ne. Friend, first know this, that, as we seem, we are—
Greeks. For of this thou wouldst be satisfied.

  Phil. O welcome speech! O rapture, but to hear
The voice of such an one, unheard so long!
What need, my son, what impulse, what kind wind,
Guided thy bark and led thee to these shores?
Speak, tell me all, instruct me who thou art.

  Ne. The wave-washed Scyros is my birthplace: homeward
I sail: my name is Neoptolemus,   240
My sire Achilles. I have told thee all.

  Phil. O son of country dear, and dearest sire,
O foster-child of Lycomedes old,
What errand brings thee here? whence dost thou sail?

  Ne. From Ilium my present course I hold.

  Phil. How? surely thou wast not aboard the fleet,
When at the first toward Ilium we sailed?

  Ne. In that emprise wast thou participant?

  Phil. My son, dost thou not know whom thou beholdest?

  Ne. How should I know, on whom I ne'er set eyes?   250

  Phil. Nor yet my name, nor rumour of that grief
At all hast heard, that did consume my life?

Ne. All that thou askest is to me unknown.

Phil. O miserable, O hated by the gods,
Of whose sore plight not even to my home
Hath reached the fame, nor any Grecian land—
But they who cast me out, the impious ones,
Laugh to themselves their laughter, and my disease
Rankles alway, and grows from bad to worse.
O child, son of Achilles, see this man— 260
For I am he whose fame thou hast surely heard,
Lord of the bow of Heracles, the son
Of Poeas, Philoctetes, whom the two
Atreidae, and the Cephallenian king,
Cast out with scorn, solitary as ye see,
With a fierce malady wasting, stricken down
By the man-slaying serpent's furious bite:
But here, my son, so plagued, they cast me forth,
And left me all alone, from sea-girt Chryse 269
When with their ships they sailed, and touched this shore.
Then on the beach, beneath a sheltering rock,
Tired with long tossing on the wave, I slept:
They gladly saw, and left me and were gone,
And left with me nought but a few poor rags,
Matching my misery, and a little food,
A scant supply, may heaven give them the like!
Bethink thee, boy, what waking then was mine,
When from my sleep I rose, and they were gone!
And how I wept aloud, and shrieked reproaches,

Seeing indeed the ships with which I sailed
All gone, and no man in the place, not one   280
To help me—no one who to me, distrest,
Could minister in my sickness: all ways round
I gazed and nothing found save pain to see,
Yea, and of this great plenteousness, my son!
So passed the hours—lingeringly they passed—
And I was fain, lone, in my narrow home,
Upon myself to wait. My hunger's needs
This bow supplied, and on the wing brought down
The feathered fowls o' the air: then, what my shaft,
Sped from the tightened string, had struck, to this   290
I wretched crawled, trailing my luckless foot—
To this: and if of water I had need,
Or when the wintry ground was strewn with rime,
And faggots were to break, then would I creep
Forth, as I might, to compass this; and then
Fire I had none, but striking flint on flint
The hidden flame I found—whereby I live.
Nay, for a roof o'erhead, and fire to boot,
Gives all a man may lack—save health to me.
Come now, my son, hear what a land is this.   300
No mariner comes near it, of his will:
For haven it has none, nor mart whereat
He shall make gain of traffic, or be lodged.
Men who are wise set not their sails this way.
Yet some touch here, unwilling: for such things

Sometimes must happen in the lapse of years:
But these, my son, whene'er they come, in word
Are kind enough, and some perchance will give me
A little food or raiment, pitying me;
But this they will not, when I speak of this— 310
Convey me hence; and 'tis the tenth year now
I die this living death, poor starving wretch,
Drained of my strength by this insatiate sore.
From the Atreidae have I suffered this,
And from Odysseus: may the gods in heaven
Requite them for my wrongs like things to bear!

   Chor. Methinks that like thy former visitors
I also pity thee, O son of Poeas.

   Ne. I bear thee witness: this which thou hast spoken—
I know 'tis truth, how vile the Atreidae are, 320
And mightiness of Odysseus, having learnt.

   Phil. How then? against these cursèd sons of Atreus
Hast thou withal some grudge, by wrongs enraged?

   Ne. Oh that my hand might execute my rage:
So should Mycenae, so should Sparta learn,
A mother of valiant sons is Scyros too.

   Phil. 'Tis a good wish. But wherefore art thou come,
Against their lives denouncing thy fierce wrath?

   Ne. O son of Poeas, I know not how to tell,
But yet I will, the story of my wrongs. 330
When the death-doom upon Achilles fell——

   Phil. Alas—no more, until I first know this:

The son of Peleus—say you, he is dead?

Ne. Yea, dead; by no man slain, but by a god;
An arrow of Phoebus smote him, and he died.

Phil. Noble were both, the slayer and the slain :
Of these two things I doubt, which first to do—
More of thy wrongs inquire, or weep for him.

Ne. I think indeed that thou hast grief enough,
Ev'n of thine own—keep all thy tears for that. 340

Phil. 'Tis wisely counselled. Therefore tell thy tale—
Begin again and tell it—how wronged they thee?

Ne. Godlike Odysseus in a gay-prowed vessel
Came, and the foster-father of my sire,
To seek me, saying—but, if their tale was true
Or false, I know not—that, my sire being dead,
Troy could be taken by no arm but mine.
They with such tidings held me not long time
A lingerer from sailing with all speed—
First, as I yearned after my father slain, 350
To see him, yet unburied, whom alive
I saw not : and that promise too was fair,
If sailing I should sack the towers of Troy.
And so I sailed, and on the second day
The good ship with good winds to help drew nigh
The cape Sigeian ; and, landing, all the host
Pressed round me straight, to greet me, and they swore
They saw the dead Achilles, come to life.
He then lay dead ; and I the miserable,

When I had wept for him a little while,   360
Came to the good Atreidae, as was fit,
And asked my father's arms, and what was his:
Oh 'twas a shameless word they spoke to me:
'Son of Achilles, all else that was thy sire's
Is thine to choose—but those his arms belong
Now to another, to Laertes' son.'
But at the word, weeping, I started up,
Rage at my heart, and bitterly I spake:
'What, tyrant, have ye dared, without my leave,
To give my arms away, and not to me?'   370
Then said Odysseus, for he chanced at hand,
'Yea, boy, and rightly have they given them:
For I was there, and saved both them and him.'
I answered quick in wrath, and hurled at him
With all hard words I knew, and spared of none,
If he should take from me my arms—my own.
For all his meekness, when it came to this—
Stung at the things he heard, thus he returned:
'Thou wast not, where thy place was, there with me!
And, since thy speech is rude, I'll tell thee this—   380
Thou shalt not sail to Scyros with these arms.'
So, since I heard him scorn and flout me thus,
I sail for home, and yonder knave, fit son
Of knavish sire, Odysseus, has my arms.
But, more than him, I count the kings to blame.
The rulers make the city and the camp:

And all the mischief in the world is done
By evil teaching that bears evil fruit.
The tale is told: and, who the Atreidae hates,
To heaven, as to me, may he be dear! 390

Chor. O haunting the mountain, [*Strophe.*
        Life-sustaining of all that lives,
        Earth, mother of Zeus himself—
For whom the great Pactolus river rolls over sands of gold—
There also, mistress Mother, I called on thee—
When on this man sheer scorn the Atreidae poured—
On thee, O lady, riding on lions,
(Strong to rend bulls, but tame for thee)—
What time they gave his father's arms 400
To the son of Laertes, a peerless prize.

Phil. O good my friends, it seems ye come to me
With passport most familiar, this your grief:
Too well ye chime with me: too well appear
The Atreidae and Odysseus in your tale.
I know indeed his tongue would stick at nought,
Neither base speech nor villainy, whereby
He should achieve nought honest in the end.
No marvel this to me: but was indeed 410
Great Ajax there, and did he bear to see it?

Ne. Ajax, O friend, was dead: had Ajax lived,
I had not thus been robbed of what was mine.

Phil. How say you? Is he also dead and gone?

Ne. So deem of him—no longer in the light.

Phil. Alas the day! But Tydeus' son, and he
Whom from false Sisyphus Laertes bought—
They will not die; who better had not lived.
Ne. Not they: be sure of that. Oh no, they live,
And prosper mightily in the Argive host. 420
Phil. What of the old and good, true friend to me,
The Pylian Nestor? With sage counsels oft
Would he refrain the mischief of the rest.
Ne. A hard lot now is his: for now he mourns
For dead Antilochus, his warrior son.
Phil. Alas, two words of unmixed woe thou speakest—
Men of whose death I least had wished to hear.
Alas the day! where shall I look, when these
Are dead, and here again—Odysseus lives; 429
Where would thou hadst told me he, for them, had died!
Ne. A clever wrestler he: but clever plans,
O Philoctetes, oft are frustrated.
Phil. He whom thy father loved, Patroclus—say,
I pray thee, where in this thy need was he?
Ne. He like the rest was dead: in one short word
Take all the truth of this: an evil man
War does not love to slay, but still the brave.
Phil. Ay, there thou speakest true; and on that hint
I'll speak, and ask thee of a worthless wight,
One shrewd of tongue and clever—what now of him? 440
Ne. Who should this be if he were not Odysseus?
Phil. Not him I meant, but there was one Thersites,

Who ever chose his windiest phrase, when men
Were weariest: knowest thou if still he lives?

Ne. I saw him not, but heard that he yet lived.

Phil. He could not miss.   Never aught evil perished,
But of all such the gods take tender care.
I think the knavish and case-hardened ones
They love to turn back from the doors of death;
But still of just and good make swift despatch. 450
How should I deem of this, how praise, when I
Praising their deeds, find still the gods unjust?

Ne. But I, O son of an Oetaean sire,
Henceforth shall take good heed, Troy and the sons
Of Atreus not to see, save from afar:
And, where the worse is mightier than the good,
And brave men fail and talkers bear the sway—
The men who'd have it so, I'll not endure;
But me the rocks of Scyros shall suffice
Henceforth, nor will I seek another home. 460
Now to my ship I go.   O son of Poeas,
Farewell—thine utmost, well: and may the gods
Release thee from thy sickness as thou wouldst.
But let us go: for, whensoe'er the god
Allows our voyage, then we must depart.

Phil. Go ye, my son, so soon?

Ne.   Occasion calls us,
Not far but near, for favouring winds to watch.

Phil. O boy, for father's sake, and mother's sake,

And aught that in thy home thou holdest dear,
For pity I pray, leave me not thus alone,   470
Forsaken in what miseries ye see,
Dwelling with ills, how many ye have heard.
Make me thine afterthought. In bearing me,
I know that ye will bear a noisome freight.
Yet bear with me. Surely to noble souls
Shameful is hateful, glorious is the good.
No fair reproach thou'lt win, declining this;
Great meed of glory, doing it, my son,
To Oeta's land if I be brought alive.
Go: not one whole day does this task employ: 480
Consent; where'er thou wilt, aboard thy ship,
Set me, in hold, or stem, or stern, where least
Those in the ship my presence shall offend.
As Zeus above regards thee, hear my prayer:
Deny me not—lo, at thy knees I fall,
Maimed as I am and helpless. Leave me not,
Forsaken here, far from the haunts of men:
But either to thine own home bring me safe,
Or to Euboea's strand, Chalcodon's realm;
To Oeta thence short passage shall be mine,   490
And to the ridge Trachinian, and the fair
Spercheius stream, and to my father's sight—
My father, of whom 'tis long that I have feared
Lest he be dead. For oft by those who came
Full many a sad entreaty have I sent,

That he would send himself, and fetch me home:
But either he is dead, or else methinks
My messengers, as messengers are wont,
Made light of me (small blame?) and went their way.
But now to thee my message and myself   300
I trust—rescue me thou—pity me thou:
Seeing that all things change, and, if good hap
Or evil shall befall us, chance ordains,
We should beware of danger from afar:
And, when 'tis well with us, then most of all
Look to our lives, lest ruin lurk unseen.

   Chor. Oh pity him, prince—   [*Antistrophe*
Hearing him tell of a battle waged
With sufferings many and sore,
Whose like I pray the gods may never fall upon friend
      of mine!   310
But if, O prince, thou hatest, with bitter hate,
The sons of Atreus, I in thy place would turn
To this man's profit their misdoing,
And to the home where he longs to be
Upon our good ship swiftly hence
I would bear him, shunning the wrath of heaven.

   Ne. Take heed thou yield'st not now in facile mood,
And, when thy shipmate's sickness cleaves to thee,   320
From this consent art found dissentient then.

   Chor. It cannot be.   Nay, such reproach as this
Thou shalt not ever have cause to fling at me.

Ne. Nay then, I am ashamed to lag behind,
When thou art eager to befriend the man.
So sail we then; let him aboard with haste:
The ship will bear him—it shall not be refused.
Only may heaven help us from this land,
And whither our purpose is from hence to sail.

   Phil. O most glad day, and most beloved of men, 530
And ye, kind sailors, would that it might appear,
Even by my acts, how grateful ye have made me.
But ere we go, my son, let us salute
My home, no home, i' the rock—that thou may'st learn
On what I lived, and what I have endured.
I think that any other man than I
Would scarce have borne beholding but the sight:
But I perforce was schooled to bear my lot.

   Chor. Stay, let us learn: for hither two men come,
One from thy ship, a sailor—a stranger one— 540
Hear first their errand—afterwards go in.

   Mer. Son of Achilles, thy companion here,
Who with two more was left to guard thy ship,
I charged to tell me of thy whereabouts—
By mere good-luck, no forethought, having chanced
With thee to anchor on the selfsame shore.
For homeward now from Ilium as I sailed,
With no great fleet, but master of my ship,
To Peparethus with its clustering vines—
And heard that of thy company were all

The sailors here—so I resolved, that not 550
In silence, speaking first to thee, would I
Go forward, dealing with thee as was just.
I think thou knowest not of thine own affairs,
What new designs the Argives entertain
Concerning thee—nay, not designs, but deeds
Already in act, no longer left undone.

   Ne. My gratitude, good friend, for thy good care
Shall in all love abide, or prove me base.
But tell me all thy tidings, let me know 559
What new-hatched plot of the Argives thou hast learnt.

   Mer. The old man Phoenix and the sons of Theseus
Have hoisted sail and gone in quest of thee.

   Ne. To bring me back by force or argument?

   Mer. I know not: I but tell thee what I heard.

   Ne. Do Phoenix and the sons of Theseus this
For the Atreidae's sake so zealously?

   Mer. This thing, know well, they do, and purpose
     not.

   Ne. Was not Odysseus ready to sail forth
On his own errand? Did some fear withhold him?

   Mer. He and the son of Tydeus were about 570
To seek another man, when I set sail.

   Ne. Whom might Odysseus sail himself to seek?

   Mer. 'Twas one—But tell me first of yonder man,
Who is he? And what you say, speak not aloud.

   Ne. Thou seest the famous Philoctetes, friend.

Mer. Inquire no more of me.   Take thyself off,
And with all speed out of this land begone.
   Phil. What says he, boy? What dark words whispers he
To thee—and makes his merchandise of me?
   Ne. I know not yet: but, what he speaks, he shall 580
Speak out, for thee and me and these to hear.
   Mer. O son of Achilles, do not to the host
Accuse me, saying things that I should not:
For many a good turn, as a poor man may,
I for my doing receive again from them.
   Ne. I love not the Atreidae; and this man,
Because he hates them, is right dear to me.
Then, if thou camest as my friend, no word
Hide thou from me, of all that thou hast learnt.
   Mer. Take heed, boy, what thou doest.
   Ne.   I have considered.
   Mer. Thine be the guilt.
   Ne.   So be it, only speak.   590
   Mer. Thus then.   For this man they of whom I spake,
The son of Tydeus and Odysseus' might,
Sail hither, having sworn to bring him back,
Either by argument or strong constraint.
And this distinctly all the Achaeans heard
Odysseus promise. For he, more than the other,
Was confident that he would do this thing.
   Ne. But wherefore did the Atreidae for this man,
After so long a time, so greatly care,

Whom all these years they had cast out and left? 600
What longing fell on them, or might and wrath
Of heaven, requiting thus their evil deeds?

Mer. I, for perchance thou hast not heard this thing,
Will tell thee all.   There was a noble seer,
A son of Priam, Helenus by name :
Him, going alone i' the night, this man, of whom
Are spoken all shameful and opprobrious words,
Wily Odysseus, took, and leading captive
Showed openly to the Greeks, a goodly prize :
Who prophesied to them what else they asked, 610
And that the towers of Troy they should not sack,
Unless they should persuade this man with words,
And bring him from this island where he dwells.
And the son of Laertes, when he heard the word
O' the prophet, promised them straightway that he
Would bring the man and show him to the Greeks—
Most like, he thought, consenting to be taken,
If not, why then by force : and, if he failed,
Who would might from his shoulders take his head.
Thou hast heard all : and for thyself, be warned, 620
And any whom thou wouldst save, no time's to lose.

Phil. Alas the day !   Did he, that utter bane,
Swear to persuade and carry me to the Greeks?
As soon, once dead, persuade me to come back,
From Hades, like his father, to the light.

Mer. How that may be, I know not : but I must

Back to my ship begone, and may the god,
Ev'n with his best of help, befriend you both.

Phil. O boy, how say you, seems it not outrageous,
The son of Laertes should so fondly deem
That me with honeyed words he could convey
On shipboard hence, and shew me to the Greeks? 630
Nay, sooner my worst enemy, that serpent,
That made me thus a cripple, would I hear.
But nought will *he* not utter, nought will *he*
Not dare. And soon, I know, he will be here.
Let us be going, my son; that from the ship
Of Odysseus many a league of sea may part us.

Chor. Go we. 'Tis the good speed in the good season,
That's fraught with sleep and rest, when toil is o'er.

Ne. So let it be. Soon as the head-wind drops,
Then we will sail: for now it sets against us. 640

Phil. 'Tis ever fair sailing, when one flees from ill.

Ne. Nay, but no less to them these skies are adverse.

Phil. No wind's to pirates adverse, when there's chance
Of stealing, or of plundering by force.

Ne. Be it as thou wilt. Go, taking from within
All that thou needest or desirest most.

Phil. Some things indeed I need, though small the
    choice.

Ne. What is it that in my ship is not already?

Phil. There is a friendly herb, wherewith alway
My wound is lulled, and all its pain assuaged. 650

Ne. This then bring out—what else, now, wouldst
    thou take?

Phil. Some shaft, unnoted, may have slipped aside,
Which here I must not leave for men to find.

Ne. Is this the famous bow, that now thou holdest?

Phil. This, and no other, which my hands now wield.

Ne. May I have leave to gaze upon it close,
And handle it, and adore it as a god?

Phil. This thou shalt have, and aught that I can do,
My son, that may to thee be serviceable.

Ne. I do indeed desire it—on this wise: 660
If so I may, I would; if not, let be.

Phil. A reverent speech: 'tis granted thee, my son—
For thou alone hast given me to behold
This light o' the sun, and the Oetaean land,
My aged father, and my friends at home:
All's thine—and from beneath my enemies' feet
Thou hast uplifted me beyond them all.
Fear not: thou shalt have leave to handle these,
And give them freely back to me who gave,
And boast aloud that thou alone of men
Hast touched them, for thy kindness' sake to me.
For by a good deed I myself obtained them.   670

Ne. To have seen and proved thee friend, repents me
    not:
For, whoso knows to render good for good,
More than all wealth I count his friendship dear.

Go now within.
 Phil.   And thou shalt go with me:
For now my sickness craves thy present help.
 Chor. His fame I have heard, not seen him with my
   eyes,   [*Strophe* 1.
Who to the couch of Zeus made rash approach,
How to the circling wheel with chains
Him the almighty son of Cronos bound: 680
But of no other wight I know,
By hearing or by sight,
Who with a fate so cruel as this man here
Encountered—who, none having harmed or robbed,
An equal dealer among equal men,
Found all unworthily this lingering death:
So that I marvel how, how ever all alone,
Hearing the billows beating on the shore,
How he endured such life consumed with grief— 690
Here, his own neighbour, crippled of his feet; [*Antistr.* 1.
And mate of his misery in the place was none,
None in whose ears he might weep out
His woe, and wake response—woe that devoured
His heart with pain and drained his blood;
None who might stanch and soothe,
With healing herbs plucked from the fruitful earth,
The burning oozing issue, when it plagued
His wounded and infuriate foot.   700
But he would crawl, dragging himself along,

As helpless as a child with no kind nurse to lead,
Now here, now there, whence he might find relief—
When for a space the gnawing pain forbore.
And never for his food might he obtain   [*Strophe* 2.
Fruit of the sacred earth,
Nor aught beside, that we
Gain-getting sons of men call ours,   709
Save when with wingèd shafts from his far-shooting bow
Food for his hunger he might procure—
O wretched soul,
Who never these ten long years
Was with the juice of the vine refreshed,
But ever looked for any standing pool he knew,
Bending his steps to that.
Now meeting with a son of noble men,   [*Antistrophe* 2.
He from his grief shall win
To greatness and to bliss—   720
Meeting with one, who now at last,
After so many months, on shipboard carries him
Over the sea to his home, the haunt
Of Melian nymphs,
On banks of Spercheius, where
Lo in a glory of god-sent fire
The lord of the brazen shield a god to the gods ascends,
From Oeta's heights upborne.

   Ne. Come, if thou wilt. Say why without a cause 730
Standest thou mute, thus by amazement seized?

Phil. Ah woe is me!

Ne. What ails thee?

Phil. Heed it not. Go on, my son.

Ne. Art thou tormented by the returning pain?

Phil. Not so, but now methinks the pang is past.—
O gods!

Ne. Why on the gods dost thou cry out?

Phil. That they would help, and ease me of my pain.
Alas, woe's me!

Ne. How is't with thee? Speak out 740
And hide it not. Something's amiss, 'tis plain.

Phil. O child, I am undone: I cannot hide
This trouble from you. Ah, through me it goes,
And through, and through. Unhappy, woe is me!
O boy, I am undone, devoured by pain.
Out and alas! Now, by the gods, my son,
If ready to thy hand thou hast a sword,
Strike, and strike deep, unto my very heel:
Stay not, but smite it off: spare not my life.
Quick, O my son! 750

Ne. What is this suffering,
So fresh, so sudden, for the which thou dost
Lament thyself with such a bitter cry?

Phil. Thou knowest, child.

Ne. What is it?

Phil. Boy, thou knowest.

Ne. Say, what? I know not.

Phil. How knowest thou not?
Alas again, and evermore alas!

Ne. Dire is the burden of thy malady.

Phil. Dire truly, past all telling. But have pity.

Ne. What should I do?

Phil. Forsake me not for fear.
For this at intervals comes back, belike
With wandering when 'tis sated.

Ne. Hapless thou,
Hapless indeed in sorest suffering proved! 760
What, shall I then take hold? wouldst thou be touched?

Phil. Nay, touch me not: but, even as just now
Thou didst desire, take thou this bow, and till
This spasm of pain go by, that now has seized me,
Keep it with heed. For, when the torment passes,
A slumber steals on me: none otherwise
Is it appeased: but ye must let me sleep
Unvexed. And if meanwhile my foes should come,
By heaven I charge thee, yield not up the bow,
Nor willing nor unwilling, nor deceived 770
By trickery, to them, lest thou shouldst prove,
With me, thy suppliant, to have slain thyself.

Ne. Fear not my prudence. None but thou and I
Shall touch it. So, with good fortune, give it me.

Phil. Lo there, boy, take it: and to the jealousy
Of heaven make thou obeisance, that to thee
It may not prove full-fraught with misery,

Nor as to me and to its former lord.

Ne. Ye gods, grant to us twain these things: and grant
A swift and prosperous course, whithersoe'er 780
The god requires, and whither our sails are set.

Phil. Ah but I fear, my son, thy prayer is vain.
Again the blood wells in a sanguine tide
From my deep wound: and worse methinks will follow.
Alas! and yet again
Alas! how, O my foot, thou wilt undo me!
It creeps upon me: nearer
It comes, and nearer. Ah me, me, alas!
Ye know all now: ah nowise flee from me!
Out and alas!
O Cephallenian friend, that through thy breast 790
Such pain might pierce and fasten on thy heart!
Ah agony!
Agony yet again! O chieftains twain,
Agamemnon thou, and thou, O Menelaus,
Would that instead of me ye with your blood
Might feed, no less a time, this fell disease!
Ah me, me!
O death, death, death, how called and called again,
Each day that dawns, comest thou not at last?
O son, O noble boy, come, take me up,
And in yon Lemnian fire, the oft-invoked, 800
Consume me, as thou'rt noble: for so did I
To the son of Zeus consent, for meed of the arms

Which now thou guardest, such a boon to grant.
Speak, boy, what sayest thou?
Why art thou mute? Where are thy thoughts, my son?

Ne. My heart was heavy for thy weight of woe.

Phil. Yet, good my son, take courage: for this pain
Sudden and sharp returns, and swiftly goes.
Only, I pray thee, leave me not alone. 809

Ne. Fear not.

Phil.   Wilt thou remain?

Ne.   Be sure, I will.

Phil. I may not bind thee with an oath, my son.

Ne. I am not free to go and leave thee here.

Phil. Give me thy hand for pledge.

Ne.   That I will stay,
By this right hand I promise.

Phil.   Now yonder bring me,
Yonder.

Ne. Whither wouldst thou be brought?

Phil.   Up higher.

Ne. What now distracts thee? wherefore dost thou gaze
Upon the vault of heaven?

Phil.   Unhand, unhand me.

Ne. Whither wouldst thou go?

Phil.   Loose me, I say.

Ne.   I say
Thou shalt not.

Phil.   Thou wilt slay me with thy touch.
Ne. I loose thee then : perchance thou knowest best.
Phil. Earth, take me here and now, at point to die.
The pain no longer lets me stand upright.   820
  Ne. Methinks in no long time the man will sleep.
See how his head sinks backward to the ground.
Now over all his limbs the sweat is poured:
And lo a dark-red stream of spirting blood
Breaks from his wounded heel. Friends, come away :
In peace we'll leave him, so on sleep to fall.   [*Strophe.*
  Chor. O Sleep unlearned of sorrow, painless Sleep,
Hither, soft-breathed, we pray thee come,
Come and abide, our lord, abide :
Screen from his eyes this light   830
That now intensely glares :
Come, healer, come, we pray.—
O son, bethink thee now
Where wilt thou stand, or whither go ?
How hence resolves thy thought ?
Thou seest, now is the time.
Why should we wait to do this deed ?
Ever occasion, when it shapes the course,
Upon the instant wins great gain for men.
  Ne. But, though he nothing hears, yet I see this,
That vainly have we made our prize this bow,
If hence we sail and leave the man behind.   840
His is the glory, him the god bade bring.

Foul shame, to falsely boast a task undone!

Chor. But, O my son, let the god look to that. [*Ant.*
But, when thou answerest me again,
Breathe low, I pray thee, low, my son,
The voice of thy reply.
Sleepless is sick men's sleep,
Quick-eyed, perceiving all.
But now, far as thou canst,
Devise how secretly that task, 850
That task, thou shalt perform.
For . . . whom I mean thou knowest . . .
I name them not . . . if, urged by them,
This course thou holdest, to a prudent view
With troubles insurmountable 'tis fraught.
The wind, my son, the wind sits fair: [*Epode.*
And reft of sight, cut off from help,
The man stretched out in darkness lies,
(Sleep in the noontide heat is sound,)
Moving not hand or foot,
But robbed of all his powers—
Like one who lies at point to die, 860
With no more sight than his.
Look, if thy speech be seasonable.
For, son, if thought of mine can seize the truth,
The enterprise not fraught with fear is best.

Ne. Keep silence: start not from thy constant mind.
His eyes are opening; now he lifts his head.

Phil. O sunlight after sleep, and, by my hopes
Undreamed of, watchful care of these my friends!
For this, my son, I had not dared to boast,
Thou wouldst endure thus for my pain to wait, 870
Compassionately, with presence and with help.
Not all so easily to bear with me
Endured the Atreidae, those good generals.
But noble-natured of a noble strain
Thou, O my son, didst of these things make light,
Howe'er oppressed with clamour and with stench.
And now that all my pain has found, it seems,
Forgetfulness and respite for a while,
Now lift me, boy, thyself, upon my feet,
That, when the anguish shall release me quite, 880
We may aboard with haste, nor stay, but sail.

Ne. Right glad am I to see thee, past all hope,
Freed from thy pain, living and breathing still.
For as of one who was no more, so seemed,
Regarding then thy plight, the signs of thee.
But now lift up thyself; or, if thou wilt,
These men shall bear thee: for they will not shrink,
Since thus we are resolved, both thou and I.

Phil. My son, I thank thee; and, as thou art kind,
Lift me: let be these men, lest, ere the time, 890
They with the stench be sickened: on the ship
They'll have enough to bear, to dwell with me.

Ne. It shall be so: rise, and thyself hold fast.

Phil. Fear not : long used to this, I shall not fall.

Ne. Alas, what should I do, then, after this?

Phil. My son, what ails thee? Whither starts thy speech?

Ne. My words entangle me : what must I do?

Phil. What has perplexed thee? Say not so, my son.

Ne. It is with me already as I say.

Phil. Does then the noisomeness of my complaint 900
Make thee repent? Thou wilt not bear me hence?

Ne. Whatever is, is noisome, when a man,
False to his nature, does what he should not.

Phil. Neither in deed nor word hast thou been found
Unlike thy sire, helping a noble man.

Ne. I shall be found base : this distresses me.

Phil. Not in thy deeds : but in thy words—I doubt.

Ne. Zeus, help me now! Must I prove base again—
Hide what I should not, and speak shameful words?

Phil. This man, unless my judgment greatly errs, 910
Means to be false, and sail and leave me here.

Ne. Not leave thee—no : but, that I grieve thee more
Bearing thee hence, 'tis this that troubles me.

Phil. What meanest thou, my son? thy words are dark.

Ne. I will speak out. Thou shalt sail hence to Troy,
To the Greek camp, the Atreidae and their host.

Phil. Alas! how sayest thou?

Ne.   Grieve not, but hear.

Phil. What must I hear? what wilt thou do to me?

Ne. Rescue thee first out of this misery;
Then go, lay waste with thee the plains of Troy. 920
   Phil. Wilt thou indeed do this?
   Ne.   Much need of this
Constrains me: be not thou incensed to hear it.
   Phil. Miserable that I am, undone, betrayed!
What hast thou done? Quickly give back my bow.
   Ne. I may not do it. For to obey my chiefs
By duty and advantage I am bound.
   Phil. Fire that thou art, and monster of utter fear,
Fell knavery's most hateful masterpiece,
What hast thou done to me? how hast thou tricked me?
And art thou not ashamed to look on me,
Thy suppliant, thy petitioner—O shameless? 930
Taking my bow, thou hast robbed me of my life.
Give back, my son, I pray thee, give it back.
Nay, by our country's gods, steal not my life.
Ah me unhappy! He speaks to me no more:
His face makes answer, he will keep his prize.
O harbours, and O headlands, ye wild beasts
Of the mountain, comrades mine—and ye steep cliffs—
To you—I know not else to whom—to you,
My wonted company, I cry aloud
What things Achilles' son has done to me: 940
Swearing to bring me home, to Troy he takes me:
And, spite of pledged right hands, my sacred bow,
The bow of Heracles, whom Zeus called son,

Keeps, and to the Argive host would fain display.
Even as some mighty man, taken by his strength,
He hales me hence; and knows not that he slays
One dead already, shadow of a smoke,
Mere phantom of a man.   For in my strength
He had not taken me: since even thus
He could not, but by guile.   But now, entrapped,
Luckless, what shall I do?   Nay, but give back!
Nay, but ev'n now be master of thyself! 950
Speak to me.   Thou art silent.   I am nought . . .
. . . O two-mouthed aspect of the cave I know,
Robbed, and without the means to live, to thee
I must return, and there beneath thy shade
My lonely life shall waste itself away;
And no winged bird, no mountain-roaming beast,
These shafts shall slay, but I myself shall die,
Unhappy, and make a feast for these, whereby
I once was fed: they whom I hunted then
Shall make their prey of me, and I shall render
My life a forfeit for the lives of them—
Slain by this all so guileless-seeming man. 960
Perish—not yet: no, not until I learn
If thou wilt change thy purpose still: if not—
Miserably I pray that thou may'st die!

   Chor. What shall we do?   With thee, our prince, remains
That we should sail or hearken to his words.

Ne. A pang of pity has smitten through my heart,
Long since, not only now, because of him.

Phil. By heaven, my son, have pity, and suffer not
Reproach of men, that me thou didst deceive.

Ne. What shall I do? Would I had never left
Scyros: so grieves me this which now I bear.

Phil. Thou art not base: methinks thou hast come hither,
From base men having learnt a shameful lesson.
Leave this for others, for whom such deeds are fit,
And sail from hence, but give me back my bow.

Ne. O friends, what must we do? [*Odysseus enters.*

Od. Basest of men,
What *dost* thou? Back, and give this bow to me!

Phil. Ah, who is this? Odysseus do I hear?

Od. Odysseus, whom thou seest, doubt not, am I.

Phil. Ah, I am sold—undone! So this was he
Who trapped me thus and robbed me of my arms?

Od. 'Twas I, be sure, no other: I confess it.

Phil. O boy, give back, give up, to me the bow.

Od. That shall he not, howe'er he would. But thou
Thyself withal must go along with these,
Or they shall bring thee hence by force away.

Phil. Basest of men and boldest, me shall these
Bear hence by force?

Od. If thou go not, consenting.

Phil. O Lemnian land, and thou, all-conquering flame,

Hephaestos-kindled—how may this be borne,
That, from thy realm, this man by force should drag me?

Od. Zeus, let me tell thee, Zeus, who rules this land—
'Tis Zeus that so will have it.   Him I serve.   990

Phil. Man whom I hate, what wilt thou find to say?
Prating of gods, thy gods thou makest false.

Od. Not so, but true.   Thou must go hence with us.

Phil. I will not go.

Od.   I say thou shalt.   Obey.

Phil. Ah me, unhappy!   Plainly my father then
Begat me for a slave, and no free man.

Od. Not so, but equal with the best, with whom
Thou shalt take Troy, and lay it in the dust.

Phil. Never: not though I must endure the worst,
So long as here I stand on this high rock.   1000

Od. What wouldst thou do?

Phil.   Fling myself down from hence,
And dash my brains out on the rocks below.

Od. Lay hold of him.   Disarm him of his threats.

Phil. O hands, what things ye suffer, since I lack
My own good bow, bound by this man his prey.
O thou most base and most ungenerous,
How hast thou stolen upon me—snared me how—
Skulking behind this boy, whom I knew not—
Too good for thee, but not for me too good—
Who knew not save to do the task enjoined;   1010
But even now conceals not his remorse,

Both for his own fault and the wrong to me.
But thy base soul, still from its ambush peering,
Taught him too well, albeit unapt and loth,
To play his ill part with the proper craft.
And now, wretch, wilt thou bind me hand and foot,
And drag me from this shore, whereon 'twas thou,
Friendless, forsaken, citiless didst fling me,
Lifeless among the living? Woe is me!
Full often have I cursed, and curse thee now.
But, for the gods do nought of my desiring,   1020
A charmèd life thou leadest, and art glad;
But life itself is bitterness to me,
A piteous life, consumed with misery,
Mocked at by thee and by the sons of Atreus,
Thy two great captains, whom thou servest here.
Yet thou, ensnared and by compulsion bound,
Didst sail with them, but me, the miserable,
Who sailed of mine own choice, and seven ships
Sailed with me, me did they cast out with scorn—
It was their deed, thou sayest, but they, 'twas thine.
And now why drag ye me, why hale me hence?
Me, who am nought, and dead long since for you.   1030
O thou most impious, how am I not now
Crippled and noisome? How will ye presume,
With me o' the fleet, to offer sacrifice
To heaven, or pour libations any more?
For this was thy pretence to cast me out.

I curse you: and my curse ye shall not 'scape,
So having wronged me, if the gods love right.
Yea and I know they love it; for not else
Would ye have hither sailed for one so wretched,
But that some goad from heaven stung you for me.
O fatherland and ye regardful gods, 1040
Long-lingering, now, now let your vengeance fall,
If ye have pity of me, and spare them not!
For piteous life is mine, yet, might I see
Their ruin, healed of my sickness I should seem.

Chor. The man is wroth, Odysseus, and has spoken
A wrathful word, defiant of thy threats.

Od. Much might I say in answer to his speech,
Would time serve; now one word is all I may.
For, where such men are wanted, such am I;
And when the question is of just and good, 1050
None shall ye find more scrupulous than I,
Only my will is to be vanquished—never:
Never save now: but now have thou thy way.
Loose him, and lay no hand on him again.
Here let him bide. In truth we need thee not,
Having these arms of thine: for there with us
Is Teucer, who is perfect in this craft;
And I myself with no worse skill than thine
Could wield these shafts and speed them to their aim.
Why then, what need of thee? To pace thy Lemnos 1060
We'll leave thee, and depart. Perchance thine office

Honour, which thou hast scorned, may win for me.

Phil. Unhappy that I am, what shall I do?
What, shalt thou flaunt my arms among the Greeks?

Od. Waste not thy words: I go; gainsay me not.

Phil. Son of Achilles, wilt thou too depart
And leave me, silent, thus, without a word?

Od. Come thou: look not at him, although thy heart
Is noble, lest our fortune thou shouldst wreck.

Phil. And by you also, friends, shall I be left   1070
Thus desolate, and will ye have no pity?

Chor. This boy is captain of our crew: whate'er
He says to thee, his answer shall be ours.

Ne. Odysseus, that I know, will say of me
That I am weak. But yet remain, if so
This man desires, so long a time, until
The sailors have made ready with the ship,
And to the gods our prayer is said. Perchance
Meanwhile the man may get a better mind
Towards us. We therefore hasten hence, we twain:
And when we call, haste you, and make good speed. 1080

Phil. O chamber of the hollow rock,   [*Strophe* 1.
So hot, so freezing cold,
How, as it seems, oh wretched that I am,
I never was to leave thee, but shall die
With no companionship but thine.
Woe, woe for me!
O cave, O melancholy cave,

Most full of my distress,
What now shall be my life from day to day?
Whence shall I get, oh miserable, 1090
What hope of food to eat?
Oh would that upward through the air
On loud-resounding gale
The birds that cowered would snatch me hence:
I am defenceless now.

   Chor. Thou, thou thyself hast willed it so, [*Strophe* 2.
O thou unfortunate,
And by no other will than thine,
And no resistless strength,
Art thou condemned to suffer thus;
When, being free wisely to choose,
Thou didst reject the better fate,
And hast preferred the worse. 1100

   Phil. Oh hapless, hapless then am I, [*Antistrophe* 1.
Consumed with misery!
Who now henceforth must dwell for time to come
Here with no man to bear me company,
Alone, unfriended, till I die.
Woe, woe for me!
And I no more can get me food
With my wing'd shafts, no more,
Grasping between stout hands the friendly bow.
But unsuspected treacherous words, 1110
Masking a false intent,

Beguiled me.   Might I see him yet,
The author of this plot,
Ev'n for no less a time consigned
To anguish such as mine.

 Chor. By fate, by heaven-appointed fate, [*Ant.* 2.
Thou art afflicted thus :
It was no treacherous act of mine
That brought thee to this pass.
Let others feel, who have deserved,
Thy bitter and disastrous curse :   1120
For fain indeed were I, that thou
Shouldst not reject my love.

 Phil. Alas me, and methinks   [*Strophe* 3.
Upon the grey sea-beach
He sits and mocks at me,
Brandishing in his hand the life
Of me, ill-starred—the bow
Which no man else hath borne.
O wrested from these friendly hands,
O kindly bow, if thou
Hast any heart to feel,
Me, comrade once of Heracles,
With pity thou regardest :   1130
Who now no more in days to come
Shall handle thee; but thou shalt play thy part
With, for thy new-found lord,
A lord of trickery,

And on base stratagems must look,
And on the hateful presence of my foe,
Bringing to pass by shameful means
His projects—numberless as were
The mischiefs that he wove for me.   1139

   Chor. Justice 'tis good for a man to praise, [*Strophe* 4.
But, having praised it, then not to shoot
Forth from his lips resentful spleen.
And he, the one, the chosen of the host,
Obeying their behest,
Served thus the common good of all his friends.

   Phil. O birds of the air, my prey,   [*Antistrophe* 3.
And tribes of bright-eyed beasts,
That in this place abide,
And on the mountains find your food,
Scared from my cave no more,
Ye will approach me now:
For now I hold not in my hands   1150
The mighty shafts of yore—
Oh helpless that I am—
But faintly warded is this place,
That you no more should fear it.
Come on: fair time is now to glut
Your retributive jaws to heart's content
Upon my quivering flesh.
For soon shall I be dead:
Where shall I find whereon to live?

Who lives with feeding thus on air,
Robbed of his former strength, and now
Of all those gifts possessing none,
From the life-giving earth that come? 1160

   Chor. If thou regardest at all a friend, [*Antistrophe* 4.
One who draws near in good will to thee,
Draw near, by heaven; and think, think well,
'Tis thine to 'scape this sickness, sad to feed,
And all unskilled to bear
The myriad weight of woe that with it dwells.

   Phil. Again dost thou remind me
Of the former grief, again—
Noblest of all men, thou,
That ever in this place set foot? 1170
Why wilt thou slay me? How hast thou undone me!

   Chor. What meanest thou?

   Phil. That thou didst hope to bring me
Hence to the hated Trojan land.

   Chor. For this, I deem, is best.

   Phil. Begone and leave me now.

   Chor. Welcome, welcome the task thou hast enjoined,
To do what I desire.
Let us go hence, go hence,
Each to our place and business in the ship. 1180

   Phil. By Zeus, who hears the curse—go not, I pray you!

   Chor. Calm thyself.

   Phil.   Friends, in heaven's name, remain!

Chor. Why dost thou call on us?

Phil. Alas my fate! my fate, alas!
Unhappy, I am undone!
O foot, my foot, now in the life that follows,
What shall I make of thee, ill-starred?
O friends, come back, retrace your steps! 1190

Chor. What should we do, of contrary intent
To that thou didst enjoin on us before?

Phil. Small cause for anger,
If one with tempestuous grief distraught
Shall sometimes speak a senseless word.

Chor. Come with us, hapless one, as we exhort thee.

Phil. Never, know this for a surety, never—
Not though the lord of the lightning
Comes with his blazing bolts, with the withering blast
Of his thunderous flame enwraps me:
Perish Ilium rather, 1200
And perish the host that its wall encircles—
The pitiless ones who this poor lame foot of mine
Spared not to spurn from them.
Yet, O my friends, this one prayer grant me!

Chor. What is the prayer thou wilt ask of us?

Phil. A sword can ye find for me—
Or an axe, or some dart, deny me not.

Chor. Say what rash deed wouldst thou do with it?

Phil. Strike off my head with my hand, and my limbs,
One by one: for on death, on death

Is my mind set now.

   Chor. Why wouldst thou this?

   Phil.   So my sire I might seek. 1210

   Chor. Where wouldst thou seek him?

   Phil.   In the halls of the dead:

Since in the light no more shall I find him.
O city, O land of my home,
Would I might see thee—I the unhappy—
Who thy sacred stream forsook,
And to help the Greeks, whom I hate, went forth:
Undone—undone!

   Chor. Long since I should have left thee, and returned,
And near my ship I should have been ere now,
But that I saw Odysseus drawing nigh,   1220
And coming towards us hither Achilles' son.

   Od. Wilt thou not tell me, on what errand bound
Back hither again in such hot haste thou comest?

   Ne. To undo the sin that I before committed.

   Od. Thou speakest riddles: what sin didst thou commit?

   Ne. That which, obeying thee and all the host——

   Od. What thing didst thou, that thou shouldst not have done?

   Ne. Taking a man with base deceit and guile——

   Od. What man? alas—dost thou intend some mischief?   1229

   Ne. No mischief truly; but to the son of Poeas——

Od. What wilt thou do? How am I filled with fear!
Ne. From whom I took this bow, to him again——
Od. Zeus, and what then? thou wilt not give it back?
Ne. For shamefully and wrongfully I took it.
Od. By heaven, in mockery dost thou say these things?
Ne. If it be mockery to speak the truth.
Od. What word, son of Achilles, hast thou spoken?
Ne. The same words twice and thrice shall I repeat?
Od. Would I had never heard them—no, not once!
Ne. Know now full certainly—my say is said. 1240
Od. Yet is there one, one still, who shall prevent thee.
Ne. How? who is he that shall forbid me this?
Od. All the Greek host shall do it, and I for one.
Ne. Wise is thy wit, but all unwise thy speech.
Od. Neither thy speech is wise, nor thine intent.
Ne. But if 'tis just—why, this is more than wisdom.
Od. How just, what by my counsels thou didst win,
Thou shouldst give back?
Ne. The sin that I have sinned,
For it is shameful, I would fain repair.
Od. Fearest thou not the Greek host, doing this? 1250
Ne. Justice to friend, thy terrors daunt me not.
Od. With thee, then, not with Trojans, must we fight.
Ne. But in thy hand, to do it, I put no faith.
Od. Then come what will come! Seest thou my right hand

Gripping the hilt?

Ne. But me thou too shalt see
Doing the selfsame thing, and not delaying.

Od. Nay, I will let thee be: but I will go
And tell the host, and they shall punish thee.

Ne. Thou'rt wise in time: still keep such prudent mind,
Out of harm's way perchance thou'lt keep thy foot. 1260
But thou, O son of Poeas, Philoctetes,
Leave now thy cave in the rock there, and come forth.

Phil. What means this noise of voices by my cave?
Why do ye call me, friends? What is your business?
Alas, an evil business! Are ye come,
Some great affliction to my grief to add?

Ne. Fear not, but hearken to the words I bring.

Phil. I trust thee not: since from fair words before,
Thy words, which I believed, I fared but ill.

Ne. Is there no room then for repentance now? 1270

Phil. When thou wouldst steal my bow, such wast thou then,
Plausive in speech—with mischief in thy heart.

Ne. But now not so: but this I fain would hear,
Art thou resolved persistently to stay,
Or wilt thou sail with us?

Phil. Cease, say no more;
All thou canst say shall be but wasted breath.

Ne. Thou art resolved?

Phil. More than my tongue can say.

Ne. I would thou couldst have hearkened to my words:
But, if all to no purpose they are spoken,
Why, I have done.

Phil. Thou canst but speak in vain; 1280
Thou wilt not win my thoughts to friendliness,
That didst by treachery obtain thine end,
And of my life hast robbed me—and com'st here
To advise me, thou—base son of noble sire.
Perdition light—on the Atreidae first,
Then on the son of Lartius—and on thee!

Ne. Hold off thy curse! Take from my hands the bow.

Phil. What sayest thou? Again am I deceived?

Ne. No, by the majesty of Zeus supreme! 1289

Phil. O welcome words, if what thou sayest be true!

Ne. Words that the deed shall follow, plain to see:
Reach hither thy right hand, and take thy bow.

[*Odysseus enters.*

Od. In the sight of the gods, I charge thee, give it not
In the Atreidae's name, and of the host!

Phil. My son, whose voice—Odysseus did I hear?

Od. None other: and he is near thee, in thy sight.
And he will bring thee hence by force to Troy;
Whether Achilles' son consent or no.

Phil. But not unpunished, if this shaft flies straight.

Ne. Ah, by the gods, I pray, loose not thy shaft. 1300

Phil. Nay, by the gods, fair son, loose thou my hand.
Ne. I will not.
Phil. Why of mine enemy, whom I hate,
Didst rob me, not to slay him with my bow?
Ne. For me and thee this is dishonourable.
Phil. But yet be sure of this, your chiefs of the host,
Your Grecian heralds, pursuivants of lies,
Are cowards in battle, but in words are brave.
Ne. Good now: thou hast thy bow, and hast no cause
Of anger against me, or of complaint.
Phil. No cause, my son; but thou hast shown thy nature, 1310
What strain thou'rt of—no child of Sisyphus,
But of Achilles, who, whilst yet he lived,
Had fairest fame, and now among the dead.
Ne. Sweet to my ears thy praise, both of my sire
And of myself: but hear now, what I fain
Would win from thee. The lot indeed that heaven
Awards, men cannot choose but bear: but who
On self-inflicted misery are bent,
As thou, such men deserve not sympathy,
Or any man's compassion. And thou art 1320
Grown fierce, and counsel dost reject, and if
One speaks to thee in love, advising thee,
Thou hatest him, as though he were thy foe,
And wished thee ill. Yet I will speak to thee
The truth, so help me Zeus: and what I speak,

Doubt not, but know, and write it in thy heart.
For this thy grievous sickness is from heaven,
Because the guardian snake thou didst approach,
That keeps with unseen watch the roofless shrine
Of Chrysè: and respite from this sore disease
Know that thou canst not win—howso yon sun   1330
May rise in the east, and in the west decline—
Till to the plains of Troy of thine own will
Thou comest, and, finding there Asclepius' sons
Who are with us, art of this sickness eased
By them, and, with this bow, and me, to help,
Hast sacked, in sight of all, the Trojan towers.
Now hearken, how I know that this is so.
There is with us a prisoner out of Troy,
One Helenus, a prophet without peer,
Who plainly says these things must come to pass:
And furthermore that in this present summer   1340
Must Troy be taken utterly; or else,
If he prove false in this, his life's the forfeit.
Now therefore, knowing this, of thine own will
Yield: for a goodly prize is this to win,
Being chosen, one from all the Grecian host,
Their bravest, so first into healing hands
To come, and earn withal a matchless fame,
That thou didst take this lamentable Troy.

   Phil. O hated life, why in this light of day
Holdest thou me back from the doors of death?

Ah me, what shall I do? how disobey 1350
The loving words of counsel that he spake?
Shall I then yield?   How after this shall I
Endure man's sight? or who will speak to me?
O eyes that did behold all these my wrongs,
How will ye suffer it if I consort
With Atreus' sons who flung me forth to die?
How with the son of Lartius the all-guilty?
For it is not grief afflicts me for the past,
But what I must endure from them hereafter
I think that I foresee.   The heart that once 1360
Breeds evil, teaches evil to the end.
Yea and at thee I marvel now for this.
Thou shouldst have never gone thyself to Troy,
And me thou shouldst have hindered:—whom they
    scorned,
And robbed thee of thy birthright—and adjudged,
Thy father's arms awarding, hapless Ajax
A worse man than Odysseus: yet wilt thou
Go there to fight for them, and make me go?
Not so, my son: as thou didst swear to me,
So bring me home: and thou, at Scyros tarrying,
Leave them to perish as they have deserved.
So shalt thou win a twofold thanks from me, 1370
And from my sire; and not, helping bad men,
Be deemed thyself of nature like to theirs.
    Ne. There's reason in thy speech: yet would I fain

That, trusting to the gods and to my words,
Thou, with this man to friend, wouldst sail from hence.

Phil. What! to the plains of Troy—and to my foe,
The son of Atreus—with this helpless foot?

Ne. Rather to those who of the pain will ease
Thee, and thy festering foot, and heal thy sickness.

Phil. O evil counsellor, what wilt thou say? 1380

Ne. That which, made good, is best for thee and me.

Phil. Hast thou no shame the gods should hear thee say it?

Ne. Why of a good work should I be ashamed?

Phil. What good? to the Atreidae, or to me?

Ne. To thee: I am thy friend, and speak in friendship.

Phil. How, who wouldst hand me over to my foes?

Ne. Friend, learn not in misfortune to be bold.

Phil. Thou wilt slay me: I know thee by thy words.

Ne. I slay thee not: I say thou dost not know me.

Phil. Do I not know, the Atreidae cast me out? 1390

Ne. See if they will not now deliver thee.

Phil. Not with my leave, if I must first see Troy.

Ne. What then remains to do, if by my words
I can persuade thee nothing that I say?
Easiest it were for me to cease, and leave thee
To live, with no deliverer, as thou art.

Phil. Let me endure the lot appointed me.
But what, laying thy hand on mine, thou once
Didst swear, to bring me home, this do for me,
My son, and tarry not, spend no more thought   1400
On Troy. For long enough have I made moan.
   Ne. Be it as thou wilt : let us be going.
   Phil.   O the noble speech !
   Ne. Firmly plant thy feet with mine now.
   Phil.   To the utmost of my strength.
   Ne. But the blame then of the Greeks how shall I
     shun ?
   Phil.   Think not of that.
   Ne. How if they lay waste my land for this ?
   Phil.   I will be there——
   Ne. Why, what service wilt thou render ?
   Phil.   With the shafts of Heracles——
   Ne. How ?
   Phil.   I'll keep them well at distance.
   Ne.   Kiss the earth, and come, set forth.
                   [*Heracles appears.*

   Her. Nay, son of Poeas, go not yet :
Abide, till thou hast heard my words.   1410
Know that the voice of Heracles
Sounds in thine ears, thine eyes behold
His face : for hither for thy sake,
Leaving my place in heaven, I come,
To show what Zeus intends, and from

The way thou'rt going to turn thee back:
Then hear and heed my speech.
And first of my own fortunes I will speak,
What toils I having suffered and gone through
Won deathless glory, even as thou seest. 1420
Yea, and know well, this debt is thine to pay,
Through suffering to make glorious thy life.
But to the city of Troy go with this man:
So first from thy sore sickness shalt thou cease,
And, being chosen first of all the host,
Paris, whose fault was cause of all that woe,
Thou with my arrows shalt bereave of life,
And shalt sack Troy, and carry to thy home
Spoils, having won first prize of all the Greeks,
To Poeas thy sire, and thine Oetaean heights. 1430
But from the Trojan host what spoils thou takest,
Bring to my pyre, memorials of my bow.
And thou, son of Achilles, heed my words:
For neither thou without this man may'st take
The plain of Troy, nor he apart from thee:
But, like two lions in one pasture mated,
Have thou good care of him, and he of thee.
And I will send Asclepius to Troy
To heal thy sickness; for a second time
My shafts must take it. But remember this— 1440
When ye lay waste the land, then to revere
The gods: all things my father Zeus to this

Counts second. Piety dies not with men;
But, whether they live or die, yet it endures.

Phil. O voice, how welcome to my ears,
And face so long unseen—
I shall obey thy words.

Ne. And to this sentence I agree.

Her. Then make no long delay to do it:
Occasion, as ye see,
Is urgent, and fair winds at stern. 1450

Phil. Once, ere I go, I'll greet this land.
Cave, that so long hast watched with me,
And nymphs of meadow and stream, farewell:
Farewell, the great male voice
Of the headland midst the waves—
Waves, in my cavern's farthest nook,
That, smitten by the south wind's breath,
Oft drenched me o'er from foot to head,
And often did the mount of Hermes,
When storms went over me,
Reverberate my groans. 1460
But now, O springs, and fount Lyceian,
I leave you, leave you now—
Who never hoped for this.
Farewell, O sea-girt plain of Lemnos,
And waft me hence unblamably
With favourable course,
Whither the sovereign Fate conducts,

And counsel of my friends,
And heaven's all-potent will,
That has ordained it so.
   Chor. Let us depart now all together:
Our prayer to the sea-nymphs having prayed,   1470
To come and speed us hence.

NOTES

Notes

P. 4, l. 44. 'Conference *also* of counsels prospers for men of experience more than others.' The value of experience is *sometimes* shown in the prosperous result of *united* counsels, when the experienced man (instead of relying on his own superior wisdom) confers with others. [It will be seen that, in this much-controverted passage, I agree with Professor Kennedy about ξυμφοράς, but not about ζώσας. Counsels which *live*, or *abide* (Professor Kennedy's own word), are surely contrasted with counsels which perish and are abortive.]

P. 8, l. 125. Macbeth, i. 3, 112, 'Or did *line* the rebel with hidden help and vantage.'

P. 12, l. 221. 'For (had I not been a stranger) I should have tracked it not far—not failing to find. . . .'

P. 12, l. 227. If he is afraid, let him *not* fear, but speak. 'Let him remove the charge (that hangs now over the city), denouncing himself if need be.' 'Himself against himself' let him speak out (μὴ σιωπάτω).

P. 16, l. 329. I follow Hermann, understanding a verb, 'I never will (speak),' and reading εἰπών.

P. 19, l. 420. Oedipus will flee from the house of Laius, that harbourless harbour (more storm-vext than any sea), to which fair winds, as he thought, had blown him—anywhere out of that—yes, even to the mountain solitudes of Kithaeron, there to bewail his misery : *they* shall be his haven now : he will escape, *from* Thebes, *to* them.

P. 27, l. 624. I see nothing better here than to read the line as a question, 'When you have shown what sort of thing (how unreasonable) jealousy is, then will you kill me?' *i.e.* Do you suppose that the Thebans will let you put me to death? This suits the answer of Oedipus, who understands the speech as a defiance.

P. 64, l. 1526. I read οὔ τίς, understanding ἦν from the preceding line.

P. 70, l. 76. Timon of Athens, iii. 5 :—
'He is a man, setting his fate aside,
Of comely virtues.'

P. 74, l. 185. 'Bold that you are, be bold (make up your mind) to yield.'

P. 76, l. 229. 'The fates punish no man, concerning wrongs that he is the first to suffer, for requiting them.' If I deceive you, who deceived me, the gods will pardon my deception.

P. 79, l. 309. I follow Professor Kennedy. 'May he bring a blessing to his city and to me. I need not say, to himself: he needs must do good to himself in doing good to others.' Otherwise 'To me: for do not all good men (*as well as others:* all men, none the less that they are virtuous) desire their own good?'

P. 80, l. 328-330. The lines are displaced in the MSS. ἢ τῆσδε κἀμοῦ is full of meaning after τροφαί, but nonsense after ὁμοῦ. When Oedipus asks Ismene *whom* she is pitying, with a suggestion that she does herself injustice in seeming for a moment to separate herself from her father and sister, at once, with quick instinctive appreciation of his meaning, she identifies her lot with theirs.

P. 83, l. 403. The burial of Oedipus may be said to 'chance amiss' in one sense, if he is denied due rites of burial; in another, if he is buried elsewhere than in Boeotia.

P. 88, l. 522. ἤνεγκον ἄκων μέν (MSS.) is unmetrical. ἑκών is untrue and unsuitable to the context (compare 964). Hermann suggests ἄνων (= ἀνύων). Perhaps we should read ἤνεγκ' οὖν κακότατ', ὦ ξένοι, ἤνεγκ' ἀέκων μέν (or ἤνεγκα μὲν ἄκων).

P. 89, l. 540. 'A reward the like of which never to obtain from the city did I serve her.' ἐξελέσθαι an ironical word: compare ἐξαίρετον δώρημα.

P. 89, l. 547. ἁλούς (for ἄλλους of MSS.) is a certain correction. Compare 997.

P. 90, l. 570. I read παρῆκέ μ' ὥστε βραχέα σοι δεῖσθαι λέγειν.

P. 91, l. 588. I read τοῦ: 'or *whose* opposition do you speak of?'—'Not small shall be the peril'—of course for Theseus. What then could he mean by asking, 'Who will make my difficulty? Your sons? or shall I make it for myself?'

P. 94, l. 661. Literally, 'though terrible things were emboldened to the utterance:' an expression precisely parallel to πολλαὶ ἀπειλαὶ κατηπείλησαν just before.

P. 96, l. 735. τηλικόσδε.

P. 102, l. 867. 'Such poor eyesight—*barely* eyesight—as I had when my former eyes were lost.' Disparaging, not his daughters, but his own helpless condition : an argument for pity.

P. 110, l. 1069. πώλων probably corrupt for ˘ ¯ : it may have displaced (as a gloss upon φάλαρα) some word quite unlike it ; possibly χαλῶσ' (suggested by Hermann instead of κατά) : 'fast as their bridles can hasten them (*all that their bridles can*), flinging them loose.'

P. 112, l. 1132. I read, with Hermann, πῶς σ' ἂν ἄθλιος γεγώς. Line 1134 shows that *Theseus* is the subject of θιγεῖν.

P. 116, l. 1220. ἰσοτέλεστος (which I connect with μοῖρα) is passive: 'a doom whose payment (of the tribute of their lives) falls equally on all.' Men are ἰσοτελεῖς of their lives to Pluto (τελέουσιν Ἄιδᾳ ψυχάν).

P. 116, l. 1230. 'Who wanders far to multiply vexations? What plague is not *there*?' involved in the mere fact of being young, so that there is no need to go further to seek for it.

P. 117, l. 1248. ῥιπαί unquestionably (as in El. 106) of the starlight : the only adequate meaning of 'vibrations of the night,' and required by the antithesis. All influences of sunlight and of starlight to Oedipus are fraught with sorrow.

P. 118, l. 1281. 'The many words (whatever their tenor) even from the silent wring response.' Compare with δυσχεράναντα, κατοικτίσαντα (feeling imputed to the words), Oed. Col. 659, 661 : and, for a similar 'hypallage,' 267.

P. 122, l. 1380. 'From thine altars and thy thrones' [plural expressing contempt, expressed in Greek by σὸν and σοὺς] 'my curses oust thee'—forestall your sitting (suppliant at the altar) and preoccupy your throne.

P. 122, l. 1390. 'I invoke for thy heritage (the only abode you shall inherit from me) the gloom of Tartarus, to give thee a home far off from Thebes.'

P. 125, l. 1454. I read with Hermann, ἐπεὶ μὲν ἕτερα, τὰ δ' ἐπ' ἦμαρ ... (In the Antistrophe, 1469, δέδια δ'· οὐ γὰρ ἁλί' ἀφορμᾷ ...) This gives complete correspondence of metre : and L A have τάδε πήματ'.—ἐπεὶ μέν, like ὅτε μέν, 'sometimes.' ἐπ' ἦμαρ, 'within a day' : compare Trach. 1128.

P. 128, l. 1534. Let the secret belong to the ruler only, and not be divulged to the people, who, even in the best-governed state (even, therefore, in Athens ; compare 1004), are capricious, and might be tempted, in some crisis of their history, to regard the presence of my bones among them as a pollution, and cast them out.

P. 128, l. 1536. This is the reason why it seems a light matter to commit such outrages. Men are shortsighted, all but the wisest (such as Theseus): they ignore a punishment which is far off.

P. 129, l. 1550. Compare Paradise Lost, iii. 21 :—

'Thee I revisit safe,
And *feel* thy sovran vital lamp; but thou
Revisit'st not these eyes, that roll in vain
To find thy piercing ray, and find no dawn.'

And Lear, iv. 1, 25 :—

'Might I but live to see thee *in my touch*,
I'd say I had eyes again.'

P. 135, l. 1713. There is no justification for the use of μή with ἔχρῃζες. Read ἰώ μοι, or ὤμοι. 'It was your wish; but it was sad for me to see you die, forlorn, an exile.'

P. 145, l. 124. 'The Serpent:' the ensign (or emblem) of Thebes.

P. 153, l. 326. τὰ δεινὰ κέρδη MSS. 'Your clever winnings,' on which you plume yourselves.

P. 155, l. 368. Dindorf's simple alteration παραιρῶν is probably right. I take ὑψίπολις ἄπολις together, like παντόπορος ἄπορος in the Strophe, and connect τόλμας χάριν with the following sentence. The Chorus, under cover of generalities, are denouncing Creon. It may be thought that after 366 the antithesis of the usual readings and pointing is wanted; but the warning tone of the whole Antistrophe is even more impressive without it. 'Wonderful is Man: he has put all things in subjection under his feet. And yet not all. Still Right is supreme. The wrongdoer, though he be a monarch— he is the outlaw. Let me not know a wicked person.'

P. 162, l. 556. 'No, not if my words could be unspoken:' literally, 'with my words unspoken:' *i.e.* I do not choose life, whatever I may have rashly said.

P. 164, l. 594. ὃ τέτατο. The relative seems to me indispensable; although of course νιν refers to ῥίζαν, not φάος. The broken sentence is expressive. 'For now the light of hope that shone so brightly about the life of Antigone, last root of the fated house'—[not 'that light is out,' but] 'the axe is laid to that root; no trace of life remains.' I retain κόνις, and understand 'The bloodstained dust of the gods below levels the root of the house of Oedipus' to mean 'The gods below have levelled bloodstained dust over the root.

Lastly, 'the rash speech and frantic purpose' (mind possessed by an Erinys) of Antigone are said to have co-operated in the work of destruction.

P. 164, l. 607. Donaldson's θέοντες is highly probable; and either παγκρατής (Don.) for παντογήρως (which, however, is a fine word, and could hardly have come from a blunder); or, instead of ἀκάματοι, ἄκοποι (Dind.), which as a rarer word might have been replaced by an explanation.

P. 164, l. 613, 614. It is very doubtful whether the true reading can be recovered here: οὐδὲν ἕρπει and ἐκτὸς ἄτας being possibly stopgaps borrowed from lines 625, 618. But this is not very likely, and it is worth considering whether the lines may not stand with the substitution of ἄτα for ἄτας, and perhaps οὔποθ' (or οὐδάμ') for οὐδέν. 'Nowise doth universal woe avoid the life of man.' βιότῳ dative, as after ἐκποδών; or possibly βιότου.

P. 166, l. 664-667. καὶ τοῦ**** . . . παραστάτην. These lines were transposed by Hermann (whom other editors have followed), and placed after 671 (τἀναντία). Two obvious difficulties are created by the change: (1) The reference of τοῦτον τὸν ἄνδρα (664) to the obedient subject, with τοῦτον just before (οὐκ ἔστ' ἐπαίνου τοῦτον ἐξ ἐμοῦ τυχεῖν) meaning the disobedient one. (2) A false antithesis, between *good ruler* and *bad subject*. 'He who governs his household will be a righteous ruler of the state. But a subject who sets himself above the laws and above his rulers shall have no praise of mine.' Whereas the other way the connection is natural and true. 'The qualities which make a man a righteous ruler alike of his household and the state would also make him a loyal subject. Disloyal subjects I cannot praise:' *i.e.* 'I, Creon, the just ruler, should in your place loyally obey, and therefore I cannot praise you if you are disobedient.'

P. 171, l. 782. The language is that of war. ἐμπίπτειν is 'to attack.' χρήματα, I believe, is metaphorical: men become the property of Love the Conqueror. Love 'wins the fight and divides the spoil' (literally, 'falls on the gear').

P. 171, l. 784. Compare Coriolanus, iii. 2, 116, 'the smiles of knaves tent in my cheeks.'

P. 182, l. 1062. ἤδη, scil. ἐρεῖν. 'Forthwith methinks I shall speak as you require—so far as you are concerned:' *i.e.* I shall speak the truth, not seeking reward—at least from *you*.

P. 204, l. 244. εἰ γὰρ ὁ μὲν θανών. 'If (whereas Agamemnon

was slain and *is* no more) his murderers shall not pay their blood for his.' That only the second member of the sentence is hypothetical (compare δεινὰ ἂν εἴην εἰργασμένος, εἰ τότε μὲν ἔμενον, νῦν δὲ λίποιμι τὴν τάξιν) is marked by the negatives, οὐδέν in the first, μή in the second. (γᾶ τε καὶ οὐδέν = '*pulvis et umbra.*')

P. 209, l. 363. 'My meat and drink.' Here, and in too many other passages of the 'Electra' and of the 'Ajax,' too many to be noted, (I may mention, however, as flagrant examples, El. 445, Aj. 1285), I have been indebted to the not-to-be-surpassed translations in Professor Jebb's editions of these plays. I translated these two plays some time ago, in the course of school-work, with no thought of publication, and therefore plagiarized freely. In some cases I have altered: but in far more I have shrunk from deliberately substituting worse for better.

P. 211, l. 417-420. I should like to substitute for these lines the following:—

> 'I hear them say, revisiting the light,
> Her father's very presence as he lived
> She saw; and that he took, and on the hearth
> Planted, that sceptre which he wielded once.'

P. 215, l. 445. 'By this act, meaning "his blood be upon his own head," the murderess washes her hands of the guilt' (Professor Jebb): though, literally, I think it is '*He took* the bloodstains' (the *print* of the axe), the active being quite sufficiently justified by the Homeric ἀναμάσσειν: if ἀναμάσσειν, why not ἐκμάσσειν?

P. 212, l. 452. ἀλιπαρῆ, with a certain pathetic irony, 'uneloquent,' 'unpetitionary.' 'How should my father regard the supplication of this poor, coarse, faded hair of mine; so unlike that of Chrysothemis, which no grief has aged?' Compare 1378, λιπαρεῖ χερί.

P. 214, l. 496. 'Never shall we see (and lament to see) this portent come near to the murderer and his paramour undeprecated (by them).' Certainly it will come nearer and nearer to them, and they will not lack cause to rue its coming.

P. 215, l. 534. I cannot agree with Professor Jebb in thinking that τίνων is the interrogative. The expression is to be compared with ἄγγελλε δ' ὅρκῳ προστιθείς: literally, 'as a kindness to whom— paying it? (for whose sake—as a debt?):' the construction is complete without τίνων, but τίνων is added to emphasize Clytaemnestra's meaning, which is, that no one *had a right to claim* such kindness.

P. 216, l. 551. I connect γνώμην δικαίαν σχοῦσα with τοὺς πέλας ψέγε. 'Are you so clear of injustice that you can pass judgment upon me?'

P. 216, l. 564. 'The rushing winds.' [πολὺς ῥεῖ ὁ ποταμός, πνεῖ ὁ ἄνεμος.] So strong they would have been; but Artemis checked them, and becalmed the Greeks. Exactly like '*celeres* obruit otio ventos.'

P. 236, l. 1087. 'Having armed and made ready the unlovely deed.' ὁπλίζειν is used in Homer of making ready anything, especially meat and drink : and Eurip. Ion 1124, θυσίαν θεοῖς. The point of the expression is that Electra has resolved to do a deed which, till it is done, looks to all eyes, as to those of Chrysothemis, unlovely and a crime ; but, having done it, she knows that the universal voice will approve alike her wisdom and her piety. Professor Jebb (who thinks that σοφά τ' ἄριστα τε παῖς κεκλῆσθαι is what Chrysothemis desires, and that Electra knows that the two things are incompatible) seems to me to have confused 'wisdom' with 'caution.' Chrysothemis is cautious, but Electra is, and one day will be acknowledged to be, wise. (Compare τοὺς ἄνωθεν φρονιμωτάτους οἰωνοὺς at the beginning of the ode.)

P. 249, l. 1413. Read σοι for σε. To alter φθίνει into φθίνειν is to commit Sophocles (at this moment most inopportunely) to the Aeschylean view of the vengeance as a new crime in the series of crimes. Orestes is the καθαρτής of the house of Pelops (70). The day is breaking at last (17-19). The house is rid of the curse (1508-1510).

P. 251, l. 1449. I do not like the suggestion of an alternative construction of τῆς φιλτάτης in agreement with συμφορᾶς. Probably τῆς φιλτάτης is meant to be, to Aegisthus, a surprise for τοῦ φιλτάτου. What Electra means by speaking of the "misfortune" of Clytaemnestra rather than of Orestes, it is for him to make out as he can.

P. 251. l. 1451. Probably φίλης προξένου κατήνυσαν is to be explained in the first instance as an aposiopesis—understanding φόνον. κατανύσαι αἷμα would hardly justify κατανύσαι τινὰ (meaning 'to murder'); and the two meanings of the words must both lie in προξένου (not one in προξένου, the other in an implied πρόξενον) κατήνυσαν. Moreover, κανανύσαι προξένου, meaning 'to arrive' (compare ἀνύσειν 'Αΐδαν, Aj. 607, where 'to accomplish'='to reach') *is itself an elliptical expression* (scil. οἶκον). The meaning, therefore, depends upon the word *supplied*: Aegisthus will supply οἶκον, the audience φόνον. 'They accomplished { to the house / the murder } of a loving hostess.'

P. 261, l. 100. The Chorus know that Heracles has been in Asia, and that he is either in Euboea or on his way thither. Perhaps he is crossing the Aegaean; perhaps he is preparing to come, as Xerxes came, by land, and is now passing the Hellespont. Sophocles seems to me to have used and *adapted* a Homeric phrase. Compare κεκλιμένος πόντῳ, Il. xv. 740; λίμνῃ κεκλιμένος, v. 709; 'Ἀλφέου πόρῳ κλιθείς, Pind. Olymp. i. 92 (of the tomb of Pelops at Olympia), where the participle means 'living' (or 'encamped' or 'buried') 'on a slope towards' (looking down upon) the sea, or lake, or river. So here—regarding the sea (in Greek fashion; compare μετέωρος) as an eminence sloping to the shore—'midway between the continents,' 'looking down upon the coast of either.'

P. 268, l. 281. Compare Browning, 'Caliban,' 'Letting the rank tongue blossom into speech.'

P. 279, l. 554. I follow Hermann's interpretation (in his first edition), which accounts for τῇδε, and gives an excellent antithesis between ὀργαίνειν and λυτήριον λύπημα : '*angry* it is not well for me to be, but hear how (not for vengeance, but to rid myself of her) I mean to *vex* this maiden :' 'angry I am not, but vex her soul I shall.'

P. 283, l. 653. The best emendation seems οἱ στρωθείς. One MS., *Ven.* (thirteenth century), has οἰστρωθείς. But οἰστρηθείς may be right: 'a frenzy-fit of Ares proves (to Deianeira) release from weary days,' this war with Eurytus being, the Chorus hope, the last of the toils and dangers of Heracles.

P. 283, l. 662. θηρὸς is corrupt, as the metre shows, and παγχρίστῳ can hardly stand alone as a substantive. Moreover, ἐπὶ προφάσει θηρὸς gives the wrong meaning. The Chorus do not distrust the Centaur. They mean that the πρόφασις assigned by Deianeira will induce Heracles, so they hope, to put on the robe, and so to become subject to the spell which is to draw him home. συγκραθείς κ.τ.λ. —'having drunk through every vein' the magic chrism 'upon a pretext' (*i.e.* having been induced by specious reasons to put on the robe). If so, then the word wanted is a substantive—in meaning and metre = πέπλῳ. Possibly φάρει (ἄ as *inf.* 916). 'Clasped by' (welded, made one with) the robe which Persuasion has anointed; 'the robe anointed all over' (or 'supremely anointed') 'by Persuasion :' compare such expressions as διδακταὶ ἀνθρώπων ἀρεταί.

Notice that both συγκραθείς and ἐπὶ προφάσει are unconsciously prophetic, and to the spectators ominous, of the horror so near at hand, fitly followed on the instant by the entrance of Deianeira, distracted with fear. (Compare the ominous word προσαρμόσαι, *supra*, 494). 'Penetrated' indeed by the Centaur's blood, 'welded and made one' with the robe which she had smeared, was Heracles to be, in another sense than she had dreamed of. A 'specious' robe indeed it was to prove; and, whilst she thought that by her harmless πρόφασις she was winning back to herself her husband's love, she little thought, but the spectators knew, how the πρόφασις of Nessus had deceived *her*, to work his death.

P. 285, l. 724. Whatever reason to fear the worst, fortune may interfere, and all will yet be well. 'We ought not to reckon our hopes and fears' (ἐλπὶs = forecast) 'as of more account (of more avail) than fortune.' For the sense of πάρος, compare Oed. Col. 418, πάρος τοὐμοῦ πόθου προύθεντο τὴν τυραννίδα: and Heracl. 200, ἡ γὰρ αἰσχύνη πάρος [Reiske for βάρος] τοῦ ζῆν παρ' ἐσθλοῖς ἀνδράσιν νομίζεται.

P. 290, l. 837. The torture of the treachery, mixed with the pangs of the poison. I read with Hermann ὑποφόνια δολόμυθα κέντρ' [and in Strophe (830) ἔτι ποτ' ἔτ' ἐπίπονόν γ' ἔχοι]: μελάγχαιτα without article being put for a substantive, 'more epicorum:' and ὑποφόνια (attested by Harpocration) = 'caedem expiantia.'

P. 290, l. 843. 'Concerning which' (*i.e.* the destruction of Heracles) 'partly indeed she was heedless' (for προσέβαλε = προσέσχε, scil. νοῦν, compare 580)—and so far she cannot be acquitted of blame; 'but partly it came . . . of a policy not her own' (μολόντα governed by στένει) 'and now she repents it with bitter tears.' ὀλεθρίαισι συναλλαγαῖς, dative of manner; 'it came to pass (she did the deed) from a fatal desire to win back her husband's love' (ταῦτ' ἐποίησεν ὀλεθρίως πρὸς τὸν πόσιν συναλλαττομένη): a sense of συναλλαγὴ justified by Aj. 732, where it means 'mediation.'

P. 293, l. 911. I read τῆs ἀπαιδος (for τὰs ἀπαιδας). The plural οὐσίας seems to me indefensible. I understand τῆs ἀπαιδος οὐσίας as genitive after ἔκλαιεν: [for gen. after words expressing emotion, compare Oed. R. 234, Phil. 715, Hec. 1256, Hippol. 1400: and for similar combination of constructions (noun and verb) Oed. Col. 1357, and *inf.* 936, οὔτ' ὀδυρμάτων . . . οὔτ' ἀμφιπίπτων:] 'lamented . . . crying out upon her own hard fate, and for her childless state henceforth.' ἄπαις οὐσία, '*called* mother of many children, *really* mother of none;' all her children would disown her, as Hyllus had already. The alteration of τῆs ἀπαιδος into τὰs ἀπαιδας might easily have been made by some one who did not see that the genitive was to be *coupled* with ἀνακαλουμένη, and thought that ἀνακαλουμένη ought to have another object.

P. 297, l. 1018. None of the proposed emendations convince me; the words may be translated as they stand, and the metre does not invite corruption. To say that the sight of Hyllus is undimmed (ἔμπλεον) is not an unnatural way of saying that he is young. ἤ= μᾶλλον ἤ: compare Herod. ix. 26. The construction seems to be condensed from ἔμπλεον σώζειν (=ὥστε σώζειν) τὸν πατέρα μᾶλλον ἤ ὥστε αὐτὸν δι' ἐμοῦ σώζεσθαι; so that ἤ δι' ἐμοῦ is interposed between σώζειν and ἔμπλεον on which it depends.

P. 298, l. 1046. Bothe's conjecture κοὐ λόγῳ κακὰ has been generally adopted: but Cicero's translation, 'O multa dictu gravia, perpessu aspera,' seems to show that he at any rate read what our MSS. have, καὶ λόγῳ κακὰ: and this makes good sense—λόγῳ in a sort of opposition to χερσὶ and νώτοισι in the next line.

P. 301, l. 1127. Hyllus had meant, 'It ill becomes me, as *her* son, to keep silence; not to plead my mother's cause.' 'It ill becomes you as *my* son,' says Heracles, 'to keep silence of her fault.' '(What she has done now, I know not; but) such silence indeed on your part *beseems not her former fault*.' Hyllus replies, 'Nor what she has done this day (does silence beseem)—thou shalt confess.'

P. 313, l. 68. = μίμνε, μὴ συμφορὰν δεχόμενος, τὸν ἄνδρα. Compare Prom. v. 339, πάντων μετασχὼν καὶ τετολμηκὼς ἐμοί, where καὶ τετολμηκὼς = τολμηρῶς.

P. 316, l. 128. Compare Merchant of Venice, i. 1, 123 :—
'How much I have disabled mine estate
By something *showing* a more *swelling port*
Than my faint means would grant continuance.'

P. 318, l. 176. 'Perchance in fruitless recompense for some victory—either because she was disappointed of battle-spoils, or because of a hunting of the stag when she was unrewarded.' The victory was ἄδωρος (to Artemis), and therefore its recompense is ἀκάρπωτος (to Ajax).

P. 319, l. 207. For 'stream' read 'storm.'

P. 327, l. 430. 'Am I not fitly called *Aias*, having such cause to cry *Ai ai?*'

P. 329, l. 475. To such monotony (of incurring and avoiding by turns the danger of death) a man's existence is reduced when honour is lost, and there is nothing left to live for but a little more life.

P. 333, l. 582. θρηνεῖν ἐπῳδάς: 'to use the spell of lamentation' ('to lament for a spell'): *i.e.* to lament when action is needed is like using charms when the knife is needed, playing the enchanter over what needs the surgeon.

P. 334, l. 603. Ἰδαῖα μίμνων λειμῶνι' ἄποινα μηνῶν ἀνήριθμος αἰὲν εὐνῶμαι.

P. 336, l. 651. A sword-blade wants two things—to be sharp, and to be flexible. By heating it, and then dipping it in water, it is hardened, so that it will take an edge. But it cannot be used in this state; it is very hard, and therefore very brittle. Now it wants to be *reduced*, to be made flexible. This is done by plunging it, while still warm, into a bath of hot oil, so hot as to ignite. Sophocles refers to this *second* dipping in the hot bath, and this follows, without need of explanation, from the use of περισκελεῖς two lines before. For περισκελεῖς is 'over-hardened' (compare Antig. 474), and describes the state of the steel after the first process, when it is ready to take the edge (στόμα), but when it is also so hard as to be brittle—the temper that will break rather than bend.

No doubt the speech of Ajax is meant to deceive, the motive of the deception being a proud reserve and avoidance of all appeal, where appeal would be vain, to the sympathy of Tecmessa and the sailors; no doubt at the same time nothing is said that is not *true* —true in its deeper and hidden meaning. The deliverance, the purging away of his stains, the escape from the wrath of Athene, even the respectful homage to be paid to the Atreidae, point clearly enough, to us who have the clue, to his death. And when he speaks of the wonders that time can work—how there is nothing it cannot overthrow, not even the most stubborn will, and how the edge of his own resolve has grown flexible (not *dull*), so that 'it pities him' to leave Tecmessa and his child, all this is true. The Chorus think that he has abandoned his intention of killing himself, but he says nothing of the kind. He only says that, whereas he was hard, now he is softened, so that he feels pity. The sword-blade is not less, but more, efficient because it bends. The edge of Ajax' purpose is not less keen because in his heart he pities those whom that purpose requires him to forsake.

P. 336, l. 666. Compare Lear, iv. 6, 34 :—

'O you mighty gods!
This world I do renounce, and in your sights
Shake patiently my great affliction off:

If I could bear it longer, and not fall
To quarrel with your great opposeless wills,
My snuff and loathèd part of nature should
Burn itself out.'

P. 359, l. 1285. See note on El. 209.

P. 385, l. 417. The enemies of Odysseus said (according to the post-Homeric story) that he was the son of Sisyphus, transferred with his mother, while still unborn, by Sisyphus to Laertes.

P. 392, l. 625. Sisyphus, 'before he died, desired his wife not to bury him. She having complied with his request, he complained of her neglect, and asked Pluto, or Persephone, to allow him to return to the upper world to punish his wife. When this request was granted, he refused to return to the lower world, until Hermes carried him off by force' (Dict. Biog.).

P. 395, l. 676. Ixion.

P. 402, l. 852. I read ὧν αὐδῶμαι, εἰ ταύταν τούτων. . . . 'But —you know whom I mean—if as by *them* advised you counsel thus' . . . ('if of them you have this for your plan ').

P. 402, l. 858. I read ἀλέης (=ἀλέας): like αἰθρίας, νυκτός, θέρους, etc.

P. 402, l. 864. The safer course is the wiser one : to carry off the bow and arrows and leave Philoctetes behind.

P. 422, l. 1329. ἐντυχεῖν MSS. Read ἂν τυχών (not τυχεῖν).

P. 422, l. 1330. αὐτός MSS. Read αὑτός.

ὡς ἄν, 'however :' compare Ajax, 1117, 1369, Oed. Col. 1361, Trach. 715 : 'however day may succeed to day,' 'however the sun may rise and set (but still the same sun pursuing the same course), no day will bring relief.'

P. 426, l. 1443. We must read, with Hermann and other editors, οὐ γὰρ εὐσέβεια (or ηὐσέβεια). "Follows men in death and does not die when they die" is out of the question. The MSS. are very faulty in this part of the play : *e.g.* in 1441 both L and A have ὅταν πορθεῖτε; in 1429, ἐκλαβών; here, ἡ γάρ.

www.ingramcontent.com/pod-product-compliance
Lightning Source LLC
Chambersburg PA
CBHW022138300426
44115CB00006B/252